75 SEARCH AND RESCUE STORIES
by Shaun Roundy, MA

© 2011 University of Life Press
www.UofLIFE.com

D1452787

For Tom & UCSSAR teammates
past and present,
and for volunteer rescuers
everywhere.

CHAPTERS

FOREWORD

Search and Rescue is an easy job. When the pager goes off, you simply drop everything you are doing to go help someone you probably don't even know. You leave the birthday party. Get up from the restaurant while celebrating your anniversary. You leave church. Leave Thanksgiving dinner. You leave yard work unfinished or leave your son's baseball game. The calls even come on Christmas. Really, search and rescue is an easy job.

At least that's what most people think. What they don't see is the hours that search and rescue members spend while training, the hours spent in meetings, the hours spent on the mountain honing skills, the hours spent toiling in adverse conditions, such as freezing weather, freezing water, or on dangerous cliff bands, so they can rescue the next victim. Snow, ice, sun and sweat are familiar to us. Also unseen are the credit card charges or the checkbook entry listing all of the fuel, the equipment, and vehicle repairs that every search and rescue volunteer pays on their own dime.

And the recipients of all of this generosity? Ah, yes, the victim. The victim of unforeseen circumstances. The victim of poor planning. The victim of peer pressure. Those who exceed their own personal limitations for the sake of thrill, for the adrenaline rush, to quash the peer pressure, or those who simply make a mistake and need help. We see them all, both young and old, the brave and the afraid. Some who should know better. Some who simply don't care. But they do share one common thread. They know - and expect - search and rescue to respond when they are in trouble. And we do.

During my tenure with the Utah County Sheriff's Office Search and Rescue team I have truly become a believer. First and foremost, a believer in people. Those people who choose to serve mankind. But more importantly, perhaps, I have become a believer in miracles. Because I have witnessed firsthand the miracles performed by volunteer search and rescue members. I have witnessed the silent sacrifice, dedication, compassion and humanity that they possess. I have observed, proudly, the spirit in their hearts as they toil to serve their fellow man.

In Utah County, we have a widely varied topography, and outdoor recreation is a constant here. From ten peaks over 11,000 feet to the barren desert. From a raging river to the darkened cave. From a 100,000-acre freshwater lake, to a dangerous cliff-band twenty miles away. From a majestic waterfall to a hiking trail. From avalanche country to an alpine meadow. And for each of the above places mentioned, we go. We go to help.

We respond to calls involving injured hikers, ice rescues, swift water rescue, a boater in distress, a person bucked off a horse, the ATV rollover, the drowning victim, victims of suicide, the fall victim, those stuck on ledges, those who have fallen into moats, or the child swept away by rushing waters. And we go to help.

Many people ask me what it takes to be a search and rescue volunteer. They ask what skills they need, what equipment they need, and how much it will cost them. They ask me if we get called out a lot, or what the Sheriff's Office gives them. They want to know if they have to respond to all of the calls. And they want to know if they get paid. Sadly, they receive no pay. And, for the record, I tell everyone who asks these questions what they need: compassion and dedication. We can't train for those two components. They need to come from within.

So, why do they do it then? These men and women from all walks of life - from the state senator to the housewife. From the graphic artist to the writer of books. From the small businessman to the pilot. From the mechanic to the nurse. Why do they do search and rescue? Although I can't speak for all SAR members when I answer this, I can tell you this much. They do it for the handshake they receive from an appreciative father when his child is carried down the trail. For the hug they receive from a loving mother. And for the many - often unspoken - thank you's they receive.

They do it while witnessing tears of joy, or sorrow, from a happy or grieving family member. They stand by, solemn and respectful, as a family wails over an opened body bag while gazing down at a loved one. They do it because they care. And they do it because they are incredible, compassionate men and women whose reward is the satisfaction they receive because they made a difference. They don't care who gets the credit, for they are a team. But individually, they are heroes. Each and every one of them.

For all of those who read this book, you should give thanks. Thanks to all of those who sacrifice to help you. I have been very fortunate in my career to rub shoulders with the men and women of search and rescue. There are no finer people out there. This job is not for everyone. Not everyone we bring onto the team still serves with us. Sometimes the work is too hard. The time commitment too large. Or the personal or financial cost too much a burden. But we thank all of those who try, and are sincerely grateful to those who continue to serve.

And I speak for our team when I thank all of those we have helped, and their loving families. That's why search and rescue is easy. When you have appreciative people who care as much as you do. I also thank Shaun Roundy, who both humbled and honored me, with a request to write a foreword to his book.

Sgt. Tom Hodgson
Utah County Sheriff's Office

1 EXPERIENCE

When I joined one of the world's best search and rescue teams a dozen years ago, I wanted to know everything about it - what to expect, how things worked, what to do and not to do, and what to think about the commitment I just signed up for. In short, I wanted to hear stories.

Now I look in the eyes of this year's probies and see the same hunger. They can hardly wait for the pager to go off. They want to get sent up the mountain or underground or into the river or onto the lake to help someone. They want experience, and there are only two ways to get it.

Usually you have to learn the hard way. Trial and error, successes and failures. This sort of experience takes time and errors can prove costly. "Experience is what you get," they say, "when you don't have experience."

A quicker and safer way to gain experience is to get it vicariously through stories. Stories provide concrete lessons that can be readily applied to real world situations. They also have the benefit of hindsight to further draw out the important details.

I wanted to write this book for a long time. I wondered how to take a series of relatively disconnected events with changing characters from the past twelve years and weave them into a single, fluid tapestry. I pondered how I could arrange the events to build tension in a steady crescendo to a single climax and denouement. Then one day as I related one of the stories to friends, I realized that I didn't need to turn the book into a classic novel or Oscar-worthy Hollywood movie script. I can simply tell the stories. They stand on their own just fine. Between the lines and between the individual events, they deliver all the themes and development that I hoped to include.

So here I give you 75 of my best SAR stories gathered over the past twelve years. You'll read about people stranded between cliffs hundreds of feet tall, and others who accidentally or intentionally fell off. You'll read about stuck cavers; capsized boats with missing swimmers; lost, injured, and hypothermic hikers, bikers and climbers; avalanche survivors and fatalities; airplane and helicopter rescues and crashes; boat, four wheeler, motorcycle, and snowmobile problems, rescues that gained national media attention and documentaries made; and more.

You'll also get a good look at how search and rescue works in our county and how it feels to experience a rescue mission from either end - as rescuer or the victim being rescued.

You'll get an accurate perspective on the risks and costs - both physical and emotional - of participating on search and rescue. It's not always just fun and adventure. Sometimes rescuing means inconvenient hours, inclement weather, fatigue, with occasional frustration and disappointment. Sometimes the failures leave lasting scars.

I've read some of these stories to friends and neighbors and their reactions have surprised me. Some stories they found unsettling. Others, informative and exciting. The one consistent reaction I've observed as I lowered the pages at the end of a story and looked up at their faces is rapt attention. Having lived through the actual experiences, I take these tales for granted. I forget just how gripping the events were during the long moments as rescue missions played out. I'm pleased to discover that I've captured those emotions in the telling.

2 DISCLAIMER

From the outset, you should understand that the following 75 stories are told from a single person's perspective: mine. It's the only one I have.

I might describe the elephant's trunk while others had a completely different experience near the tail. I may have omitted minor details and equivocated others. Most significantly, I have taken the liberty of filling in broad gaps by inventing details that I have no way of knowing - I've told victims' back stories the way I imagine they might have happened, based on the few facts I had at my disposal.

I did this, ironically, in order to deliver the most accurate possible reading experience - accurate in the sense that had I not fabricated back stories and personalities for our victims, you could hardly imagine them as real people. You would not care about them enough, you would not sense the urgency they must have experienced, and thus your experience of the story could never be true to life.

That said, I did my best to stay true to whatever facts I know about the events (other than names, which I have changed in most instances to respect the privacy of people who never intended to need our help).

I never meet most victims until after their world falls apart. I will never meet most of them again afterward, and if I do, they'll be just another face in the crowd. Without my helmet, radio, and the blinding safety-yellow t-shirt with a sheriff star over the heart, they won't recognize me either. So why does it matter if I get their side of the story exactly right? I'm not writing a newspaper expose. I'm not writing their personal history. I'm writing mine.

Besides, these stories repeat endlessly over the years with new people in new places, and the overall experience remains the same. That's what matters most. That's what I've tried to capture and share. I'm content with this goal and hope you will find it exceptionally informative and enjoyable.

3 ALL ABOUT SAR

There's no way to convey "all" about SAR in a brief chapter (let alone an entire book), but here's a quick overview for orientation so the following stories will make more sense.

Most rescue teams consist of professional volunteers organized by county sheriffs. "Professional" means we train hard and are the premiere experts at what we do. "Volunteer" means we don't get paid, and often pay annual dues for the privilege of waking up in the middle of the night and spending hours in the worst weather imaginable to save the life of a stranger we've never met and will never see again. Add to that the hours of training to maintain top-notch skills and thousands of dollars to equip ourselves with required gear and fill our gas tanks before driving back and forth across the county and you begin to get the idea of what our being a professional volunteer entails.

As our Sheriff often reminds us, there's no way taxes could ever pay for the services we provide to county citizens and visitors. Only the Coast Guard and National Park Service handle anywhere near the volume of rescue work donated by volunteers. National organizations like the Mountain Rescue Association (MRA) and National Association for Search and Rescue (NASAR) support local teams where the rubber meets the road (or trail or river or lake).

Two separate organizational structures direct the organization.

The Incident Command System (**ICS**) defines the chain of command during rescue missions. This consists of the Sheriff Sgt Tom Hodgson, other deputies, and volunteers appointed by the Sheriff's Office (**SO**) as team commander and ICS members.

Membership in ICS requires the ability to deal with a tremendous amount of incoming information (often over multiple radio channels) while turning it around and sending it back out to keep things organized. Such leadership holds a degree of prestige, but most SAR members would rather get sent up the mountain or onto the lake than sit in the parking lot and coordinate.

ICS generally sets up a Command Post (**CP**) from which ICS directs rescue missions, assigns SAR members to teams, and provides support for field teams. CP may be an ICS member's vehicle or, for complex and extended missions, the high-tech Multi-Agency Command Center (MACC) with its meeting rooms and satellite internet, or other locations may be employed.

Each team is assigned a **Team Leader** and given a specific search area or other responsibilities such as setting up rope systems or transporting gear. Hasty teams are dispatched to locate victims and provide initial, minimal care. Subsequent teams are numbered Team One, Team Two, etc.

A team member may also be designated as the **On-Scene Commander** to oversee and direct the rescue first hand rather than merely from information communicated over the radio. Both team leaders and on-scene commanders should stand back, out of the action, make assignments, and ensure that the operation runs smoothly. A safety officer may also be assigned whose sole duty is to see that all safety precautions are observed.

When not involved in a rescue mission, the **Board of Directors**, consisting of the president, vice president, secretary, treasurer, and quartermaster, are charged with day to day operation of our nonprofit 501(c)(3) organization (your tax-deductible donations are welcome! Visit ucssar.org/donate today). Board members are elected annually by the membership.

The Board further assigns **Sergeant** positions to coordinate training and make sure the team stays up to date in their discipline. Sergeant positions include training, new member training, fundraising and publicity, and each of the **Special Teams**: Mountain Rescue, Swiftwater, K9, Singletrack (motorcycles), Communications & ELT (downed aircraft), Open Water/Flat Ice, Dive, Cave, Medical, Mass Casualty, Fleet, and Tracking.

In other counties, SAR members may belong to and participate on a single special team, but in Utah County, all 50 members are expected to maintain proficiency in the most common disciplines and may train and qualify for any additional special teams.

New member information and applications can be found on our website at ucssar.org/join, and interviews are usually held in October. The exciting and challenging nature of SAR attracts its share of driven A-type personalities, so some degree of friction is unavoidable. Not everyone sees eye to eye on every opportunity and challenge. Despite this fact, dedication to the organization's core purpose of selfless service to strangers smooths out most differences and we all get along remarkably well.

Thanks to ongoing training, high levels of personal dedication, and around 100 rescue missions every year, our skills remain sharp and our team enjoys a reputation for excellence throughout the region. Such preparedness increases team pride and individual satisfaction, and experience shows that those who dedicate themselves to the highest standards tend to last longest and enjoy SAR most.

SAR poses with a Life Flight helicopter crew above Aspen Grove in 2006

4 Welcome to Utah County

Utah County's varied and extreme topography makes it a perfect location for search and rescue - if you like excitement and challenge, that is.

Scattered across 2,000 square miles stretches the southern terminus of the Wasatch Range. 11,750' Mount Timpanogos and 10,908' Cascade Peak sometimes seem built of half rock and the other half stone. Cliffs pile one atop another as mountains shed altitude in their own version of a crash diet. Crystal streams tumble down gullies and ravines, while pine and aspen grow in terraced layers like a boy scout's dream birthday cake.

Elk Point cliffs in the Primrose Cirque

At 4,489' above sea level, the lowest point of the valley floor towers above state high points of 25 other states.

Stack another 7,439' atop that for the county's high point - Mount Nebo's 11,928' cone - and only a dozen states stand taller (including Utah's 13,528 King's Peak).

Yet Utah County doesn't only go up. Beneath the surface, caves plunge deep into the earth's crust. The West Desert has Utah's 9th deepest known cave. Timpanogos Cave National Monument travels half a mile through the north end of the mountain and features tens of thousands of stalactites, stalagmites, helictites, and other formations.

American Fork, Provo, Hobble Creek, Spanish Fork, Payson and many other canyons wind deep into the mountains and lead to thousands of miles of dirt roads and singletrack hiking, biking, horse and motorcycle trails.

Between the roads and trails lie untracked expanses filled with airy mountain ridges, windblown ravines and lush valleys; pine, aspen and scrub oak forests and mountain deserts; birds, squirrels, deer, elk, moose, cougars and bears; breathtaking beauty and deadly dangers.

Resting atop the topography, four full seasons blow an ever-changing atmosphere ranging between 100°+ scorchers to well-below-zero deep freezes. Over 500 inches of snow falls in upper elevations. Violent storm fronts pass through all seasons, bringing gale-force winds that rip shingles from roofs and kick up four-foot waves on the lake in fifteen minutes.

150-square-mile Utah Lake, the third largest freshwater lake west of the Mississippi, is less than 12' deep. It freezes over most winters and sometimes stacks enormous piles of ice on shore when storms coincide with the spring thaw. The lake attracts duck hunters, fishers, waterskiers, sailors, and others.

550,000 county residents can't avoid catching a glimpse of nature's majesty every time they step outside. Steep mountain ridges catch the morning sun

A sailboat waits for a breeze on Utah Lake

and make them feel like they live in a postcard every time they look up. Canyon breezes tempt commuters to skip work and go for a hike. Afternoon sunlight shimmers like a million diamonds on the lake and calls students from two major universities to take time out for a dip in the lake's murky but refreshing ripples and waves.

Some resist Mother Nature's temptations, others yield. Eventually, inevitably, something goes wrong. People get lost, stranded, hurt, or killed.

Entropy is a law of nature. It's the one predicting that "things fall apart." Spend enough time in nature and it happens to everyone, regardless of whether they have prepared or not.

That's why we're here. Search and Rescue volunteers are on call 24/7/365 to pick up the pieces and, as much as possible, glue them together again.

Backlit spindrift blows off the mountain during a winter morning commute

Timpanogos Glacier and Emerald Lake "Lodge" in early spring with less than 2' of roof protruding from the snow

An ice pile forms near Bird Island with Utah Lake frozen over

Olin gets first tracks in backcountry powder on a "training" day

The lower portion of Stewart Falls above Sundance during a training exercise

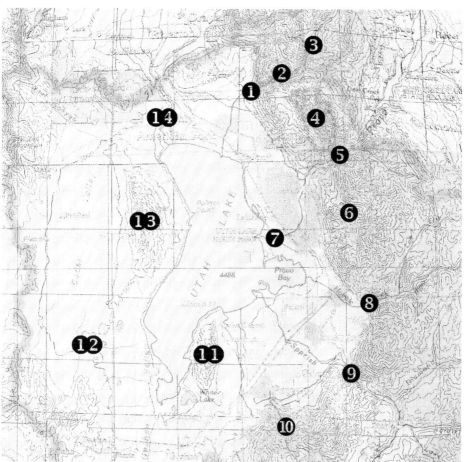

1. American Fork Canyon
2. Timpanogos Cave National Monument
3. Tibble Fork Reservoir. Mineral Basin continues up to the right
4. Mount Timpanogos. Moving clockwise around it:
        1:00 Timpooneke Trail
        3:00 Horse Flats, Robert's Horn, Primrose Cirque, Elk Point
        5:00 Sundance
        8:00 Dry Canyon
        9:00 Battle Creek Canyon
        10:00 Grove Creek Canyon
5. Provo Canyon, Bridal Veil Falls, Stairway to Heaven. Upper Falls to the right
6. Squaw Peak.
        3:00 Cascade Mountain
        6:00 Rock Canyon, Y Mountain
7. Utah Lake State Park to the left
8. Hobble Creek Canyon
9. Spanish Fork Canyon
10. Payson Canyon. Mount Nebo off the map to the south
11. West Mountain. Lincoln Point to the north
12. West Desert and Nutty Putty Cave
13. Lake Mountain, Pelican Point to the right
14. Jordan River

The back side of Mount Timpanogos from Heber Valley in early June

Elk Point floats above clouds in the Primrose Cirque

First Falls in the Primrose Cirque in October

Valley view from a steep slope high up Mount Timpanogos

Bull moose along the Alpine Loop's Ridge Trail

Mount Timpanogos from my front porch in Orem

Delicate helictites inside Timpanogos Cave National Monument

Spring snow and waterfalls decorate the upper Primrose Cirque in early June

5 GLOSSARY

In order to add to the realism of the stories you're about to read, I often use jargon that needs explanation. This glossary of abbreviations and terms should help.

SAR: Search and Rescue. Pronounced like 'star' minus the 't'. This is how we refer to ourselves, though you'll occasionally see it written S&R.

ESAR: Explorer Search and Rescue. Within a BSA explorer post, youth aged approximately 16-21 train SAR skills and sometimes get called out for missions. The group hopes to groom future SAR members.

Proby: First-year team member who has not yet passed the exam and been approved by the board and membership as full members. Other than holding administrative positions, they may participate as fully as other members as long as their skills are adequate and known to ICS. Probies are typically enthusiastic and eager for action. They want to get involved, make a contribution, and get some experience under their belt.

LZ: Helicopter landing zone. This area should have a flat or gentle slope, be free of obstructions and dangers, and be kept free of people. An LZ coordinator is assigned to manage the area and provide GPS coordinates to approaching aircraft.

DPS: Department of Public Safety. Their helicopter, Star 7, has a Highway Patrol emblem on its nose and often assists on search and rescue missions.

ELT: Emergency Locator Transmitter. These units are attached to aircraft and transmit a signal when bumped hard enough (such as when a plane crashes). They may also be set off by a hard landing, rough handling, or for absolutely no reason after sitting stationery for years in someone's attic.

The signals are picked up by the SARSAT satellite which zeroes in on the signal location with each pass across the sky every 100 minutes. They may also set off our mountain top repeater. Teams then **DF** (direction find) the source of the signal with **L-PER**s (an ELT tracking device).

PLB: Personal locator beacon. Hand-held version of ELT that cause many SAR veterans to fear that people will get deeper over their heads due to the perception that they will get located and rescued immediately if they ever get into trouble. This is not necessarily the case.

PLS: Place last seen. Knowing the last known position of a victim helps us know not only where to search from, but how big of a search radius is needed based on how long he or she has been missing and how fast s/he could travel.

RP: Reporting party. Whoever reports an incident. We try to keep these people around to gather additional information or clarify old information as needed.

200'er, 75'er: The length of ropes most commonly used on the mountain. All team members are assigned a 75' rope, while some members are given 200'ers as well.

Webbing: 1/2" wide nylon strand used to tie anchors around trees, rocks, etc, improvised harnesses, and other uses.

Brake Rack: A collection of metal bars through which a rope is weaved in order to create friction. This friction allows a belayer to control and lower hundreds of pounds with very little effort.

PFD: Personal flotation device. Life jacket. SAR members always wear a whistle, knife, and flashing beacon on their PFDs.

PWC: Personal watercraft. Often called wave runners or jet skis. Usually referred to as watercraft in this book.

Avy: short for 'avalanche.'

Scree: A field of loose, broken rock ranging in size from about an inch to six inches. Scree slopes sometimes slide downhill when walked on. Thus going downhill can turn into fun "rock skiing," or can prove strenuous due to fighting to maintain footing and balance. Hiking up scree can be taxing when each step up the mountain is followed by sliding half a step back down.

Talus: see "scree."

An ice climber lowers off the fourth pitch of Stairway to Heaven

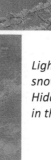

New snow clings to a tree against a bluebird sky

Light October snow cover near the Hidden Lakes breakover in the Primrose Cirque

6 Mechanical Advantage

Here's one last concept that plays a part in a few of the following stories and which I'll explain briefly before getting started.

Mechanical advantage helps by dividing a load. With a 2-to-1 system, five pounds of force moves a ten pound load. On the down side, pulling ten feet on a 2-to-1 system only moves the load five feet.

3-to-1 is the most common system used in SAR due to its balance between advantage and speed and because it takes less rope than a 2-to-1. 5-to-1 is the most I've used on a rescue. It wasn't fast, but I don't know if we could have succeeded without it.

The system illustrated here is a 2-to-1 used to control a boogie board, rescuer and patient in the river. Along with controlling the load's position up and down the river, teams on either bank can pull the load side to side. Even with the mechanical advantage, it still takes at least three people to reel them in.

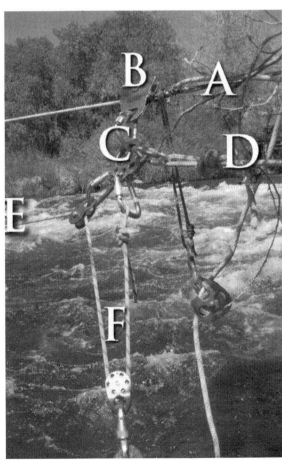

A. Highline with prusik to tension it.

B. This pulley lets the system slide back and forth along the highline.

C. Bear Claw allows for multiple attachments without crossloading carabiners (whose strength is reduced by pulling on them the wrong way or in multiple directions at once).

D. River-left control line. Always say "river right" or "river left" facing downstream (from the current's point of view) to avoid confusion.

E. River right control line.

F. 2-to-1 mechanical advantage.

7 WHEN HEAVEN FREEZES OVER

On December 7, 1999, I attended my first SAR meeting as a new member. That Saturday came the monthly team training for avalanche evaluation and search, and a week later, ten minutes before the work day ended, an ice climber, climbing alone on Provo Canyon's *Stairway to Heaven*, lost his purchase on the ice and took a 60' fall.

Stairway to Heaven

I didn't yet know what happened. All I got was a numeric page reading 05-30-52. I checked my reference card and translated the numbers to "Canyon-Bridal Veil Falls-Medical Problem." I packed up my computer, hurried to my car, and called in on the radio. Little by little, the details filled in. I didn't know exactly what to expect or what role I would play, but I could hardly wait to find out.

The sun dipped behind Lake Mountain and disappeared as I drove to the freeway. Fifteen minutes later found me donning pant shells and strapping ice tools to my pack in the parking lot below the incident. I hurried up the snow-covered River Trail and strapped on my crampons at the base of the talus slope leading to the fallen climber. I tried to look prepared and hoped to get sent up the mountain.

I knew the area and had climbed here before. *Stairway to Heaven* is an 800' frozen waterfall - the tallest free-flowing vertical ice in the Lower 48. Standing in the center of the 200' wide ice sheet gives the impression that time has stopped a frothy waterfall. You might glance around half expecting to see a salmon caught mid leap up the falls, or a grizzly bear standing half submerged, stretching out its toothy snout to catch the fish for dinner.

The ice came and went, waxing and waning, throughout the winter, depending on the air temperature. Cold temps turned the ice thick but brittle. Warm spells gnawed away at the ice and sometimes sent huge columns crashing down the mountainside.

An ICS member walked by and checked my gear. "Avalanche beacon? Probe and shovel?" I nodded and spun to show the shovel strapped to my pack. "Okay, you're on team three. What's your number?"

"750," I answered, trying to conceal my eagerness to get hiking. He wrote it down and turned to evaluate another proby.

The trail up to the ice is steep and covered in frozen dirt and boulders of various sizes. Team 3 hiked quickly for a hundred yards, then paused to catch our breath. I moved to the top of the group before stopping.

We caught up with team 2 at the second lowering station being tied to stubby trees and boulders, and I again moved to the top of the group before stopping.

"Team two, team one," a dozen radios squawked.

"Go for team two," the team leader replied.

"We could use four more people up here, and does anyone have extra blankets?"

"I have blankets," I reported quickly, still trying not to show how badly I wanted to get sent up. I feared that overeagerness would diminish my credibility. Better to appear level headed and calm.

"Go," the team leader said, pointing to me, then designating three others.

We climbed quickly and steadily the last forty yards to a small mass of rescuers huddled around the fallen climber. To my left, the massive ice block towered up into the darkening night sky. All around lay large chunks of ice knocked loose by climbers or the varying weather. I dropped my pack and pulled out two blankets which I lay across our patient, trying to stay out of the way of medics checking vital signs and attaching a c-collar to stabilize his neck.

Our victim had fallen from possibly sixty feet up, bounced off the narrow ledge atop the first pitch, then sailed another forty feet to the sloped boulder field below and slid fifteen or twenty feet down the ice and snow. EMTs found multiple tender spots during their rapid assessment, but what concerned them most was the lower back. We took extra care to keep it from moving and risk spinal injury.

Other team members finished rigging a lowering system by wrapping nylon webbing several times around a large rock, then attaching carabiners and a brake rack. They ran a 200' rope through the rack and attached it to more webbing tied to the litter. Someone got a plastic backboard ready to slide underneath the victim.

"Will you do spinal stabilization?" CJ asked, looking me in the eye.

"Okay," I replied. "What's that?"

CJ explained how to hold our victim's head to keep it inline with his body while we rolled him onto his side and slipped the backboard under him. I nodded.

"You call it," he told me. "On three."

I nodded again. I felt excited to be doing something useful on my very first rescue. My heart was pounding in my chest but I paid no attention, staying focused on my assignment.

"Ready?" I asked. Everyone nodded. "One. Two. Three!"

I held our victim's head and neck in alignment as we lifted him and someone slid the plastic backboard below him. We rolled him back down and velcro spider straps soon fastened him securely before lifting him again and sliding the waiting litter into place.

Soon eight rescuers gripped the steel rail of the litter and lifted. "Down slow," someone commanded, and we carried the fallen climber down the rugged slope to the next station. Fresh hands eager to help took over and carried the climber to the third station and on down toward the ambulance parked on the river trail.

Once we cleaned up the lowering stations and made our way back to the River Trail, loitering journalists, and a grateful family, the climber's grandfather shook our hands heartily and said, "I don't know what we'd do without you guys!"

If I had stopped to reflect at that moment, I may have discovered why I do search and rescue. It's not for the thanks, though that can be nice. It's not for the prestige of wearing a sheriff star and being a member of an elite team; that's cool but not a big deal. It's not for the excitement and adventure, though that's a major part of it. I think it's mostly because an important job needs doing and I want to do it. I want to experience everything and understand. I want to look back, after years of service, and be able to say, "I know how that feels."

The gathering on the River Trail was interrupted when an ELT then went off in the valley, signalling a downed aircraft. ICS dispatched six team members with ELPERs to investigate, but it turned out to be a false alarm.

So that was it. Our job was over. I hurried home and turned on the television, eager to watch us on the news.

8 INDY

In January, I attended my second team business meeting. I glanced around the room at my new teammates. Members included Utah Senator John Valentine, a founding member of the team; Commander Alan Wakefield who, with over twenty years experience, had mastered the complex art of organizing searches and other ICS functions; Board of Directors President CJ who would earn my deep respect and become a mentor with his admirable example of competence, respectful leadership, and calm, confidence-inspiring demeanor; Sheriff Sergeant Tom Hodgson, who took the reigns of Search and Rescue a few months earlier and whose leadership and support would ensure that our team remained one of the most respected in the region for the next decade and beyond; and many others.

Following an hour of training, a review of last month's call outs, announcements of the upcoming Saturday training, and information about various conditions around the county like the thickness of the ice developing on Utah Lake, someone requested that the new probies stand and introduce themselves again. President CJ nodded and we began.

Olin went first. His technical savvy and calm, accepting nature would make him a trusted favorite on the team. Everyone likes Olin, and everyone knows it. We would remain friends for many years to come. Three years later we would serve on the Board of Directors together, he as quartermaster and me as secretary. Later he would train the probies and I would advance to vice president. We would ride motorcycles for hundreds of miles of trails both in and out of the county. We would be the only two of our proby group to last over five years on the team.

Lora had been an ESAR member and joined SAR after turning 21. She and I would take an EMT class together and remain close friends until she married someone from ESAR and moved to the East Coast.

Shawn went next. He would last three or four years, till a demanding work schedule made it too difficult to keep up. His two boys would remain active on ESAR for many years and join SAR briefly afterward.

Karen was a diver and medic and would last three or four years until Olin and I booted her from the team for low attendance due to traveling out of the country frequently. She wasn't very happy about that, but that year's board had gotten serious about enforcing the bylaws as a means to maintaining high team standards.

Two other probies introduced themselves, and then came my turn.

As I stood and opened my mouth to tell my name, my cell phone rang in my pocket. My ringtone was the tune from *Indiana Jones*. "Daa ta-ta-taa, daa ta-taa."

CJ cocked his head slightly and his jaw dropped enviously. "I want my own theme music!" he exclaimed.

SAR agencies from several counties assist in a search following a massive avalanche in the backcountry near The Canyons resort

9 WHITE CHRISTMAS

The crisp chirping of 50 pagers around the valley interrupted dancing visions of sugar plums at 4:12 a.m. Christmas morning. Dreams of a white Christmas had come abundantly true and stranded a couple's truck in deep snow at Fifth Water in Sheep Creek, above the Diamond Fork hot pots.

Over a dozen SAR members responded, rolling out of bed and dressing groggily, then driving 17 miles up Spanish Fork Canyon and riding snowmobiles through a blizzard to bring the stranded couple out. Their truck would have to wait. Merry Christmas from Search and Rescue! In this case, we judged it better to give than to be the ones in trouble receiving the gift of rescue.

By evening, the day's second call arrived. A back country skier had gone missing somewhere in the high mountains between Salt Lake and Utah Counties. Search and Rescue again responded, driving carefully up a dangerously slick American Fork Canyon while road crews worked to clear the roads as the storm continued dumping snow on the Wasatch Range.

Because of the numerous small avalanches spilling onto the road, most SAR members were sent to the canyon mouth to wait while a few snowmobiles were dispatched up Mineral Basin.

The skier was located on the Salt Lake County side before midnight, and only half a dozen team members stuck around with a few more sleds to make sure the first volunteers returned safely.

We expected the holiday action to stop there. Winter usually means the quiet season for Utah County SAR. Colder temperatures persuade most folks to stay indoors. Besides, most of our mountains are too steep – with too many avalanches – for much backcountry skiing.

The majority of an average year's 100 calls come during the warmer months - sometimes every few days, sometimes weeks apart, and occasionally over half a dozen stacked into a single afternoon. The only certainty is that there is no certainty. You never know when someone will get in trouble and need our help.

After so much new snow and due to extreme avalanche danger, Sundance closed the day after Christmas, but brand new skis and snowboards, combined with the allure of deep Utah powder, made at least a dozen skiers and riders impatient to make tracks.

Rather than drive to one of the many avalanche-controlled Salt Lake or Park City resorts, they continued three miles past Sundance to the Primrose Cirque trailhead above Aspen Grove. Just around the corner from the parking lot, a steep chute descends from Elk Point and looked like the perfect spot to hike up and ride down the deep fresh 'pow.'

Deep in their minds, they knew better. They even discussed the avalanche danger, but good judgment yielded to adrenaline, youthful illusions of immortality, and the promise of a momentary thrill ride down the steep, deep & fresh Utah powder slowly settling out on the slopes.

Unfortunately, Elk Point is one of the worst avalanche zones in the county. Above the steep ravine hangs a thousand feet of rocky cliff. Few anchors pin the snow to the rock, and it slides often, sometimes leaving piles of snow and shattered trees over fifty feet deep by springtime.

The lower Primrose Cirque, Elk Point to the left

Five members of the group had climbed half way up the chute around 4:30 in the afternoon and had just stopped to take a break when the first wind slab a thousand feet above them grew too heavy to hold together and broke loose. The rumbling thunder grew louder as the slide entrained more and more snow, crashing down against rocks and tumbling over cliffs.

The hikers looked up. "Uh, oh," one muttered. Another turned and ran downslope as fast as he could, but it was no use. The giant wall of snow caught them all and washed them away like toys left on the beach at high tide.

As the slide spread out across the wide apron, it grew shallower, and by the time it rolled to a stop, it had swept the hikers nearly half a mile and one hiker was buried up to his neck. Another's body was mostly buried under a foot of snow. Other hikers who had been farther downslope and avoided the main blast, rushed to their aid and helped them dig out.

"Wahoo!" one shrieked with delight, raising his arms in victory once he got free. "That was *so* wild!"

"Shit!" another cried as he dug frantically away at the hard snow still piled around his legs. "Let's get the hell outta here!" They hadn't gotten off the slide path when another cornice broke free from it's lofty perch and came crashing toward them in a second wall of pure white.

The slide caught them and carried them farther downslope. By now no one was celebrating. The seriousness and urgency of the situation had fully set in. This was not the thrill ride they had anticipated. They dug out frantically and ran off the slide path as quickly as possible.

After the third avalanche broke loose and sped down the mountainside, crossing the entire basin before coming to rest, no one could be seen moving in the debris. Two of the five hikers, along with all others in the area, had gotten clear of the slides, and three had vanished. None had avalanche beacons and there was no way to find them in the growing debris pile.

Four more avalanches crashed down over the debris within the next fifteen minutes, for a total of seven.

After the first slide, a hiker on the far side of the cirque dialed 911. You can hear several slides crashing down in the background on the emergency dispatch recording of the call.

When finished, the slide path was nearly 2,000' long and 1,000' feet wide, and snow piled over 30 feet deep in spots. SAR arrived with snowmobiles, shovels, probes, and dogs, but the chance of finding any of the missing hikers alive had already dropped to near zero.

Evening had fallen and clouds covered the mountain peaks above. Over 300 avalanche starting zones hung above us, and after a quick up-close look at the slide, Incident Command opted not to risk further lives by putting anyone on the mountain in such dangerous circumstances.

In coming weeks, the avalanche garnered national attention. Various rescue agencies offered their support in the search for the missing bodies.

Probe lines made their systematic way up and down the slope, marking the areas searched with spray paint and tiny flags. Nine-foot-tall aluminum probes were broken and replaced. Dogs sniffed and holes were dug wherever they showed interest. Location of hats, gloves, poles, and other items were marked to suggest possible trajectories and predict victim locations. Ground Penetrating Radar dragged back and forth across the slide, mapping out endless layers of ice and pine limbs. Psychics contacted us who pinpointed the location of the victims somewhere in the 40 acre debris pile. Friends from as far as Virginia phoned to tell me they saw me on tv.

One body was located half way down the slope two days later. The second turned up near the lower end of the slide a week or two later. After that, periodic K9 searches continued into the spring, but the area was simply too massive and the snow too deep to justify an all-out search by the many teams who had already donated thousands of hours to the search.

We had searched everywhere - and searched most places at least twice. We had done all we could, for now. We'd just have to wait for the snow to melt. Searchers went back to their families, jobs, and lives, for now.

An autumn view down Rock Canyon from Lightning Pass

10 He is Risen

I left church on Easter Sunday and walked across the street to my car. A perfect blue sky shone overhead and the grassy green field before me beautifully echoed the theme of the renewal of life. Spring had arrived, emerging from its tomb to conquer winter's death-like grip over the world.

Halfway across the street, my pager went off. I pressed the green button and read its message. "Report to Aspen Grove for body recovery. No radio traffic."

One of my university students had been hiking that afternoon with friends when one spotted an object in the snow near some aspens just emerging from the melting snowpack.

"Oh, look!" he exclaimed, "a glove." He picked up the glove and saw something more. "Oh, look," he added, "a glove liner." He tugged on the glove liner and something still remained. "Oh, look. A hand."

They called 911 and the page went out soon afterward.

The body belonged to the third young man killed by a massive avalanche the day after Christmas. We initially searched for over a week, poking holes in the entire snowpack with long aluminum poles and repeatedly running dogs, RECCO, and ground penetrating radar across the slide area.

Other SAR teams, search dog groups, and other agencies assisted in the search, but this last victim had been buried too deep to reach. K9 teams now visited the slide every week or two for yet another try. At long last, the search would end.

Radio traffic would draw the press, who kept their scanners tuned to our frequencies, and we wanted to let the family have this moment in peace.

At the trailhead, Tom assigned me to handle safety check ins. Before going into the field, everyone had to be checked for probe, shovel, and a functioning avalanche beacon. I recorded everyone's team number so that if another avalanche occurred, we would know when everyone was accounted for.

I reluctantly accepted the assignment. I had only spent a few years on the team and was eager to experience absolutely everything. I wanted to help dig up the body and see what three months in a deep freeze would do to it.

Twenty minutes later, a team member showed up who was less eager to go into the field and took over my safety assignment. He checked me for avalanche gear and I headed up the trail.

The young man had been mostly exhumed from the snowpack grave. One arm reached out above and slightly behind him. Perhaps the force of the slide had pushed it back, or perhaps he was doing as avalanche experts teach - to raise a hand as the avalanche slows and sets up in case the hand makes it out of the snow and helps someone to rescue him. If so, it worked, just three months too late.

For the most part, the dead boy looked great. His skin was pale with a barely discernible blue tint and a light bruise across his right temple. Other than that, he looked like he could have been buried yesterday.

We carefully finished digging him out and stood back while a deputy snapped photos for his report, then lifted the boy into a body bag and lay him on a litter.

We moved the litter away from the three-foot deep hole and then, in a less dramatic setting, we retreated while Tom invited the family to come forward and spend some private time with their once-lost, now-found (but still lost) son, brother, fiancé, and father to an unborn child.

A fallen horse rider is carried to an air ambulance in Payson Canyon

SAR members ski above Sundance with UDOT avalanche forecasters to check current conditions

11 Y MOUNTAIN

Laying against the steep front-range mountainside above BYU campus aptly known as Y Mountain sprawls a giant cement letter Y. The steep switchbacking trail to its base is a favorite part of hikers' exercise routine, and running all the way up earns bragging rights for trail runners.

One summer when the low scrub oak and wild grasses on Y Mountain caught fire from a lightning strike, Forest Service tankers flew in to dump fire retardant to douse the blaze. As the tiny lead plane led the larger tankers in steep dives down the mountain face, anxious fire crews - which consisted less of BYU cougars and more of BYU's rival Utah Utes, whose school color is red - keyed their radio mics and shouted frantically, "Hit the Y!!! Hit the Y!!! Hit the Y!!!"

By altering course a mere 50 yards and bombing the gigantic white cement letter with red-orange retardant, the pilot would have lost his job, perhaps his license, and gone down in the Ute hall of fame as the greatest school hero of all time.

From the top of the Y, a trail leads southeast and up into Slide Canyon. The canyon splits the mountaintop five hundred feet below its summit and creates a passage to the taller range directly behind it, with several peaks towering above 10,000'.

A BYU student hiked into this area one November and spent three days without shelter before being found. How she didn't find her way out on her own remains a mystery. When she visited team meeting to thank us for our efforts with home made treats, she gave us a hint as to why the search took so long.

When a helicopter flew directly overhead, for example, she got beneath a pine tree and shook it vigorously as a signal.

She shared other interesting survival tips like burning her denim pants back pocket and sandwich for heat. She did other things right like staying warm at night by stomping down the snow and walking in a circle to keep moving.

We accepted her thanks, told her we were glad she survived, and enjoyed her delicious, gooey, chocolate chip cookies.

12 WINTER OLYMPICS

I joined the team two years before the Salt Lake Winter Olympic Games. During my interview, my language skills – fluency in Spanish and French, with some Chinese and limited ability in a few others – were considered an asset and one more reason to accept my application.

As the games approached, some expert (I assume) drummed up the number to expect five rescues per day statewide. Considering the quarter-million visitors expected, our towering mountains, the greatest snow on earth, cliffs, snowy roads, and other dangers, that number sounded reasonable.

I looked forward to these rescues. I anticipated finding foreigners from all over the world and putting a positive spin on the most memorable vacation they would ever experience.

SAR teams across the Wasatch Front and Back trained together to work out interagency communication and logistics kinks before the real thing arrived and caught us off guard.

Finally, the Olympics arrived. Massive fireworks displays lit up the valleys and illuminated the snow-covered mountains. Visitors landed at the Salt Lake International Airport and filled hotels and Olympic venues for the next 17 days.

We woke up, went to work, came home, kept our pagers near, and waited. And waited.

And waited. The calls never materialized. The Olympic spectators turned out to be just that. They didn't come to Utah to ski or hike or climb, but to watch.

Finally, after half the games had slipped by, half the races won, medals awarded, podiums occupied while national anthems from around the world played in the background, the pager finally went off.

A car had been found in the Jordan River.

We arrived on scene and divers checked for bodies in the vehicle but found nothing. While others towed the car from the water, Lora and I along with other teams scouted the muddy river banks, looking for tracks of anyone who had climbed out.

With the car out of the river, a deputy ran the plates and found that the car had been stolen and abandoned.

The rest of the Olympics passed without incident.

13 CABLES

The world looks different from the air, and blatant geographical features like telephone poles and wires - which can hardly be missed from the ground as they jut upward and slice the sky into pieces - can look practically invisible from a helicopter.

Many years ago, before a spring avalanche demolished most of the tram at Bridal Veil Falls, before an autumn fire burned down the building at the top, and before the Sheriff required the tram owners to cut down the remaining cable which hung in the sky, a catastrophe was averted only by an act of God.

Someone was seriously injured near the falls and a medical chopper landed in the Bridal Veil parking lot for quick transportation to a trauma center.

Medical helicopters are flown by expert pilots, often with military experience, and their extensive competence allows them to handle situations which may prove too dangerous for lesser pilots. We know this and it inspires confidence when we trust our lives to their care as they sometimes shuttle us up and down the mountain or donate many hours of flight time to search efforts.

Once on the ground, a team member spoke to the pilot, his respect and admiration glowing from his face as he raised an eyebrow and nodded upward toward the sky.

"That was some pretty fancy flying up there," he said, nodding upward, "passing right between those two sets of cables like that." The gap barely left room for the aircraft's spinning rotors.

The pilot's face blanched. "What TWO sets?"

We never used that spot for a landing zone again.

Gazing up
Provo Canyon's
Bridal Veil Falls

14 FIREWORKS

By mid-summer of my third year on the team, I had begun to question whether I should stay. I only recently began to learn how to say "no" to every enticing opportunity that came knocking and I needed to scale back on my commitments. I was a real estate agent, a real estate appraiser, a university English teacher, and a few other things on the side. I felt busy and stressed and started looking for a way to lighten the load.

Besides, I wasn't sure how much difference I made on the team. I could count on one hand the times I made a difference in a rescue that someone else couldn't have done just as well had I not been around. Nearly all rescues are team efforts and rarely does any single person make a significant difference on their own.

Then something happened that changed my mind, and I decided to stay.

July 24 is a Utah holiday – Pioneer Day. Parades full of marching bands, floats, and covered wagons surrounded by pioneers in period dress march down Main Streets, and families picnic, hike, and go to the lake.

My new friend Amy and I took my Hobie 16 sailboat to Bird Island on Utah Lake. Winds blew steadily enough to scoot us across the lake's rippled surface, but not stoutly enough to fly one of the long aqua-blue pontoons as the boat heeled against the breeze.

After a few hours of sailing and exploring the tiny island, we headed back south toward Lincoln Marina. The southwest wind meant that heading directly back to the marina, almost directly into the wind, would be slow and uneventful, so we took our time on long east-west tacks as the wind mounted ahead of an oncoming frontal passage.

As we turned west for our final tack, a monster crawled out of the West Desert. It towered hundreds of feet into the sky and consisted of thick brown-and-gray dust clouds blown up by powerful

Bird Island and sailing Utah Lake

winds. Clearly, this was one big storm front - the kind that rips shingles from houses and fills the sky with them like flocks of giant, drunken bats. The kind that builds four foot waves in twenty minutes. The kind whose potential microbursts wreak havoc with structures and knock over decades-old stands of trees.

The mounting wind sang in the wires that vibrated and hummed as it passed. Amy and I sat along the port edge of the raised trampoline canvas as our speed climbed above 20 knots - wonderfully fast for a sailboat. Sitting mere inches above the waves made our velocity even more apparent and Amy screamed her excitement into the wind.

I wasn't worried. *What's the worst that could happen?* I thought, but decided to take one more tack closer to shore just in case. Then we could hop out and walk the boat to the beach to wait out the frontal passage if we wanted. If things got bad.

"Ready about?" I quizzed. I had already taught Amy all the necessary sailing jargon and she knew just what to do.

"Ready!" she assured me.

"Coming about!" I cried, and jammed the tiller to starboard, turning the bows into the wind as Amy scooted toward the center of the boat and ducked the boom as it swung overhead toward us.

Unfortunately, Hobies don't come about very well. The sharp dual hulls dig into the water like knives and don't spin around as easily as normal, wider, flatter, dish-like sailboat hulls. The boat stalled without rounding enough to backfill the jib and finish our direction change.

"Let's try that again," I said, and let the wind blow us back perpendicular to its course to build up speed and give it another go.

Unfortunately, I forgot to remind Amy to scoot back to the boat's edge with me, and unfortunately, that's when a powerful burst of wind struck the sails.

It must have been quite a gust as everything happened very quickly. I don't even remember flying through the air and splashing into the water near the sail. The next thing I remember is laughing and sputtering a bit as we rose to the surface. The boat lay on its side, the tip of the mast in the water, one pontoon floating on the lake surface with the other six feet in the air.

"Woohoo!" Amy shouted as she wiped the water from her eyes, then grabbed hold of the mast and pulled herself through the water toward me. I laughed and felt impressed at how well she was taking our little mishap.

Tipping over a Hobie Cat is not a problem. They're made to do that. If you never capsize, you're probably not sailing hard enough or in enough wind to fully enjoy the craft's potential. To right it, you simply spin the bows into the wind and lean back on the righting line. The sails slowly spill any water piled on top of them and the boat pops upright before you know it.

The thing to watch out for is turtling - tipping all the way upside down. That's trickier to get out of. You can install an anti-turtle device which prevents turtling with extra flotation on the tip of the mast, but that's hardly necessary in Utah Lake. After all, the mast is 26 feet tall, and the lake only 12 feet deep.

Unfortunately, that introduces another problem. When the stout winds pushed against the raised pontoon and canvas trampoline, the mast rotated down into the water and jammed in the mud. Two-foot waves hammered it deeper with every stroke. Before I realized it, the mast was hopelessly stuck in the clay lake bottom.

After half an hour of struggling, of following the wire stays up the mast and trying to lift and break it free by kicking my feet futiley against the water, I finally admitted we might be in a bit of trouble. I considered taking off my PFD and diving underwater to dig out the mast, but something about the dark, murky depths made me uncomfortable, and taking off my PFD in the middle of the lake didn't seem like the best idea. Better to play it safe.

I finally unscrewed the hatch cover in one hull and pulled out my radio. I turned it on and spoke. "Any unit, 750."

"This is 706, go ahead 750."

"Would you mind sending out a couple of wave runners a mile due east of Lincoln Beach?"

Unfortunately, the team rarely does limited responses and everyone loves lake rescues. A page sent half the team and half a dozen watercraft in our direction. Mercifully, my radio batteries soon died and I missed out the abundant teasing that probably continued nonstop. At least I was first on scene and no one could take that accomplishment away.

Even after radioing for help, I kept trying. I didn't want to give up. I hoped to work everything out before anyone arrived and not need their help after all.

"Give me your hand," Amy finally said, sitting on the lower pontoon with her legs dangling comfortably in the warm water.

"Do you want a hand up?" I asked.

"I want you to sit down."

I smiled and obeyed. She was right. The mast wasn't going anywhere. I may as well relax.

Night soon fell and we watched the sunset reflect on the water to the west and the city lights rise to the north and east. Fireworks celebrations in several cities began just after dark, and brilliant red, blue and green explosions shimmered on smooth waves, the front having passed long ago and the wind dying completely. Amy and I talked and her sharp, sarcastic wit kept me laughing and enjoying our evening together.

At last I saw a set of lights head north from the marina. I stood up so they could see the flashing beacon attached to the shoulder of my PFD, and they turned and drove toward us.

As Jared's watercraft slowed and settled into the water alongside the boat, I was struck by how *impressive* he looked! Others arrived immediately after, their headlights shining in the night as they slowed and stopped nearby.

One team member urgently wanted to load us up and rush us back to the marina.

"No!" I objected. "Help me get my boat up."

There was no hurry. The night was warm and pleasant. Amy and I were comfortable and had plenty of food and water aboard. We could stay out all night if we wanted. We could easily swim to shore and walk to the marina if we chose.

And then it struck me. *If SAR looks that cool and we're not even in trouble, how must we look to people enduring the worst day of their lives?* The injured people in great pain or distress or who would die without us? *This is important,* I thought. *This matters. I'm staying.*

From that moment on, I never considered quitting SAR again.

SAR to the rescue

15 DIY

In hindsight, I shouldn't have called for help, but I didn't know any better. "Experience is what you get," they say, "just after you need it."

When Jared's watercraft arrived, I swam over and climbed aboard. I held a wire side stay running up the sailboat's mast and walked myself up it, lifting hard, and with the watercraft's flotation, slowly broke the mast tip free from the clay lake bottom.

With no wind to sail back with, someone tossed me a throw bag and Amy climbed aboard Ken's watercraft while I got towed and steered the boat.

"So," Ken asked as we got underway, "are you ever going out with Shaun again?"

"I don't know about Shaun," Amy replied coyly, "but what about you? Want to go get lost?"

Back at the Marina, Alan asked her the same question. "*Shaun?!*" she exclaimed in mock surprise. "He said his name was François and he'd get me a part in a movie if I sailed to Bird Island with him!"

Amy's charisma took the heat off me for the evening, but that would not be the end of it. To our victims, even ones who demonstrate poor judgment, we offer the courtesy of not mocking them. Maybe we crack a joke or two amongst ourselves, but then we let it go and forget about it. The same rules don't necessarily apply to each other.

Three or four team members have been rescued in the past. Some do stupid things and they get forgotten. Others becoming running jokes that continue long after the humor has been wrung out.

For a long time, I simply didn't react when teammates made lame jokes about the event, hoping they'd grow tired of the subject, but it didn't work. All these years later, Olin still likes to joke about "The Roundy Triangle." The tale grows taller with every telling.

"Shut up," I say, "that was funny about five years ago."

In hindsight, I should have taken off my PFD, dived to the murky lake bottom and dug the mast free of the clay mud. On a five-week sailing trip I later took from Aruba, through the Panama Canal, and up to Acapulco, my captain said that sailing is really about "moving from port to port, fixing things." It's about improvisation - making things work with whatever you've got on hand, because there's no other choice.

I should have handled the situation myself. I should have taken a lesson from the wise SAR member who once walked down a mountain with a broken leg rather than call on the team for help.

Ah, hindsight, why must you always come too late? Maybe someday I'll get sick of the lame jokes and quit the team after all.

16 CRAZY FOR SAR

A BYU student asked to attend our monthly business meeting and conduct a survey for a paper she was writing. She wanted to discover what motivates us to devote so much time, effort and our own money to SAR when the only reward we expect is the opportunity to trade in a good portion of holidays, weekends, days and nights for training, hard work, a few adventures, possibly getting out of a speeding ticket by an appreciative police officer, and the occasional heart-felt thank you from victims, their families, and strangers.

She passed out her survey and we began filling them out. The questions proved more difficult to answer than we anticipated.

Some questions asked if we were lonely. Others asked if we had any friends outside the organization and how often we participated in various risky behaviors. It seemed the only options her survey offered, the only assumptions she anticipated to explain our motivation, were that we were either social outcasts or crazy.

One by one, team members sat up straighter, backing away from the survey on the desk before them, and exchanged incredulous glances.

Perhaps she was a psychology student. Perhaps she was Freudian. After all, Freud postulated that life's top goal is survival, therefore any activity that puts life at risk is, by definition, insane.

Modern research shows that Freud's rudimentary understanding of human motivation left gaping holes. For example, psychologists now link the act of participating in sports to ancient survival-related activities like hunting.

They recognize that activity enhances mood, which, along with better health, makes us more attractive, thus increasing our chances at producing offspring, another survival impulse.

Numerous other studies show that, once basic needs are met, one of the largest motivational forces is to contribute to a cause bigger than oneself and make a positive difference in the world.

All these explanations may be true, but I'm content to enjoy the camaraderie, adventure, satisfaction of challenging work and an important job well done, and poetic expressions about the soul's need to explore, experience, expand and accomplish.

For example, even blind and deaf Helen Keller demonstrated keener insight than Freud when she famously quipped that "Life is either a daring adventure or nothing."

Do these kids look crazy for climbing a tree and risking a fall? Well, maybe a little.

17 ONWARD, UPWARD

Onward, upward,
Into the clouds we go,
Kicking hard steps
    Into summer-packed snow of
    Long-dormant avalanche beds.
Into the sky we climb,
Searching rocky cliffs,
    Thick, dark forest,
    Rivers, caves, and hidden nooks.
Grasses bend and show the way.
Dust in a meadow marks a passing.
We've never felt so glad
    To find a tiny piece of garbage
    A candy wrapper
    Littering nature's living room
    And leading us ever onward, upward.
Somewhere ahead,
Somewhere above,
A small boy is lost
    And alone,
    Afraid in the dark.
We are afraid, too.
    That it's already too late.
    That the boy moves too fast for us
    Escaping into the sky
    Before we can catch up
    And stop his soul from leaving.
Airy peaks scrape dark cloud bellies
    Drawing out heavy raindrops
    And itchy electric charges that
        Crack the sky in two,
        Blind the eyes,
        Deafen the ears,
        Momentarily or forever.

Hiking up the Primrose Cirque

We rush onward, upward
Hoping to arrive in time
    To stop a young spirit
    From leaving his body behind
    For his mother to cry over.
Onward, upward,
Kicking steps through dirt and weeds,
    Water and wood,
    On the off chance
    That nothing has yet been written
    In stone.

18 THE OLD COUPLE

"What's the toughest call you've ever been on?" a proby asked Olin.

Olin thought for a minute, then began his answer. "There was a couple in their 70s," he began, and several of us rolled our eyes and nodded our heads, recalling the incident and reliving the memory of our suffering that night.

"They climbed Timpanogos – made it all the way to the top!" Olin explained, his tone of voice revealing a note of admiration for their accomplishment, "but it took them over 24 hours. Their kids got worried after night fell, so they called us."

Olin went on to tell how we found the couple just a few miles up the Timpooneke Trail, shuffling along slowly in the dark, their flashlight batteries having died.

We greeted them amicably and gave them our backup headlamps. They shared fun sized candy bars with us and we continued a friendly conversation as we walked slowly down the trail.

"That was when we realized we were in trouble. When I say 'slowly,' I mean really, really, really slowly."

More nods and sighs from the crowd as if Olin were describing the last leg of a thousand-mile race.

"I thought I was going to lose my mind. We offered to carry them down in the litter, but they wanted to walk."

At this point in the rescue, I was walking behind Olin, taking up the rear of the shuffling crowd. I opened my chest pack looking for a piece of candy or anything to take my mind off the maddeningly slow pace.

Olin's face brightened as he reached the end of the story. "Then suddenly I heard Shaun's harmonica behind me."

My first song was about pioneer children who walked thousands of miles across the plains to Utah. I adjusted the tune's tempo to emphasize our predicament: "Pioneer children sang as they walked, and wallllllked, aaaaaannnnnddd wwwaaaaaaaaaallllllkked...."

"That literally saved my life," Olin said with a deep sigh.

19 Do Hard Things

If you ask me to list my all-time favorite call outs, the list will include two types of missions: fun and hard.

Fun calls include zipping across the lake on a watercraft on a bluebird summer afternoon and pulling an attractive girl from the water moments before she sinks below the waves where her boat capsized. She would catch her breath, discover a brand new perspective on life, and we would become fast friends on the ride back to the marina with her arms wrapped tightly around my waist. We would go on a picnic that weekend, fall madly in love, and live happily ever after.

Nothing remotely like this has ever happened to me, but I won't complain if it does.

Hard calls are not always fun. Their rewards come at the expense of fatigue, endurance, and technical challenges. They may include rushing up tall, steep mountains in dark, inclement weather, carrying a heavy pack filled with ropes, hardware, medical and survival gear on my back. They may include severely wounded victims who we must quickly transport through challenging terrain, knowing they will die if we don't. The next story, Upper Falls, makes a perfect example of all these.

I didn't always like hard things. I wanted everything easy and comfortable - who doesn't? But then something happened. I did hard things because I could not avoid them, and I learned. I changed my mind. I discovered the exciting, deeply-satisfying appeal of the word "challenge."

Sometimes the reward of doing difficult things comes in the act. There's a certain thrill in rock climbing, for example, when you stick a tiny hold and reach the next bolt or gear placement without falling.

More often, the reward happens after the fact. When I reached the 13,770' summit of the Grand Teton after climbing the full Exum Ridge, I had a splitting headache from dehydration. I looked down at Lupine Meadows and the anticipated elation did not materialize. I merely felt tired and uncomfortable. While planning the expedition, I often wished aloud that the Grand was a little taller to make it the highest point in the state. "Do you still wish it was 35' higher?" Chad asked as we sat down on the summit block.

My climbing partner reaches Wall Street on the Grand Teton

"This is high enough," I answered as I lay back and closed my eyes.

After returning to camp, packing up, dropping 7,000' and slowly swinging my 45 pound pack from my stiff and sore shoulders at the dirt parking lot, after taking a short nap in the shade while waiting for the rest of the climbing party to catch up, and after climbing into the car and starting down the highway toward home, I looked up. I saw what we had just accomplished. I noticed how thick the air was below 7,000', that I no longer had to catch my breath after a drink of water or saying a long sentence.

And I felt *good*. Happy. The hard part was over, the suffering and fatigue already fading from memory, and only the satisfaction of doing hard things remained.

Becoming converted to doing hard things doesn't mean I actively seek out difficulty and danger, but perhaps I'm wrong and my perspective has grown skewed. After solo climbing an extremely steep route 7,000' up Mount Timpanogos one spring, Chad asked me if it was hard. "Not really," I replied, "you just have to keep going."

"You never think anything's hard," he responded, "unless you can barely do it."

Maybe so. Maybe he's right. Maybe I hardly know the meaning of the word "hard" anymore. If that's true, I can't say that I mind the delusion.

11,000' on Timpanogos' steep west face

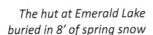

The hut at Emerald Lake buried in 8' of spring snow

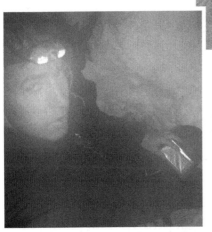

Camping in the Emerald Lake hut after digging in through the snow, and with only a foil blanket for a sleeping bag

Mount Timpanogos summit hut

Avalanches smooth out the cliffs below Timpanogos' summit

20 Upper Falls

Half a mile up canyon from Bridal Veil Falls, another dramatic multi-step waterfall spills down Cascade Peak's impressive north slope. Upper Falls ends with an 80' waterfall, while upstream, two drainages dump frothy-white water over dozens of waterfalls of all sizes.

"This place is *amazing!*" Laura said for the twentieth time. "Why don't people ever come here?"

"Duh!" answered Jesse with a mocking smile. The answer was obvious. No easy trail led up the rugged ravine. What trail existed crossed over exposed, sloped limestone slabs and up cliffs, scary enough to turn back most hikers. They scaled the first 20' cliff with the help of thick tree trunks and roots, and without ropes and trad gear to affix the rope to cracks in the rock, they'd never have reached the top of the 50' cliff where Patrick now belayed Jesse to the top.

Jesse found new hand and footholds on the cliff face, then crawled onto the wide ledge where Patrick stood next to a stout pine tree where he had tied a webbing anchor to belay from.

"It *is* amazing, though," he agreed. He stood up and untied the rope from his harness, then grabbed another rock hold to climb over the final four foot step to where Laura stood ten feet away on flatter ground. As he pulled, the rock popped free, and Jesse fell backward.

Laura gasped and reached out her hand uselessly, her eyes widening instinctively.

"Help me!" Jesse cried as he toppled over backward, but Patrick was facing the anchor and hadn't seen him, and so Jesse did not stop until he had fallen completely off the ledge, summersaulted backward through 50 feet of cool mountain air, and landed, on his face, on the jagged, broken rock below.

Laura stood frozen in her tracks. He eyes did not blink and she could only take shallow, rapid breaths. Meanwhile, Patrick immediately sprung into action. He tied off the rope securely to the anchor, said, "Don't move!" To Laura in a commanding voice, then jumped off the ledge toward Jesse's crumpled form below.

Patrick's belay device was still attached to the rope and his harness, and he rappelled down in seconds, pushing away from the cliff face with his feet, then letting the rope slide swiftly through his gear, and slowing again to make one more push away from the wall before landing on the rock below.

"Jesse!" he shouted as he disconnected from the rope and ran toward his friend.

Jesse moaned. The fall - or rather, the landing - had knocked him momentarily unconscious, and as he came around, he discovered sharp and intense pain filling his face, his neck, and what seemed like the rest of his body, too. Several bones in his face were broken, from his jaw to the orbit around his eye, and one eye was already too swollen to open more than just a slit.

"Where does it hurt, dude?" Patrick demanded.

"E'erywhere," Jesse muttered softly without opening his eyes or moving his jaw. He wanted to think through the rest of his body part by part to find out if anything else seemed broken, but the piercing, burning, throbbing pain in his face drew all his attention and he could barely focus on anything else.

"That's good! That's good! That's very good!" Patrick assured him.

"Cause I' ali'e?" Jesse breathed out, trying not to work his broken mandible.

"Yeah!" assured Patrick. "Alive and...not paralyzed. Don't move!"

Despite Patrick's instructions, Jesse flexed the fingers on both hands and wiggled his toes. They all seemed to work. At least nothing had broken off.

Patrick hiked down the ravine until he got a cell signal and dialed 911. He climbed back up the cliff and lowered Laura down, then walked her all the way to base of Upper Falls after checking on Jesse.

In the parking lot, I filled my pack with ropes and other technical gear, plus extra water, clothing, lights, and other essentials. ICS assigned me as on-scene command, and Patrick led us up the trail with North Fork Fire paramedics who would take charge of medical.

We climbed the steep trail as fast as we could manage. We followed Patrick over exposed, sloped ledges and up small cliffs. As we arrived on scene, a news helicopter hovered high overhead and splashed images of us dropping our packs and beginning to assess our patient on hundreds of thousands of glowing television screens tuned in to the evening news in warm, cozy living rooms around the state.

Jesse's face looked bad. He wore a mask of dark-crimson crusted blood, and heavy bruising left his face almost entirely black and blue. On the other hand, he could talk. He was alert and coherent. Once we established that he wasn't bleeding into his mouth, we worried less about the obvious external injuries though we couldn't be sure about any hidden internal injuries. Vital signs seemed strong enough and NFF would continue to monitor them to make sure they didn't turn downhill.

While Kenny and others finished up initial treatment and packaged Jesse in the litter that the next team had brought up the mountain, taking extra care to immobilize his spine and surrounding him with blankets and sleeping bags while maintaining easy access to the blood pressure cuff and IV, I evaluated the terrain.

I didn't want to carry him out the way we hiked in. We had climbed steeply sloped rock with virtually no protection available. The twenty-foot cliff choked with tree limbs would also prove extremely difficult to manage. A route straight down the bottom of the canyon would be the better choice.

Six cliffs complete with waterfalls separated us from the highway and the waiting ambulance. A carry out would present significant technical challenges, but we could deal with that.

Best of all, of course, would be to have Life Flight lift Jesse out with their hoist, but evening was falling hard and the day didn't have enough light left for a helicopter to negotiate the narrow canyon. If we wanted an air lift, we'd have to wait till morning.

We could choose to sit and wait, monitoring vital signs to make sure they didn't trend down; but if Jesse began to crash, there wasn't a whole lot we could do to save him this high on the mountain. If our patient died of hidden internal injuries, I would have a difficult time ever forgiving myself for not trying harder.

The decision didn't take long to make. "CP, on scene command," I called into the radio, "we're coming down. We could use all the help and two-hundred footers we can get up here."

By the time we had our first lowering station tied to rocks and tree roots and started down the mountain, the last few minutes of light were draining from the sky. Six rescuers picked up the litter and the attendant near Jesse's head made the calls.

"Down slow," he commanded.

"Down slow," repeated the team member at the lowering station who then loosened his grip on the rope and let it slip slowly through the steel bars of the brake rack. Everyone walked carefully down the loose rock as the rope played out.

The first pitch proved relatively easy and set a good tone for the rest of the night. We dropped over a small cliff and stopped atop a steeper slope where a stream tumbled down mossy rock and fallen logs. We transferred the rope to the second lowering station tied to a pine tree just up the slope. When I noticed a hint of confusion among the new team members who tied the anchor, I assigned an experienced mountaineer as safety officer, charged with double checking all systems.

The second pitch took us down a forty-five-degree slope. Once again, six of us gripped the rail and began to walk slowly down to the next station. We chose our path around the steepest dirt slopes and thick wild roses and their tiny thorns. We navigated slippery moss-covered slabs and debris piled up by avalanches.

"Watch out for the log," someone said, warning other attendants of approaching obstacles.

"Thanks," I replied, stepping carefully over the obstruction. CJ, one of my SAR mentors, once taught me that polite words like "please" and "thank you" can significantly decrease tension in stressful situations and I put his advice to good use.

The team continued communicating clearly as we navigated obstacles and steadily made our way down. "Let's move to the left around this spot," someone requested. "I have to let go for a second - you guys got it?" someone asked. "Got it," others answered. "Go ahead." This continued for over a hundred feet.

"You guys did *perfect!*" I told everyone once we reached the next station and set the litter on a small, flat ledge. "That couldn't have gone any more smoothly!"

Then we reaped an unexpected reward for our care and communication. A muffled voice called out from deep inside the litter package. "I love you guys!" Jesse exclaimed.

I tried to imagine how helpless and vulnerable he must feel, completely immobilized while being jostled down a treacherous slope in the dark. Even if we hadn't covered his face to protect him from any potential rock fall, the darkness would prevent him from seeing anything but headlamps and a few distant stars. The throbbing pain he must be experiencing wouldn't help, either. All he had to guide him were our comforting voices, our reassurance that things were going according to plan.

Hours passed quickly as we worked on through the night. Team members set up lowering stations above each waterfall, the rest of which went vertical, with each drop higher than the last - twenty, forty, then sixty feet. Before the last two cliffs, another drainage joined ours and the flow of the stream tripled.

We managed challenges like keeping the litter out of the water's spray when the terrain didn't allow us to set up far away from the falls, shuffling rescuers forward down the ropes to carry the litter to the next station, working short handed where a dozen more hands would have lightened the load considerably, and clearing edges from potential rock fall that would endanger victim and attendant during a lower.

The last carry crossed such a steep side slope that we set up a rope to prevent catastrophic failure if we happened to slip in the hard dirt. This carry was the most exhausting, both due to the terrain and because it came after eight or nine hours of constant exertion.

Olin had rigged the final lowering station around a four-foot-wide pine tree for the last eighty foot cliff, and I sent Jesse over the edge with a medic to a fresh crew at the base of the falls. A tag line affixed to the litter would pull them clear of the stream at the base of the falls, and new hands would then carry him down the rocky trail to a waiting ambulance.

Once everyone below had moved clear of any potential rock fall, the mountain crew rappelled, one after another, down the cliff. As I awaited my turn - the last to go - I looked up and saw the first faint light of dawn appearing in the slice of sky above. My job had finally ended and I took a deep, relaxing breath. Only then did I notice how thoroughly tired I felt.

By the time I rappelled down, pulled the ropes, and hiked down the trail to the parking lot, the ambulance and most team members had gone home. It was time for breakfast, a shower, and another day at work. To the world around us, it was just another day. To those of us who spent ten hours on the mountain, the days blurred together into one.

The sky was painted a clear, even light blue and the sun would rise soon. I tossed my pack into the back seat of my 4Runner and climbed wearily into the driver's seat.

I felt tired but satisfied. I loved this mission because it was hard. Because it was technically and physically challenging. I loved the smooth, effective teamwork. I loved that I got to make a contribution, to make a difference, and the fact that everything worked out so well in the end.

I turned the key and started the engine, and found the radio tuned to a local high school station that runs no commercials but lots of public service announcements. A PSA had just begun encouraging listeners to donate blood.

"Today, I mowed the lawn," said a man's voice. "I cleaned my room," announced a teenage girl. "I ran five miles and finished reading a book," a woman's voice added, and then, "Oh," her voice appended, as if it were merely an afterthought, "and I saved a life." "I saved a life," repeated the teen and man.

So did I, I thought, and it felt pretty darn good.

21 THAT SINKING FEELING

A boater called 911 from Utah Lake and reported that his boat was sinking. "We're in three feet of water!" he said urgently.

The day was sunny and calm, and even though we didn't think of three feet of water as a serious threat, we took our mission seriously and scrambled watercraft and boat teams racing around the hundred-mile perimeter of the lake looking for a boat in three feet of water.

Suddenly I saw Chris veer away from us and head toward the center of the lake. I stopped my PWC so I could hear my radio and verified that he knew something I didn't. He did.

It turns out the boat was three or four miles out, in the middle of the lake. The three feet of water described was INSIDE the boat! Outside, the depth was ten to twelve feet, the average depth of the entire lake.

State Parks arrived on scene and took all passengers aboard their Boston Whaler, and we towed the sinking boat back to the harbor, which fortunately managed to remain upright and even drained some water as the forward motion lifted the hull several inches higher above the lake surface.

22 THE 19 ESSENTIALS

"The Ten Essentials" lists items that help keep you safe and comfortable in the great outdoors. It originated in the 30's and you can find many variations of the list today. Lists often contain more than ten items.

The "ten" essentials can't prevent all accidents, but even when things go wrong that a band aid or signal mirror won't solve, these items can keep you safer and more comfortable while you deal with the emergency or wait for rescue.

If we have to rescue you and you're reasonably well prepared, you'll enjoy our sincere compliments rather than possibly feeling dorky for not heeding this advice.

1. Map: if you're hiking along the face of Mount Timpanogos where you can look down and spot your house at any moment, a map might not be that useful. If you don't know how to find north, triangulate landmarks, or understand all those wavy lines and green splotches on a topographical map, it also won't help. But if you're deep in the back country and you lose the trail, a map can stop you from marching for miles in the wrong direction.

Deep in the mountains, every little ridge and peak can look the same and you can easily find yourself disoriented. A map can point you in the right direction and add enough confidence to keep you calm as you make your way back to the car.

2. Compass: one nice thing about compasses is that they never run out of batteries. Even if you don't know where you are, you can at least keep from walking in circles.

3. GPS: Global Positioning Satellite receivers not only tell you where you are, but point out where other things are, how long it will take to get there, and where you've been. Look up waypoints and load them into your unit before leaving on your hike.

What GPS may not tell you is where cliffs and other obstacles are. They also don't work well in narrow canyons where they don't have a clear view of the open sky.

4. Extra batteries: unless you have an analog GPS (open the cover and look at the ground through a hole labeled "You Are Here ->"), they'll eventually need new batteries. So will your flashlight. Be prepared.

5. Sunscreen: sunburn not only hurts, but it drains your energy and can make you feel sick and weak. Sunscreen also prevents one of the most dangerous types of cancer - which is the last thing you want to get while hiking!

6. Sunglasses: sunburned eyes HURT! Take care of those baby blues... or greens or browns or whatever you've got. Also, sunglasses prevent premature wrinkles and make you look cool.

7. Food: bring more than you think you'll need. Calories keep you energized and warm.

8. Water: some hikers resist drinking water on the trail because the only bathrooms look like rocks and pine trees. Yeah, that's the great outdoors for you. Totally uncivilized. But if you venture here, you must abide by the rules. If you don't drink enough water, you can get weak, cramped, and suffer miserable headaches. Drink! Even in cool weather when you don't feel thirsty, your body still needs liquids to function.

The 8 oz per day rule that you hear has no identifiable source. It may be a good rule of thumb when you're sitting around your office and living room all day, but strenuous hiking may require much more.

You may also have heard that soft drinks and juices don't count, but again, no official medical research supports this assertion.

If you have a water filter, make sure you're aware of water sources along your route.

9: Extra clothing: The day may be warm and sunny in the parking lot, but the evening at altitude may be cool or downright miserable. Weather can change quickly and threaten your life more easily than you think if you're not prepared.

It's not just about bringing along a jacket or rain slicker - also pay attention to the materials. Cotton is known as "killer cloth" on the mountain. When wet, either from rain, puddle jumping, or sweat, it draws heat away from the body in order to dry, and it dries very slowly. Wool retains thermal protection when wet, but can be too warm when not needed. Synthetics like nylon and polyester, including fleece for jackets, are advisable in most circumstances.

Shoes also deserve mention. Flower-covered flip flops may be cute, but are not designed for rugged hiking. Wear something more appropriate.

10. Flashlight: you may PLAN to get back before dark, but things don't always work out that way. What if you get lost? What if you twist your ankle? What if you discover an ancient Spanish cache of Inca gold in a hidden cave? You'll be glad you were prepared. Also see Batteries.

11. First Aid Kit: athletic tape is my favorite first aid item. It can support twisted ankles, cover hot spots to prevent them from turning into full blown blisters (if you've got a blister, cover it with something before applying the tape so the tape won't rip that skin off), and even perform first aid on back packs and other items. Aspirin, band aids, gauze, and other items are also nice. Benadryl caplets can be opened and applied directly to the skin for rashes from bug or plant allergens.

12. Fire starters: matches are great, but can get wet. Lighters are fantastic but butane doesn't burn well in extreme cold. My favorite backup is a flint and steel kit along with a film canister packed with vaseline-soaked cotton balls. Spread out a piece of cotton so there's plenty of air in it, and a single spark delivers a flame that will burn long enough to ignite kindling.

13: Knife: knives do all sorts of things. They build shelters, spread peanut butter, and more.

14: Cell phone: you'd be surprised how many back country areas get reception. If you need to make a call, try hiking up an easy hill to check for even a single bar. Because your battery wears down faster if the phone is always looking for a connection, turn your phone off when out of range.

Even if your phone doesn't have a service plan, it will still work for calls to 911. Just make sure the battery is charged.

Cell phones often work well as emergency flashlights, and its screen can be seen from over a mile away. Several times we've asked victims to flash their phone toward us to help spot them on a dark, distant cliff. Helicopters with night vision can also spot the light from a long ways off.

If you come home long overdue and your mom is known to worry about you, be sure to call and let her know you're safe. That's to be kind to her after all she's done for you, and kind to us, since we may otherwise spend all night outside looking for you.

15: Whistle: a whistle can be heard much farther than shouting. Three quick blasts in succession means emergency. If you hear us blowing a whistle to get your attention and you have a whistle, blast that thing like crazy and we'll find you a whole lot faster.

16: Signal mirror: you'd be surprised how blindlingly brilliant a small mirror reflects the sun toward a search plane or helicopter. If your signal mirror has a tiny hole in the center, then look through that hole at whoever's attention you're trying to get. Hold out one thumb toward the plane and adjust the mirror until the sun reflects against it. You'll then know that whatever's directly behind your thumb is also getting flashed.

17: Toilet paper: TP can be worth its weight in gold - or twinkies or granola bars if someone else forgot to bring some. It prevents you from needing to rely on nature's alternatives: leaves (be sure to know your poisonous plants), rocks, snow.... In most cases, bury your waste 3-6" deep. In heavily trafficked areas, pack your paper (or everything) out with you.

18: PFD: if you're in any kind of water, a Personal Flotation Device can save your life. It's the one thing that would have prevented more of the fatal accidents I've seen in all my years of SAR than any other protective gear. Don't just have it nearby, wear it, and PLEASE make sure your kids do, too.

19: Your brain: don't just carry your brain with you, keep it turned on. Don't let bluebird skies and perfect temperatures skew your judgment about what's safe and what's not. Think. Evaluate. Don't take dangerous risks just to impress your friends or that hot guy/girl. If "everyone else is doing it," they'll need someone to return home and tell the sad story of whatever happened to them.

*SST riders take a break near the top of Big Springs
on the way to Lightning Pass*

A sailboat irons out the ripples on a calm Utah Lake

23 Rescue Mode

Josh stood atop the 400' cliff at the mouth of Provo Canyon. His heart ached. Beth, his girlfriend of nine months, had left him, and the migraine heartache that followed left him an utter wreck.

He couldn't sleep. His appetite all but vanished. Nothing seemed fun or interesting, and some days he couldn't seem to drag himself out of bed to go to work. After a series of warnings, his manager finally let him go.

Josh's whole world was splintering and crashing down around his feet. He had nothing left to live for and the very concept of 'hope' became so foreign that he couldn't imagine it would ever return. He couldn't imagine the pain would ever end, and he just couldn't take it anymore.

A light canyon breeze tousled his hair, blowing it from before his eyes, and he looked down. Every time he glanced down, the fear leapt into his throat - it was the first emotion other than exquisite heartache that he had experienced for weeks, and it felt good. It felt like relief.

His took a small step forward, his toes now two or three inches from the edge of the world, and felt his blood pressure rise and heart beating wildly in his throat. It felt good. It felt better than the pain.

If only he could cry and let it all out! If only he could scream and shout out all the anguish pent up inside. Maybe then all the heart-wrenching ache would go away! But the feelings got trapped inside and wouldn't come out. They felt like someone had crammed a giant, splinter-filled stake down his throat and straight through his heart. They felt sharp and raw and he just couldn't take it anymore.

Josh had stood on the cliff edge for over an hour now, deciding. There was no pro and con list. No rational back and forth arguing. No words, even; only feelings. Only sensing the heartache rise and the fear beat it back down. Only waiting for one side or the other - win or die, jump or go home - to determine his next step. Either way, it would be the first step of the rest of his life.

Going home meant the suffering would continue. Maybe not forever, but how could he know that? Jumping meant the pain would end. Oh, there might be a moment of a new kind of pain, but it wouldn't last long.

Another hour passed and at last the truth grew clear. He wanted to jump. He was only waiting for the courage or commitment to go through with it.

With that decision made, his brain returned to a more rational state. *I should at least say goodbye,* he thought. He wanted to call Beth, but she never answered the phone anyway. She was tired of his whining, she had told him. "Get over it," were her last words as she hung up the phone. He wanted to call his little brother and tell him how much he loved him, but he couldn't face talking to him and telling him he was a quitter. He couldn't call Mom, she'd freak out and blame herself when she failed to talk him out of going through with it. He didn't want to call his friends, either. He had blown them off for weeks, ignoring their calls and leaving messages unanswered, and it seemed rude to only call now. Besides, admitting that he was about to kill himself because he felt bad made him sound so pathetic.

Josh stood with his phone in his hand for several minutes wondering who would want to talk to him, and then it came to him. He dialed 911.

"I'm going to jump," he announced when the dispatcher answered.

The voice on the end of the line remained calm. He appreciated that. "Will you talk with someone first?" she asked in level tones.

"Okay," Josh agreed. The dispatcher asked a few questions about his name and location and then promised to connect him to someone to talk to.

"Josh," a man's voice came on the line, "I hear you're going through some tough times."

"Yeah," Josh agreed.

"I understand," the man assured him. "Shit happens. We all go through a little of that. Do you want to tell me about it?"

Josh thought over what to say. His girlfriend dumped him. He lost his job. He felt bad. It all sounded so trite. He felt like a fool for making such a big deal about it. "I don't know," he finally said. "Everything sucks. I can't take it anymore."

"I see," said the voice on the phone. "Yeah, I remember days like that."

"It's not just days!" Josh shouted into the phone. "It's months! And it's not getting any better!" Maybe it was a mistake to call the cops. What could they do, anyway? What did they know?

"What was her name?" the voice guessed. The question caught Josh off guard.

"Beth," he answered reluctantly.

"Was she pretty?"

"Yeah."

And thus began a two hour conversation. Josh sensed that the cop was just buying time, trying to keep him busy until he calmed down and changed his mind about jumping. He didn't care. He had time. After a while, he spotted the police cruiser park alongside the highway and the blue-uniformed officer stroll down the River Trail until he stood, one hand holding a phone to his ear, looking straight up the cliff toward his silhouette.

"Look Josh," the detective finally said, "I don't know everything, but one thing I do know - everyone goes through tough times, but they always pass. *Always!* Yours will, too."

"I don't know that!" Josh cried, his emotion finally breaking. "I don't know if they will!"

"Why don't you come down and talk to me. I can help you find a great job and introduce you to some girls. There are hundreds of pretty girls around here, ya know?"

That thought made everything worse. The idea of loving again, of opening his heart and risking another javelin being tossed through it sent a surge of fear rising up in his throat. *Love always turns into pain,* he thought. *Always!*

"I can't do it," Josh told the detective. "I'm sorry, I just can't. Tell everyone I'm sorry."

"Josh, listen to me," the detective tried, sensing the sudden change in tone, but Josh had stopped listening.

"Tell my mom that I love her. And tell Beth I love her more than she'll ever know. And my brother Cody, I love him, too, and he can have my motorcycle. And tell him I'm sorry, I'm so sorry, and that he should never quit like me."

"If you jump off that cliff, you will hurt them much worse than Beth hurt you!" the detective said urgently, trying a new tactic.

"Don't say that!" Josh cried. "I don't want to hear that!"

"It doesn't matter if I say it or not, Josh; it's the truth, and you're the only one who can save them."

"Shut up!" Josh commanded. "Leave me alone! You can't stop me!"

"You know this is a bad idea, Josh! You're in no state to make a decision like this right now!" the detective shouted into the phone, but the only sound on the other end now was a rush of wind as the phone fell and fell and fell and finally broke against the talus slope below.

Standing at the top of the cliff, Josh's heart beat wildly. Adrenaline raced through his arteries but it wouldn't remove the pain anymore. "I just want it to end!" he cried, and stepped out onto the breeze.

As his body passed the point of no return, a series of bright memories flashed before his mind's eye.

A summer afternoon as a child. A green lawn in front of a yellow house with aluminum siding. His father held the hose and sprayed cold water as he and his brother ran shrieking for cover. His mother stood smiling on the porch. Seven-year-old Josh ran around the corner of the house laughing.

He had forgotten all about those long-past happy days. Life had grown so much more complicated than it seemed back then. Josh would have taken a step backward, but the grey, broken limestone cliff face was flying past him now, the cool evening breeze whistling in his ears and blinding his eyes with tears.

Another memory.

Deep blue water and sky cut in half by red sandstone cliffs. A ski boat at Lake Powell. Josh stood on the transom and raised his deeply tanned and muscular arms into the air. The sun felt warm against his sunburned neck and back.

"I'll show you idiots how it's done!" he bragged to his friends, then bent his knees and dove forward into the lake, landing perfectly and barely making a splash. "Throw me the wake board," he commanded as he surfaced twenty feet from the boat. "And get your cameras ready, because you're about to witness a perfect back flip!"

The Lake Powell memory vanished when Josh grazed the cement edge of the water pipe ledge after 200' of freefall. From there everything happened very quickly. He hit the sloped cliff below and tumbled another 200' to stop on a wide ledge. His thoughts and memories vanished long before his limp body rolled to a stop.

When I climbed to the spot where Josh's body lay in a small pool of blood, an Orem fire fighter and police officer stood next to him and took pictures for their report. The fifteen-foot-wide ledge stood atop another fifty foot sheer cliff of black and orange quartzite.

Down on the River Trail, news cameras pointed toward us, but I knew they would not air this story. Perhaps due to its sensitive nature. Perhaps out of respect to the family. Perhaps because they know that when suicides get publicized, others follow suit, and no one wants that. Also perhaps because they understand that the law enforcement agencies involved don't want this news aired, and the news stations' cooperation would ensure continued access to future news events.

I glanced at Josh's hollow stare and experienced a fleeting uneasy sensation. I was unaccustomed to seeing a human face without sensing the soul living behind it. Josh's eyes were open, but empty and cold. The living part of him had gone. I looked away.

When I looked back, the awkwardness was gone. My mode had changed.

A coworker's son, after hearing about some of the unsettling situations I encounter on search and rescue, once asked his mother how I managed. "Is there something wrong with him? Does he have feelings?"

My solution for dealing with queasy situations is a mindset I call 'rescue mode.' Something switches in my brain and I only see the task at hand, the job to do. Everything else gets tuned out.

In this case, the only thing that mattered now was the surviving family, and our job was to bring Josh down with all the dignity possible.

When a few more SAR members made their way to the cliff, we zipped Josh into a thick plastic body bag and strapped him into the litter, then rigged a simple lowering system tied to trees next to the cliff seventy feet away. Four of us carried his body across the wide ledge, then let the rope ease us down the steep, loose slope to the canyon floor.

Once we reached the flatter ground on the canyon floor, Josh's brother approached the group. His face remained determinedly stoic, but his eyes burned with a fiery combination of grief, love, loss, and a determination to help, to serve his lost brother in the last way he would ever have the chance to do.

I knew what lay in wait for this loving, anguished brother. Pain, regret, and probably pointless self incrimination would give way to days of anger and blame before acceptance arrived; and, possibly, eventually, peace.

I stepped away from my place on the litter and let the brother take my place.

Olin and I soon drove to the top of the cliff, tied off a pair of 200' ropes to our vehicles, and rappelled the cliff, breaking away loose rock as we went so the rope would jar nothing loose and send it down onto our helmets. We searched the slope for Josh's missing wallet and keys, but found nothing but the disturbed, blood-speckled dirt and talus where an aching young man threw his life away.

Rappelling 400' looking for evidence

24 DEATH

An email from Tom following the drowning of an eight-year-old boy:

Good morning everyone,

First of all, I want to reaffirm to each and every one of you how incredible it is to work with a team such as ours.

Secondly, I would like to thank each of you for the professionalism and respect you displayed during last evening's tragic call. What you do, each and every day, touches the life of someone that you may not even know.

Such was the case last night, with the tragic drowning of yet another small child. I have been involved in law enforcement work for over thirty years now, 25 of them here at the Sheriff's Office, and I can tell you, firsthand, that it simply doesn't get any easier to deal with what you endured last night. Death affects each of us. And, oftentimes, there is simply no easy way to deal with it. For me, as with many of you, the death of a child simply magnifies our emotions and thoughts.

While the child, Landon, was being brought out of the river last night, I saw several of you, both veteran members and new support members assisting silently with whatever task your were doing. I saw some troubled faces. I saw that some of you, myself included, were dealing with some emotions we don't like to visit. We've all heard the adage that it's "human nature" to have those feelings and emotions. And though that may be certainly true, scenarios that we deal with in search and rescue sometimes leave us wounded. We carry the emotional scars of things that we see, and things that we do. As David Lynton stated in his earlier email, what is not healthy is holding these emotions in.

We all deal with issues in different ways. And quite often, just talking to a spouse or loved one can remedy what you are dealing with. However, sometimes that is not enough. Therefore, I would like to remind all of you that the Sheriff's Office can offer assistance if you need it. You don't have to talk to Collin or I, but if you make the call to me I can steer you in the right direction to much better trained people than myself to help you.

Thanks again everyone. And on behalf of all of those people who you help, for the unselfish services you provide, and for the spirit in your hearts, I thank you. As does the Sheriff's Office. I am proud of this team.

Again, please don't hesitate for a moment to call me if you need additional resources to assist you. Our health, both physical and emotional, is a true gift. I want to make sure yours remains intact. Or you simply call me if you wish, because believe it or not, I have sometimes been accused of being a good listener....

I am in awe of each of you, and thank you for giving me the honor to work alongside you....

Tom

Looking down through Rock Canyon from Lightning Pass

Near the top of Lightning Pass

25 THOROUGH

Fire fighters and SAR search differently than police, a mentor once explained to me. We search for victims, they search for threats.

When two little girls went missing from a Springville home one summer afternoon, CJ arrived first and insisted on searching the house.

"We already checked it," the police assured him.

"I'd like to check it again," CJ explained.

We learned our lesson a few months earlier in a three-day search for a missing autistic boy in a Pleasant Grove neighborhood. Local officials assured us they had searched all nearby cars, but that's where we found the boy, alive though severely dehydrated, in the trunk of a car that had been parked elsewhere during the initial search.

Sure enough, CJ found the girls asleep in a closet under a pile of laundry.

When an octogenarian went missing from his Provo Bench home in early autumn, I found another reason to conduct a thorough search. Various reports had seen the man shuffling along the River Trail, and we combed every square inch of river, woods, canals, hills, parking lots, out buildings, and other features for miles and turned up nothing.

That night, Singletrack Special Team members were assigned to check the dirt roads and trails winding through the foothills above. I knew these trails intimately from dozens of afternoons spent hiking and mountain biking up and down their smooth contours. If the trails weren't closed to motorized vehicles, I would ride them on my motorcycle several times a week, but only emergencies like this allowed us to ride here, and not many people got lost in plain view of the highway running down the center of the canyon.

Despite reports that the missing man could barely shuffle along paved trail, much less climb high into the foothills, I thought it wise to check them thoroughly just in case. You never know, and we had nothing better to do.

Our headlights illuminated the narrow trail ahead and we effortlessly climbed the hillsides that gave my heart, lungs, and legs such a workout on a mountain bike. The night breeze caressed my face through my open helmet while rocketing along the straightaways, and I enjoyed the thrill of precise control while slowing and shifting my weight from one footpeg to the other as we rounded curve after curve, handlebars scraping thick scrub oak choking the trail from both sides, and occasionally stomping on the brakes to avoid running over a bird that had stopped to sleep in the trail.

We stopped to check any track traps like pools or dust or mud puddles left from recent rain, and continued to climb higher and higher into the foothills. We passed the dirt road that split the bowl horizontally and continued upward toward Little Baldy. Eventually, after thoroughly covering most of my favorite trails, we turned back and returned to CP.

At the MACC, Jared took our GPSs and downloaded our electronic cookie crumb trail to the cumulative map documenting everywhere we had searched, then stepped outside to return our electronics.

"You were certainly thorough," he observed.

"Naturally," I answered.

The next day, a passing motorist spotted an arm waving in the tall grass on a hillside in town that had been assigned to a police department to search. The old man had stumbled there and tumbled down the hillside, then couldn't get up. We rushed teams over with a litter to carry him up to an ambulance on the road, and the search ended.

A Singletrack rider on spring snow (above) and crossing Diamond Fork River (below) with an AED for a cardiac problem at the hot pots

26 STANDING WAVE

A fierce cold front blew through the valley one December evening, piling up five-foot waves on the lake and sinking a shallow-draft hunting boat, stranding its occupants, a father and son, on Bird Island.

I've heard of storms blowing so hard and long that the lake boundary moved a full mile inland, skewering carp on broken willow limbs three feet off the ground, and taking several days to drain and return the lake to its proper place.

We sent watercraft from Lincoln Beach to retrieve the stranded hunters. CJ and Jared covered the two miles to the island, driving more slowly than usual to avoid jumping each wave crest and slamming hard into the next one.

Besides, most watercraft seem designed in such a way that they project several gallons of water directly into the rider's eyes with enough force to knock the eyeballs loose from their sockets whenever the bow dives below the surface. Better to slow down and avoid such an inconvenience.

After circling the island, they located the hunters and loaded them onto the seats behind them. The boat would have to wait for better weather for retrieval. Turning back for Lincoln Beach, they enjoyed a smoother, faster ride with the trailing winds.

Until.

Until billions of gallons of lake water blown by the front to the south end of the lake came rushing back out of the darkness in a five-foot-tall standing wave.

CJ and Jared couldn't see the wave coming in the darkness. When it suddenly appeared in their headlamp beams, it loomed above them, all frothy white and churning. They had no time to react. The wave face was too steep for the watercraft to climb, and the cold water rolled clear over their heads in what must have been a very surprising moment for both riders and passengers.

The hunters held on tight and were not swept off the watercraft despite sputtering and coughing up lake water as they continued, wet and cold, toward waiting cars with warm heaters and blankets.

I was out of town that night, and this is one of the missions that make me jealous that I didn't get to experience. It sounds like fun and I want to know exactly how it looked and felt. I want to remember it every time I look toward the south end of the lake.

27 EMERGENCY

Mount Timpanogos' proximity to Utah Valley's half million residents, along with it's quality trails and scenic views, make it one of the most-visited peaks in the Rockies.

That doesn't make it *easy*. The most popular route climbs nearly 5,000 feet from Aspen Grove to a lofty 11,750' summit atop a 1,300' cliff.

Hikers often turn around at Emerald Lake, a shimmering gem at the base of the summit cliff and glacier, rather than continuing into the increasingly thin air to the top.

Such was the case with an obese woman who reached the lake one hot summer afternoon. Sheer determination had carried her up the long trail, and she didn't have the stamina to hike back down. She called 911 for help.

We hiked up the trail and found her among the small crowd at the rock hut overlooking the lake.

"We can only bring helicopters to wilderness areas for emergencies," we explained when she expressed her wishes to fly down.

"This *is* an emergency!" she argued.

We just smiled and offered to help her down the mountain.

SAR and NFF walk an ill, hypothermic patient down the Primrose Cirque

28 FALLEN HERO

"This is world-class rescue," I thought as another fist-sized rock careened down the narrow gully, ricocheting off quartzite walls, and zinged by overhead. Darkness fell half an hour ago and all I saw now were smooth, vertical cliffs to either side and the ten-foot-wide, forty-five-degree slope we climbed toward the probably-dead Russian hero.

Who could say how far up the ravine the rockfall originated? Every time we heard it coming, crashing like tiny cannonballs shot recklessly down a castle hallway, we ducked behind a boulder, deflected them with the plastic backboard, or pressed our bodies against shallow corners in the ravine walls, hoping they would provide enough shelter from the shooting gallery. We moved from shelter to shelter, exposing ourselves to the occasional rockfall as infrequently as possible.

I admit that I enjoyed this aspect of the operation. The extreme terrain - where I would never venture without good reason like tonight's - made my life feel like an action/adventure movie. I got to witness stunning views that I would never forget. I got to put up my skills and caution against challenge and risk and it felt good to win the gamble. It felt even better to do it for a good cause, and to do what most people couldn't, or wouldn't, and most certainly shouldn't even attempt.

The girl was safe by now. The eight year old who stepped off the cave trail while looking into her bag of chips. She slid a ways down a steep dirt and rock slope and came to rest before the first big cliff. Bystanders and rangers persuaded her not to move until either a helicopter winch or roped rescuer was able to reach her and return her to safety.

The Russian - who happened to work for the girl's father - was less fortunate. He didn't think twice about hopping off the trail to go after the girl, but without solid footing, he could not control his momentum. He slid toward the cliff edge and sailed over it. The terror he must have felt - if he didn't immediately go into shock - did not last long.

The gallant would-be rescuer fell a total of 600 feet, stopping where the gully narrows to fifteen feet across and momentarily relaxes its angle slightly, and just above the next 15' cliff. With a little more momentum, gravity might have dragged him nearly all the way down the mountain. Judging by his uncomfortable-looking body position and visible trauma, he died long before coming to rest.

Considering the nature of the cave trail, it's surprising how few people have fallen off it. It's a mile and a half long, with tiny brass circles marking every hundred feet from the cave entrance. It climbs 1,065 feet elevation, up to 6,730' above sea level, leading to several heart attacks among hikers who should have taken it more slowly. It's five feet wide and topped with asphalt, and has no hand rails and sometimes drops off in sheer cliffs up to a hundred feet high. Daily rockfall peppers the trail, and after heavy rainfall, rocks can bury the trail up to 6' deep. Red stripes along the trail mark rockfall danger and hikers should not stop to catch their breath in these stretches. Asphalt patches show where particularly violent avalanches and rock fall damaged the trail, and the spring thaw sometimes reveals mangled benches even in non-red stripe areas.

70,000 annual visitors - many of them elementary and middle school children - are asked to walk, not run up and down the trail, because even a momentary stumble could have deadly results. Such was the case - albeit indirectly - with the little girl.

After climbing the last 15' cliff, I took several photos for the Sheriff report, and we got busy cleaning up. We stationed Olin above us to set an anchor and warn of rockfall, and after donning latex gloves for our protection, we tied the victim to a nearby tree to make sure he didn't slide over the cliff and down the ravine.

Maneuvering him into the body bag without tearing it in such awkward circumstances took a bit of work, but we soon had him strapped into the litter with two ropes attached - one for the main lowering line, and another as a backup belay in case the main line failed. These lines attached to nearby trees and connected to the rope with a brake rack or double prussiks through which attendants would allow the rope to pass, slowly lowering the package down the gully to the next belay station on a snowfield below.

Before starting down, we called for radio silence so no other traffic would interfere with commands between me and the other rescuer accompanying the litter down the ravine and the attendants controlling our descent from above.

"Down slow," we commanded, and the litter slid slowly over the cliff edge. We steered our package over the lip and guided it to prevent it from catching in narrow crevices. "A little faster," we requested as the way flattened out and the going grew more straight forward. Faster and slower we continued, following the easiest route for 200', until we reached the snowfield where the second lowering station attached to the litter and took over the operation. A third station followed by a six-person carry over rough but flatter terrain brought the man to the cave trail and on down to an ambulance where the coroner officially pronounced him dead.

Thus ended this phase of a sad, sad story about a brave, selfless man who traveled half way around the world from his family, then perished while trying to help another. I didn't let myself dwell on such facts. Even as I write this story, many years later, I don't allow myself that privilege. I didn't know him and my part in the drama is not personal. Others must grieve his loss while I must not. Everyone in the equation - and all future equations - is best served if I merely enjoy the adventure and satisfaction of contributing my time and skills to his needs.

In following years, park rangers who were also expert climbers drilled bolt anchors at key spots along the trail to facilitate rescue should it ever be needed again. Considering the extreme terrain, it was only a matter of time.

29 DON'T MOVE!

The trail to the base of Bridal Veil Falls offers a perfect escape from summer afternoon heat. The spring-fed waterfall runs year-round and its cool spray is refreshing from a distance, while standing directly in the cold shower of the falls is breath taking.

Pinned to the rock at the falls is a sign that reads "Thank you for visiting

Bridal Veil Falls. Enjoy the refreshing spray. No climbing beyond this point."

Hikers sometimes continue upward despite the warning, and if they discover the passage above the major cliff band, they reach narrow, exposed trails with a 200' fall waiting for anyone who trips. Whenever I see kids hiking above the falls, it surprises me that more people don't fall to their deaths there.

I went hiking above the falls myself one day to better familiarize myself with the terrain when I heard a loud *whap* above me. 150' up the slope where no one had been hiking, the top of a blond head, its part still perfectly combed, lay motionless in the dirt.

"Hey!" I shouted. "Are you okay?" The boy did not answer or move.

The place he must have fallen from was a cliff band 60' above. I thought back to half an hour earlier and remembered two boys hiking past me. I then thought of his friend, probably frozen with shock and fear on the cliff band above.

"Don't move!" I shouted as loudly as I could. "We'll come and get you soon!"

I scampered up the steep, loose dirt to the fallen boy. I had a radio in my pack and I should have called for help first to get people on the way with medical gear - if it wasn't already too late - and the ropes and gear we'd need to bring the body - if it was already too late - and the remaining boy down safely.

As I scrambled up the steep slope to the unmoving body, something looked wrong. It wasn't until I got within 15 feet that I realized what.

It wasn't a boy at all.

A log had split and curled and its rough contour looked exactly like the top of a blond head. I backed down ten feet and even knowing what it was, it still looked convincingly like a boy's head.

A rock, blown slowly by the wind, must have fallen and made the *whap* sound I heard. If I had gotten on the radio before investigating like I should have done, I might still be hearing about it today.

30 Christmas in July

Marvin and his family hiked above Horse Flats one July afternoon, then followed the trail up the steep ridge toward Robert's Horn. Cliffs and ridges fell away in all directions and mountains rolled continuously toward the distant horizon, creating stunning views and making Marvin feel more alive and better than he could remember for a long time.

But the hiking was steep and his young family soon tired.

"Why don't we start down," his wife Debbie said, indicating herself and the children, "and you can catch up with us in a little while?"

Marvin smiled gratefully. Debbie understood him and he appreciated her support and flexibility. "I'll meet you at the car in an hour or two," he promised as he kissed her goodbye.

The cool, dry, fresh air tasted sweet as Marvin climbed above 9,000', and he sucked it deep into his lungs. His sense of satisfaction increased as he reached a minor peak and stopped to take in the world-class view. "This belongs on a calendar!" he thought out loud.

Marvin considered turning around, but the next small peak looked so close, and it probably held an even better view. He would check it out and then turn around, he promised himself.

The peak turned out to be a false summit with a higher peak a hundred yards farther up. From that point, another called his name and he marched on for another forty five minutes before finally deciding to turn back. The sun had dropped over Timpanogos' summit ridge, but plenty of daylight remained. He had no reason to worry.

Even when he lost the faint trail and missed a switchback back to Horse Flats, he didn't worry. He wasn't lost, that would be impossible - he could see the Timpooneke trailhead. As long as he went down, he would eventually run across a trail or road.

And so down he went. The slope was steep, but abundant pines let him grab their branches to control his descent. Sheer limestone cliffs began to appear and grow ever taller, but dirt and choss-filled gullies made an easy path between them.

Meanwhile, the air grew cooler. Previously light cloud cover grew dark and heavy, and wind began to moan through old-growth forests in the drainage below. Marvin wished he had brought more clothing than just shorts and a light windbreaker, but he would reach the road soon and everything would turn out fine.

Evening fell and a hint of red glowed from within the dark clouds. Enough light remained for Marvin to pick his way down the slope, but not enough to see farther than a few yards with any clarity.

Half way down the mountainside, Marvin encountered his first impassible barrier. His gully turned into a sheer cliff. He didn't dare approach the edge to see how far down it went, so he picked up a rock and tossed it. He held his breath and listened. One one thousand, two one thousand, three one thousand, four one thousand. Marvin took a breath and bent over to pick up a bigger rock. Apparently the first one was too small to make enough noise to hear when it landed below.

Marvin felt his first hint of dread when he heard the first rock smash against rock far below and continue skipping down the mountainside. His stomach tightened uneasily as he imagined himself falling that far. His knees turned to jelly as he took several slow steps away from the edge.

I'd better retrace my steps, he thought as his anxiety rose. He turned away from the loose rock below that suddenly looked as if it could break free and cascade over the brink with the slightest prod.

As Marvin looked uphill, however, he was shocked to see what he had just downclimbed. The tree-laced gully was steeper than he remembered, with tiny cliff bands criss crossing his path. The anxiety and adrenaline rose higher in his throat as he visualized the consequences of a single slip.

A narrow ledge ran along the cliff edge to his left, but he didn't dare traverse that. Dirt and rocks piled high along the four-foot-wide ledge, creating such a steep angle that his stomach tied into a tight knot at the very thought of trying to traverse it. Besides, he couldn't see where it led. It could peter out and leave him in a worse spot than he already was.

I'm not going to take any chances, he promised himself. *I have to get back to my family and I'm not going to take any more chances.*

A mournful wind howled through the forest just then, darkening Marvin's mood even more, and then the rain began to fall. He took cover under an overhanging portion of the cliff to his left, and tried to think.

I'll wait for the rain to pass, he thought, *then crawl my way back up very carefully and traverse toward better terrain as soon as possible.*

And so he waited.

The rain fell harder and harder and saturated the ground until the ground could take no more and water ran freely down the gully. Retracing his steps suddenly didn't sound like such a good plan.

Marvin could do nothing more than stand under the overhang and watch. He wrapped his arms around himself and bounced up and down to generate heat, then sat down and wrapped his arms around his legs to reduce surface area and retain body heat.

Night fell and the darkness of the clouds became total. After midnight, the rain finally stopped falling when it turned to snow. Big, wet flakes that soon began to stick to the ground and accumulate. The cloud level dropped and Marvin could taste the thick humidity with every breath.

Unbeknownst to him, Debbie had waited patiently for hours. She began to worry a little when the first pitter patter of rain began to fall where she waited with the children in the car. She said a silent prayer for her husband's safety, and when the rain began to fall in giant, round drops, they all bowed their heads and implored heaven to protect their husband and daddy.

Debbie grabbed a jacket, left the kids in the car, and hiked back up the trail to find him. She didn't get far beyond Horse Flats when she passed a pair of hikers running down the trail to escape the weather. They had hiked the entire ridge and found no one there.

Debbie returned to the car and thought through what might have happened. She knew how Marvin had a difficult time stopping, how he liked to say, "Just a bit farther." Maybe he hiked the entire ridge and continued down one of the two main trails rather than retracing his steps. She thought about the faint trail and wondered if he had lost it and decided to bushwhack his way out. She knew how much he enjoyed that, too.

Debbie drove to both trailheads and found no one. She interviewed returning hikers, describing her husband, but no one had seen him.

By midnight, Debbie was approaching panic. It finally occurred to her that something had gone seriously wrong and she needed to call for help.

Thus search and rescue members all over the county rolled out of bed, dressed, and drove to the command post at the Timpooneke trailhead. Snow fell for much of the night, and clouds obscured the stars and dark mountains as teams explored the area, stopping to shout Marvin's name every few hundred yards and whenever the wind died enough to hear over better.

ICS wanted more help than they had on hand and called on Salt Lake County SAR for assistance. Half a dozen experienced team members showed up and ICS assigned them to teams.

The unseasonably cold weather took some SAR members by surprise, and two of them were forced to return to CP to warm up in the MIC before returning to search.

By first light, hopes of a successful rescue had dimmed considerably for several reasons. First, the area was full of tall cliffs. A fall from many of them would be instantly fatal.

Second, the weather and Marvin's light clothing seemed unlikely to protect him from severe hypothermia through the night's cold weather.

Third, we had searched much of the high-probability areas, and though we couldn't see much of it due to low clouds, nor hear well above the wind, we wondered if we would have heard each other had we approached anywhere near our victim.

And then we got a break. The breeze died momentarily. Field teams shouted and heard Marvin shout back. He had survived after all. The cloud ceiling

broke and we spotted him huddled above 400 feet of sheer cliff.

Now the question arose of how to reach him. ICS was about to dispatch me with a team to come in above him from Horse Flats when team members from Utah and Salt Lake Counties reached the sloped, exposed, 200-foot-long ledge leading to Marvin's position and made their way across. They dressed him in warm clothing and put a harness on him to prepare him to be lowered over the edge, which would be much safer than walking him across the ledge without ropes from above to prevent any possible slip.

I instead delivered warm pizza to the field teams while the heroes du jour fixed lines and lowered Marvin over the cliffs. He was surprisingly lucid and warm, which made the task far easier since we didn't need to strap him into a litter.

Teams made their way to the base of the cliff and pulled Marvin under a protective overhang once he arrived, then walked him down the steep scree field to the meadow and trail below. Rather than carrying him out, we kept him moving to generate heat and prevent further hypothermia.

The lesson learned? Never give up. You never know what can happen. Marvin and his little family's July Christmas wish came true.

...then walk him down the steep gully to the trail below >

< SAR teams wait for Marvin to be lowered to them...

31 LOST AND FOUND

Life is hard. It's hard for everyone at times, regardless of the brave, happy face they may wear for the world to see. People often suffer alone, bearing their burden in silence when they should reach out for support. Eventually, the struggle wears them thin or crushes them completely.

I don't know if any such feelings drove a young Utah County man to give up the fight one October night. All I know is that he wrote a note and left it with his watch and wallet along the River Trail near the lake, shot up heroin, and stepped into the current.

We searched the river the following day when someone found the note. We checked strainers and probed deep eddies and holes where endlessly rushing water carved out the land and swept it downstream. The nearby-lake backs up the lower river and its still waters run deep. Giant cottonwoods lining the banks age, decay, and topple, often into the river, leaving logs and branches to catch objects and complicate our efforts.

We didn't find the body, and eventually called off the search and forgot about the boy.

For a while.

During summer, bodies lost in the lake usually float within a few days. The cold winter river water slowed the process of decay and gas generation that brings corpses to the surface. We finally found him six months later when he floated and lodged in sticks stacked in the current ten feet from shore.

A fire department was ready to go into the river and retrieve the body when I arrived on scene with other rescuers who were able to leave work that afternoon. Whichever agency was in charge of the operation changed the plans and sent SAR into the water to do the job instead.

The Achilles raft was launched from a nearby boat ramp and motored upstream. We fixed a line to a large tree on our side of the river, and the boat carried the rope across the river to another team who attached that side, sixty or seventy feet away.

Two SAR members manned the raft and held it in place just upstream of the body. Three others climbed into the river and, holding onto the raft to avoid getting swept downstream, carefully wrapped a body bag around the man. His body had remained intact over the past six months, but we didn't dare tug on an arm or even his waist, having no idea how much pressure the decaying body could handle.

While his face had retained all its features, I had the sense that he would be difficult to recognize, even by those who once knew him best. Part of one ear seemed missing and other features looked softened, perhaps waterlogged and slightly bloated.

Once secure in the bag, we left it in the water and pulled the boat to shore where we let the excess water drain from the bag, then lifted and carried it to the ambulance that would transport him to the morgue. The entire operation went smoothly and relatively fast.

"We couldn't have done it that well," a fire fighter admitted to CP while others sprayed off our dry suits to eliminate any risk of exposure to biohazard.

Life Flight takes off from American Fork Canyon

A SAR member is lowered next to Stewart Falls during a training exercise

Climbing in Provo Canyon's Old Glory area

A SAR member's Hummer atop West Mountain

32 FLARE

Despite being an elite racer, the adventure race did not begin or end well for Scott. As he paddled out of the Utah Lake State Park marina, he turned south and found most of the other 36 teams far ahead of him. They had carried their boats over the jetty rather than paddle through the marina entrance on the northwest corner. It wasn't cheating. The race rules only required that racers pass each checkpoint, and the next checkpoint was at Lincoln Beach on the south end of the lake.

Even so far behind, Scott was not ready to give up. He paddled hard, playing catch up for seven miles, then paddled back against three-foot waves.

Back at the marina, racers roller bladed and mountain biked to the Timpanogos foothills. They rappelled a cliff in Dry Canyon where the racer right in front of Scott nearly fell to her death. She was using a "shunt" rappel device which requires the user to let go in order to grip the rope and control the descent. The racer panicked and gripped the shunt instead, sending into a free fall. The rope burned through her leather gloves and her scream lasted five full seconds before she finally let go and stopped ten feet above the deck.

Scott rappelled, then climbed back on his bike and pushed himself hard up the Curly Springs Trail. He had pushed himself hard and his efforts were paying off. Only seven racers remained in front of him. But his efforts also came at a cost – he had been racing on the edge of his ability and by the time the sun dropped behind the western horizon, his thighs felt like mush while his calves cramped painfully. If he wanted to win this race, he could not afford to let up. He pedaled hard, switching gears as the zig-zagging trail rose and fell through scrub oak and half-buried boulders.

The trail topped a small ridge and then dropped suddenly for two hundred feet. Scott put gravity to work in his favor, for once, as he milked the downhill stretch for all the speed it would feed him. His race number flapped in the refreshingly cool breeze and he pedaled hard as the trail rose again in a steep climb.

At the end of the climb, the trail ended in a sheer 80' cliff. "Snap!" Scott muttered under his breath while laying on the brakes almost hard enough to lock up his wheels. He should have known better. He had studied the map carefully and he should have known that the turn into Battle Creek Canyon was coming up. He rode right past without even seeing it.

Now he couldn't afford to waste precious time and energy turning around. He had no idea how far back the trail turned off. Instead, he pushed his bike into the brush, steering between clumps of scrub oak, knowing his path would eventually intersect the trail. Behind him, other racers came panting their way up the trail, only half a minute away.

Scott cursed his judgment as the brush grew thicker, but then a side passage suddenly before him. Dead leaves covered the grassy ground and it felt soft underfoot. He could run without branches scraping tiny gashes across his arms and legs. Now he had to make a decision.

He had examined this spot on the map and wondered what to do. The trail he was looking for continued up-canyon another quarter mile before joining the main Battle Creek Canyon trail and turning back down toward the next checkpoint. At this point, however, it ran only one or two hundred yards away from that lower path. If he cut left now, he could carry his bike down the slope and shave off half a mile of riding. It might prove just what he needed to capture the lead.

Scott thought of the other racers whose heels he had nipped at for the entire ride. He took a deep breath and made up his mind. He threw his bike over one shoulder and charged down the mountain, eager to disappear into the brush before other racers spotted him and copied his strategy.

Everything looked good at first and Scott congratulated himself on his cunning plan. The racers in front of him would never know what happened!

The slope grew steeper soon and dirt turned to loose talus. Scott slowed a bit, digging his heels into the scree and letting gravity ski him down the slope. He leapt over a fallen log and set his heel again in the talus when it slid away more easily than anticipated and he slipped and fell.

That's when it happened. The bike over his shoulder made his balance awkward, and he couldn't reach out a hand to catch himself. Instead, he landed on his elbow and the sudden force fractured an upper corner of his humerus and tore his axillary nerve as it wrenched his shoulder from its socket. A popping sound accompanied a sudden spike of pain that left him unable to breath for several seconds.

Scott squeezed his eyes shut tight and grimaced in pain, his teeth clamping together hard. He sucked in a deep breath of air that hissed through his clenched teeth. He wanted to roll over and take the weight off the dislocated arm, but the slope was steep and loose and if he relaxed, he would slide farther down the loose mountainside.

He sat up and used his left arm to lift his right, wrapping it across his body and cradling it across his chest, which lessened the pain slightly. He held it there and rocked back and forth, eyes clamped shut, breathing deeply, waiting for the sharp throbbing sensation to subside.

He knew the shoulder was dislocated, and he knew what he had to do. After a few minutes, once the pain-killing endorphins kicked in, he again used his left arm to spin his right around behind him, which made every nerve ending in his shoulder sing out in renewed objections. He pushed it further anyway, trying to position it so it would slip back into its socket. The cutting sensation took his breath away, but he continued to try for over a minute before giving up.

When it didn't work, he went to Plan B, which so far consisted of "Figure out how to get out of this mess." Just then he heard a noise not far away. A two-person team had his same idea and had cut off the trail not far from his position.

"Help!" Scott shouted through the trees, and the racers made their way to him a minute later. One racer held Scott's feet in place, and the cramps in Scott's calves and grown so tight that the other racer had to help him walk up the slope. After twenty feet, they reached the grassy meadow and Scott sat down.

After one of the good Samaritans dialed 911 to get SAR rolling, Scott explained to them how to pull traction on his arm, pulling against the spasming muscles to try to get it to pop back into place. Unfortunately, he failed to include the part about applying slow, steady pull, and when they yanked his arm as hard as they could, Scott nearly passed out.

In the canyon below, Scott faintly heard the distant grinding sound of mountain bike tires crunching over gravel and rock. He counted - one, two, three bikes. A few minutes passed and more bikes passed by. The race was lost. No use even thinking about competing anymore.

Within twenty minutes, SAR gathered in the Battle Creek parking lot and CP sent two teams up the canyon. The hasty team went quick and light. Their task was to locate Scott and guide in subsequent teams. Team One brought the wheeled litter and medical supplies, while Bruce and I were sent up the opposite side of the canyon to see if we could spot Scott's flashlight.

Before we left, Tom's phone rang. "We've got an emergency flare. Want us to use it?" Scott's two helpers asked.

"Okay," Tom instructed, "shoot the flare down canyon."

That could mean trouble, I thought.

One of the most difficult things on SAR to do an excellent job at is communication. Words are crude tools and often fail to express the clear ideas held in the mind of the speaker. Even when an idea is stated clearly, the listener can easily misunderstand, and once that happens, the brain continues to interpret everything to make it match the first impression. The two parties may never realize that the message has not been transmitted and translated accurately.

Sure enough. The injured racer aimed the flare down canyon, instead of up into the air but toward the west, and pulled the tiny chain. A burst of orange sparks erupted from his hands and flew down and away into a stand of dry pine trees.

This changed the situation from a routine carry out to an urgent mission so dangerous that it may not be wise to risk sending team members into what could erupt into a deadly blaze churning through dry timber up the hillside if the pines caught fire.

If not for the creek which immediately extinguished the flare, we'd have found out just how quickly our team could adapt to an extreme emergency.

Despite the misguided flare whose starting point no one saw, we soon located our injured racer in relatively good shape. We covered him with a sleeping bag and built a fire to keep him warm, then inserted an IV and pumped a slow trickle of morphine into his bloodstream. A team member sat back to back with him because that was the only position that didn't cause more pain.

The decision was made to fly him out in the morning (I don't know why we didn't just carry him out – perhaps because those making the decisions didn't know how easily we could have attained the trail), so we kept him company until a Life Flight helicopter arrived at first light.

The chopper hovered overhead while a paramedic dropped slowly down on the hoist cable like a giant red spider. Once on the ground, he unclipped the cable and spun his hand around in a circle telling the attendant on deck to raise the cable. The bird turned slowly and flew away, waiting for the paramedic's radio call to return.

We packaged Scott in the vacuum splint brought by the paramedic - an air mattress-size bean bag that turns rigid when a pump sucks the air from between the tiny styrofoam balls inside - and wrapped it in the netting that would attach to the hoist. We wedged Scott's helmet under his arm to attain a position of relative comfort, but the broken bone and nerve barely allowed for that. Scott wouldn't even be able to move his hand to his back pocket for months, but then, luckily, the nerve would heal.

The helicopter returned and the thin steel cable again slid down to the ground. We let it touch the ground before touching it to avoid any possible shock from static electricity generated by the helicopter. The paramedic then clipped himself and his package to the cable, and Scott grimaced in pain as the slack ran out and began to tension the system.

"That's a bit tight," he complained, tears springing to his eyes and his teeth clenching as the pressure on his shoulder increased slightly, "could you loosen it?"

The paramedic complied, letting an inch or two of strap slide through the buckle. "How's that?" he asked.

"A little more?" the patient requested.

The paramedic paused, raising one eyebrow as if to ask "Really?", then tugged the strap tighter again. "Buck up," he said, then looked upward and gave a thumbs-up signal for the helicopter to reel them in.

As the package rose into the sky, it began to spin slowly as the winch reeled it in. Through a tiny opening in the packaging, Scott watched the same mountain go by again and again and again. "I wonder if we're going to die," he wondered, then added, "I don't even care." The pain was that intense. The Life Flight paramedic would later have to take three hours off to recover from the spinning.

We all stood and watched, shielding our eyes from the dust and dry leaves sent flying by the rotor wash, until the paramedic and patient reached the open helicopter door and the sleek craft spun gracefully through the sky and flew away.

33 Life Flight Down

One week later, a tiny piece of metal in the Life Flight helicopter's tail section wore out and shattered. Without a functioning tail rotor, the wounded bird could not stop itself from going into an uncontrolled spin. The resulting crash killed the pilot and injured the flight nurse and paramedic. They had just rescued a hiker from Mount Olympus and flown her to an ambulance for care.

The entire rescue community was shaken, especially since another crash five months earlier took the lives of the pilot and paramedic. We all work closely with these dedicated and highly-skilled individuals who never fail to demonstrate enthusiasm, professionalism and friendliness. We have a deep appreciation and respect for each other.

All these years later, I still feel sorrow and regret for the loss.

A life Flight medic lowers on the hoist

Timpanogos summit ridge between the summit and the glacier

Singletrack Special Team members in Horse Flats

34 Special Teams

Some SAR teams operate purely as special teams. The dive and mountain rescue teams don't attend the same meetings, trainings, nor do they get paged to the same calls.

One of my favorite things about Utah County is that we get the chance to participate in nearly all disciplines. We're one single team, and individual members may choose to gain advanced training and certifications in specialties like K9, swiftwater, medical, dive, and others.

CJ and I got talking one spring about the endless miles of singletrack trail winding through the county's hills and mountains. These trails are too narrow for four wheelers, which meant we always attacked them on foot.

"Just think how much faster a motorcycle could cover that," CJ mused.

We had both owned dirt bikes in years past. I used to be a reasonably good rider, jumping my dad's tiny XL185 in a gravel pit near my home until the piston exploded; then steering my ancient, heavy XR500 up singletrack in Cache County where I grew up.

I had quick reactions back then. Riding 40 mph down Green Canyon one morning before class during Fall Quarter at USU, I couldn't make a turn that came up faster than expected, and my front tire went off the dirt and gravel road. When it dropped into a hole hidden by fallen leaves, I had a quarter second to react before hitting the ground and then perhaps tumbling end over end through the bushes growing up the mountainside. Rather than hitting the ground, however, I cranked the handlebars into a tight right turn. The nobby tire got a grip on the dirt and rocks and tossed the bike back up and into the center of the road. Everything happened so fast that I had no time to think about what I was doing. My muscles took over and saved me from scrapes and bruises and possibly broken bones as well. Those are the kind of reflexes required to ride fast and safe, and it was going to take some practice to get them back.

The Singletrack Special Team (SST) was born when CJ bought an XR600 and I got a 650 a few days later. It was much more powerful than my old 500, but also lighter and easier to handle. That said, both bikes are tanks and tough for novices to manage on technical singletrack. In coming years, we both moved to smaller, lighter, more agile bikes.

For our first ride, we chose Kirkman Hollow in Hobble Creek Canyon's Right Fork. In a sense, this was one of the worst choices we could have made. On the other hand, it was the best.

Kirkman begins with a short, steep, loose climb from a gravel pull out alongside the aging highway pavement winding up the canyon. We bounced our way up without any grace whatsoever, and were rewarded with a few hundred yards of easy, smooth, flat trail.

The trail gets more interesting then as it dips in and out of the draw. Our confidence grew and our old skills and comfort zones seemed to be returning. That changed when we reached the crux. The trail wound up a steep, rocky, rooty section for a hundred and fifty yards. If we didn't get our weight all the way forward, practically sitting on the gas tank, we would lose control of the front wheel. Any rock or root would send the front tire steering into the trees or sailing upward into the sky. To avoid going over backwards, we let off the gas, which inevitably resulted in stalling the bike in a very awkward position. From there, it took significant effort to keep from sliding backward down the hill until we tipped over.

Starting the bike again meant positioning it sideways, halfway off the trail, and trying to balance the bike while kicking out all the gas flooding the cylinder, then starting the engine and trying to build forward momentum again without crashing or stalling all over again.

In short, by the time we approached the upper part of the difficult section, soaked in sweat and breathing hard, we were seriously motivated to keep the bike moving. Rather than pulling in the clutch and stopping, rolling, and falling over, we feathered the clutch lever, keeping up the RPMs and fighting to maintain any momentum at all while driving slowly enough to stay on the trail.

Kirkman, being the second toughest trail in the county at the time, made it a rotten spot to break out our old skills and break in our new bikes. On the other hand, its challenge forced us to perform, and our skills increased faster than by riding an easy cruiser like nearby Packard or Pumphouse Ridge.

SST members on the Alpine Loop's Ridge Trail

35 THE RACE GOES TO THE SWIFT

The SST grew slowly at first, as ICS was concerned about potential accidents and injuries and their accompanying legal liabilities. As a former ICS commander, they trusted CJ's judgment and warmed slowly to the idea.

Brent and Olin joined, then others, and we implemented an approval system wherein new riders had to spend a considerable time riding with the SST during training and demonstrating sufficient skills and judgment before being approved to ride during rescue missions.

CJ and Brent rode on the first SST call, rushing needed gear two miles up Benny Creek so quickly that it left ICS astonished at their efficiency. Darin and I carried an AED to an accident victim at the Diamond Fork hot pots, and the SST's acceptance and prestige grew with each insertion.

In the mean time, we trained often, exploring trails at the top of the Alpine Loop, Hobble Creek Canyon, the Nebo Loop, Five Mile Pass, and elsewhere. We began training twice a year in Moab, enjoying the slickrock and building a camaraderie that quickly grew famous and even evoked a degree of jealousy among outsiders.

A competitive moment arose one summer night when two hikers got lost along the Ridge Trail atop the Alpine Loop behind Mount Timpanogos. Team members collected at the summit parking lot and CJ and I walked over to CP at Alan's truck.

Alan had a topo map open on his laptop and was studying the terrain and trails.

"They're either right there," CJ said, pointing to a spot amongst the topo's weaving black lines, then indicated another spot, "or there. Those are the only two places you can feel lost on the Ridge Trail."

"Send a team up this gravel road," I said, pointing to a dotted line on the map, six miles from where we stood. "It intersects the trail and they can hike from there."

Marc and Corey were dispatched there while three motorcycles were given the assignment to clear the entire Ridge Trail. We unloaded our bikes, donned our helmets, boots, and pads, and took off.

We had ridden the trail hundreds of times and knew our way well. We knew the rocky climbs, the dusty meadows, and the smooth stretches through old-growth pine forests when we opened our throttles and cruised along in third or fourth gear. Our headlights lit the trail before us and we stood on our pegs to fly over rough terrain, then sat and flew still faster over smooth ground. We leaned the bikes slightly into corners and let the shocks absorb the bumps. The night air felt cool and refreshing.

Our helmet communication systems allowed us to talk as we rode. We spoke of the need to maintain the prestige that the SST had accumulated over time. We mentioned the need for speed to make sure we beat the infantry, though that went without saying. We rode safely within our comfort zones, but those zones left plenty of room for the joyful thrill of competent speed.

Sheriff Lieutenant Bennett flew the department's four-seater Cessna overhead and spotted the fire that our lost party had lit. He wanted to make sure he was seeing the fire correctly and asked all ground teams to extinguish their lights. We hit our kill switches and waited several minutes for the order to continue onward.

We knew that Marc and Corey would not stop during the blackout, but continue hiking in the dark. We knew that they were gaining ground and closing the gap to the hikers while we could do nothing but wait.

Eventually Bennett told us to proceed, and as dots of light appeared below him, he assured us that all parties were moving the right direction toward the fire.

We finished the six miles to the dirt road and passed Marc's truck parked at the trail marker a few minutes later.

The trail here climbed steeply through abundant loose rock, but it barely slowed us down. We steered between the larger rocks and swerved to the edge of the trail to climb past logs placed across the trail by the Forest Service to reduce erosion. At last we caught Marc and Corey in our headlights and they graciously stepped off the trail to let us pass.

"Good evening, boys," I quipped cheerfully as I rode by. It was then that I saw the sweat glistening on their foreheads and running down their faces, and realized how hard they had been pushing themselves up the hill, determined to beat us to the punch. All in vain.

A hundred yards later, we crested the hill. A hundred yards beyond that, we saw a small fire burning amongst the low trees, exactly where CJ predicted. I arrived first and shut off my engine, with CJ right behind me.

"Are you Sarah and Linda?" I asked, and they verified that they were indeed our lost hikers. "I'm Shaun and this is Chris," I said politely, indicating CJ. "We'll be your rescuers this evening."

We talked and joked and petted their friendly dogs while they extinguished the fire. Marc and Corey arrived soon and we sent them walking down the trail together. They would give the women a ride back to their car at CP where ICS could gather a bit more information and send them on their way.

We rode our favorite trails back to our trucks and found Alan still there, with the map still glowing on his computer screen. I walked up to his open window and watched him measure the distance we rode, comparing it probably for the umpteenth time to the far shorter distance Team Two hiked. He shook his head in apparent surprise and admiration.

"Your knowledge of these trails is a real asset," he observed without looking away from the screen.

36 FROZEN

Autumn arrived and painted over summer's verdant greens with nature's annual going-away party decorations of brilliant crimson and golden hues. Fields of soft grasses turned dry and faded to light tans. October cloudscapes draped the mountains in peek-a-boo togas, then dusted them with snow.

I drove home from class one afternoon and couldn't keep my eyes off Mount Timpanogos. Its jagged ridges wore fluffy white clouds at many different levels - a few spilling over the shoulder between Baldy and Everest Ridge, others shadowing the mountain above ten or eleven thousand feet.

I didn't know that I would drive around the mountain that evening and hike up the Primrose Cirque, pushing myself and my team as fast as we could go in a desperate race to save a teenage college student's life.

The impressive mountain had also caught Jordan's eye as he left class that morning, and he decided to go for a short hike. Cooler fall weather brought a refreshing change from summer's stifling heat, and Jordan felt good. He turned his car for the canyon and drove straight to the parking lot at the Timpooneke trailhead.

The mountain air was a perfect 75 degrees as Jordan started up the trail. He walked leisurely along the trail, taking in the fall colors glowing in every direction, the fading wildflowers along the trail, and the wispy clouds floating slowly through the cirque above.

Jordan passed a series of small waterfalls and the air temperature dropped a bit, so he picked up the pace to keep warm. Rocks crunched pleasantly under his feet. He jogged now and then when the trail leveled off. The view grew better and better as he rose above the surrounding hills. He watched the approaching clouds and thought how cool it would look to catch up with one and stand inside it.

He soon achieved his goal and tasted the refreshing water droplets on his face and tongue as he inhaled deeply. The cloud was cool, though, and he hurried on to find out how it would look to climb above the cloud and look down at it.

Before long, he found himself at the meadows. The shoulder wasn't much farther, and he pushed on. How could he resist? Looking down at the city through all these clouds from the summit ridge would make an unforgettable view! The memory would sustain him during boring classes and the long, cold winter to come.

Jordan felt tired and hungry by the time he reached the shoulder, but he was not disappointed. The view was *amazing!* City streets made a plaid pattern of 90-degree corners filled with trees, buildings, and red tail lights of rush-hour traffic. Beyond the cities, the wide lake filled the rest of the valley to Lake Mountain and the West Desert beyond.

He hiked north along the ridge - away from the summit trail - to find a perfect spot to sit down and take it all in. One glance is never enough. It takes time for this sort of beauty to sink in deep.

The upper mountain was covered in a light dusting of snow. It wasn't deep enough to get into his shoes or make the mountain slope dangerous to walk on. Instead, it only added to the surrounding beauty.

Jordan soon found a large rock, brushed away the snow, and sat down. He felt chilled and cursed his spontaneity for not stopping at his apartment for a jacket. Oh, well. He wrapped his arms around himself and huddled down. He began to shiver, but that didn't matter. He would warm up again as soon as he started down. Going down would be a lot easier than climbing up. He had nothing to worry about.

He stared out over the valley. He *loved* this valley! His blessed life had filled it with so many good memories. He picked out his old high school from the pattern of squares below. Next to it lay the green field where he played soccer and Ultimate with his friends. He gazed toward West Mountain where he used to go target shooting with his dad. He watched the evening light reflect off the lake through breaks in the clouds and thought of all the blissful days spent on his best friend's ski boat. His shivering grew violent, but he knew this would only help him warm up.

After a while, he stopped shivering. Without realizing it, he had slipped into severe hypothermia. His body gave up trying to generate heat and shunted all the remaining warm blood inside to protect his brain and vital organs.

An idea began to form in his brain. It seemed distant, hard to see clearly, and hard to hold onto. Slowly, it floated closer and closer until it hung directly in front of him. He stared at it for a few minutes before its meaning finally dawned on him. "I need to get up," he said out loud, the words slurring together. "I have to get going and warm up."

Slowly, he got to his feet. His legs felt cramped and unresponsive. He took a step forward anyway and found himself unsteady. He should have felt shocked, but he didn't. He merely noticed with a hazy, detached interest.

Jordan took another step forward onto the loose shale. The rocks under his feet shifted slightly and he lost his balance. He fell. He pushed himself back to his feet and took a few more steps, then staggered and fell again.

Another thought slowly crawled its way to the front of his mind. *I'm in trouble. I need help.*

With some effort, Jordan reached into his jeans pocket and pulled out his phone. His fingers felt thick and clumsy, but he slowly dialed 911 anyway.

"911, what's your emergency?" the crisp voice on the line asked.

Jordan's answer came out slowly. "I'm...on top of the mountain," he explained. "It's cold and...I can't...walk...very well."

Dispatch notified the Emergency Services deputy on call while attempting to gather more information from Jordan about his whereabouts. But Jordan's thoughts were murky and he had a hard time describing his location.

"Can you see the city?" dispatch asked.

"No," Jordan answered slowly, "only clouds."

While SAR teams scrambled, dispatch contacted the cell phone company and obtained the approximate location that the call came from. It was not a Phase 3 GPS enabled phone that could provide more accurate coordinates and merely measured the signal off a few cell towers to triangulate Jordan's approximate location. The map showed Jordan to be on the side of Robert's Horn, a few hundred yards northeast of Emerald Lake and over half a mile from his actual location.

Kevin arrived on scene and led a two-man hasty team up the mountain to find Jordan and provide immediate care. I was assigned as Team One leader and struck out with four team members and more supplies as Olin drove around to the Timpooneke trailhead and led Team Two that way, just to cover more bases.

We hiked as quickly as we could reasonably go. We didn't want to sweat too much, which could endanger us later if we ended up staying for an extended period on the mountain, so we removed layers as we heated up. We stopped only every once in a while to catch our breath after steeper sections of trail, and even then paused only briefly before moving upward again.

After passing Second Falls and Cardiac Rock, a series of bad news came streaming in one item at a time.

First, new cell tower hits mapped Jordan not on Robert's Horn, but Timp's summit ridge somewhere north of the saddle. This location was farther away, at higher elevation, and would take more time to reach. We listened as the news came over our radios and nodded. No problem. We'd do whatever it took. We'd get the job done like we always do.

Second, a heavy storm front was blowing in from the southwest and would arrive in 45 minutes. The cloudbank would bring heavy rain showers, which could mean snow at 11,000 feet, along with strong, sustained winds, and it could last for two hours.

This news was more problematic in several ways. For one thing, we had several miles left to go and reaching Jordan in 45 minutes might not be possible, though Kevin's fast and light team had a better chance.

Furthermore, Jordan was already dangerously chilled. Exposure to rain and significant wind chill, especially if he was wearing cotton clothing, could finish him off very quickly.

Thirdly, a heavy storm or blizzard would make finding a comatose victim exponentially more difficult. If we got lucky, we would find him along the ridgeline or the faint trail running north which was probably already completely obscured by snow.

Fourth, if the front brought lightning, which was not unlikely, it would present another serious danger to deal with as the electrically polarized clouds scraped their charged bellies against the rocky mountain ridge and sent deadly bolts of electricity leaping into the sky.

"This is serious," I said to my team as we paused for a thirty-second break. They nodded in agreement.

"Let's get going," Bryan suggested, and we resumed our hike up the trail. Darkness had fallen a mile ago and we each wore headlamps now, their beams of white illuminating the trail before us and sometimes igniting tiny specs of water as clouds floated by, surrounding us momentarily in whirling wisps of thick humidity.

The fifth piece of bad news changed the situation from serious to urgent for my team.

The hasty team had gone so fast and light that they were not prepared for the coming storm. They had planned on a quick jaunt to Roberts Horn and back. The increased distance and unexpected weather put a kink in their plans. They weren't prepared to spend an extended period in heavy weather, nor did they have the extra supplies to help our victim in such circumstances.

Some discussion ensued between the hasty team and CP as to whether they should hurry forward or get off the mountain.

"This boy's life could depend on *us*," I told my team. "If we don't find him, he'll die."

"What are we waiting for?" Bryan asked, and we all quickened our pace up the trail. We no longer worried about overheating and settled into the quickest pace that our legs and lungs could sustain.

We passed the Heber Switchback and had climbed through most of the switchbacks below Hidden Lakes when our fates turned.

A piece of good news came in for a change.

Team Two, now near Scout Falls in the Timpooneke drainage, had found our boy. Olin's radio traffic came in scratchy and unintelligible from the far side of a billion tons of rock, but we pieced the information together from CP's side of the conversation.

Jordan had been able to get himself as far as the shoulder when he met another hiker. That good samaritan shared his extra clothing and a flashlight, and Jordan warmed up as he hiked. By the time Olin found him, he was moving well and in good shape.

I don't know why Jordan didn't think to call and let us know he was moving - perhaps his hypothermia was to blame, perhaps the drama of the situation - but the important fact was that he was alive and safe and we could all turn around and go home.

37 DRIVEN

Thanks to the Mountain Rescue Association, many SAR teams throughout Utah, Idaho and Montana interact regularly and are familiar with one another's skill sets.

IMSARU (Idaho Mountain Search and Rescue Unit), for example, is expert at searches, and handles complex ones all the time. Their terrain, focused in an expansive area around Boise, isn't filled with enormous cliffs, however, like Utah is, and therefore they may only perform a few technical rescues per year.

That's why, when a father and son got trapped for over 24 hours by a winter storm near Sun Valley on the summit of Thompson Peak - the highest point in the Sawtooth Range, they called on us.

Teams consisting of some of the most experienced technical rescuers from Salt Lake, Weber and Utah Counties answered the call and left within the hour. We hoped to get approval for a plane ride to get us there more quickly, but failed. Instead, four of us climbed into Lieutenant Bennett's truck for the four and a half hour drive.

Our packs held all the gear we might need - crampons, axes, nuts, cams, pickets, and extra clothing, food and water for ourselves and the victims once we reached them.

Along the way, we studied what we were up against. We downloaded photos, maps, and route descriptions. It looked like we would be able to get within a mile of the summit by snowmobile. From there, a mere thousand feet of elevation separated us from the pair who got trapped under a slight rock overhang by heavy snowfall followed by rainfall which turned the surface to a dangerous ice crust.

The upper reaches of the slope where they stood huddling together for warmth looked steep, but far from vertical. In short, everything looked doable. My excitement grew with every detail coming in. It seemed so easy! We'd get to the mountain, evaluate avy conditions as we went, place a few good snow or rock anchors, and bring them down.

Beyond the exciting rescue itself, I felt flattered to be called to help out of state. This was the kind of high adventure I signed up for! Needless to say, I was looking forward to it.

330 miles later, we pulled into the command post in a large gravel parking lot filled with RV's, outdoor lighting, and people standing around. I hopped quickly out of the truck's passenger seat and walked toward them, eager to find out exactly what was going on and get our assignment.

A man with a moustache and big smile walked toward me and extended his hand. It was the local sheriff.

"Good thing we didn't need you!" he said with a happy, friendly grin spread across his face. "Thanks for coming! Help yourself to a burger."

Grand Teton NP had flown over in their helicopter. They dangled a rescuer from a line below its belly and short-haul lifted the father and son to safety.

I tried to return the sheriff's smile and thanked him for the burger, which was wrapped in foil in a cooler full of them to feed the many volunteers involved.

A room was arranged for us at a classy local lodge and IMSARU invited us to join them for drinks at a local bar and return home in the morning, but we opted to turn around and head home instead. We had lives and obligations waiting for us and didn't want to blow half the day tomorrow driving home.

Climbing into the clouds on Timp's Everest Ridge

38 Slip Sliding Away

Best friends Paul and Jake left their families on December 31 to climb Timpanogos' Primrose Cirque on snowshoes. They had hiked the cirque in snow several times before, but never during such a heavy winter storm. The deep, soft snow, now falling at three inches per hour, made the going more strenuous, but it also made the wide bowls more beautiful and the hike more invigorating.

"This is awesome!" Paul shouted into the wind while large, white snowflakes stuck to his exposed cheeks and melted. Nothing made him feel more alive than getting outdoors into the raw elements of nature and getting his heart rate up with a little exertion.

"Are we there yet?" Jake inquired, pausing and bending over with hands on his knees to catch his breath. Even though Paul had been breaking trail for the past quarter mile, Jake was having a harder time in the high elevation. "Aren't you tired?"

"Must have been those Wheaties I ate for breakfast," Paul joked. "Come on, we're almost there!"

By "there," Paul meant the breakover at Hidden Lakes. A hundred more feet of climbing and the steep slope would level out considerably. The going would get easier and they could make their goal of reaching the hut at Emerald Lake.

After pausing for thirty seconds to let Jake catch his breath, Paul grinned and turned away, then took another step up the mountain slope. His snowshoe sank eighteen inches into the snow and he grunted while lunging forward, transferring his weight to his upper foot. Then something snapped.

Fifty feet above the snowshoers, a wide fracture line appeared in the snow surface. The dark line grew wider and everything for two hundred feet to either side began to slide down the mountain toward them.

Paul's eyes shot open wide. "Avalanche!" he shouted, but it was useless. Neither of them could do anything to avoid going for an unexpected ride. The ground beneath their feet was already in motion. The avalanche didn't so much knock them off their feet, but made them lose their balance as their whole world shattered into smaller and smaller pieces and began shaking and bouncing around them.

"Swim!" Paul shouted, recalling instructions he had heard about how to survive an avalanche. "Ya gotta stay on top!" By the time he finished the sentence, the moving slab had engulfed them. The initial crystal sound of sifting snow grew to a deafening roar. The slide disoriented them and tumbled them around like clothes in a dryer. Snow filled their eyes, mouth and nose, and packed into their ears and inside their clothing.

And then, slowly, the snowpack around them slowed and stopped, while the avalanche snout continued downward, growing exponentially as it entrained more and more snow. It sounded like monsoon thunder, and echoed from two-thousand-foot cliffs enclosing the cirque.

"Holy crap!" Jake shouted out, coughing and clearing the snow from his mouth and eye sockets. He shivered as snow inside his coat melted and ran down his back. "That was a close one!" The thunder grew fainter and fainter as the heavy snowflakes filling the sky absorbed all sound. "We are SO lucky!"

Jake rolled over and sat up in the snow. He took a deep breath. "Man!" he shouted out loud. Then he looked around.

He found himself all alone on the snow.

"Paul!" he screamed, his voice coming out pinched and high like a child's. He stood up and spun around in a panic. "PAUL!!!" he screamed again. He paused for a moment to listen for a response, then fell to his knees, digging frantically through the snow with his gloved hands.

The snow had compacted from the slide and his gloves made slow progress. Jake unstrapped one snowshoe and plunged it desperately into the pack, using it as a shovel.

After several minutes of unsuccessful digging in the direction he last saw his friend, he stood up and ran down the mountain. Not far below, a thin row of scraggly pines grew atop a small cliff band. It tapered from north to south, growing from nothing to over twenty feet high.

"PAUL!!!" Jake screamed again as he surveyed the avalanche path below for as far as he could see before it vanished in the mist of falling snow. He searched for five more minutes, then pulled out his cell phone and dialed 911.

"There's been an avalanche and I can't find my friend!" he shouted as soon as the dispatcher answered.

"What is your location?" the dispatcher asked calmly.

"We're on Timp - above Aspen Grove. We were just hiking and suddenly the whole mountain broke loose! I looked and looked and I can't find him anywhere!"

"Don't move," the dispatcher instructed him after gathering more information. "We'll have search and rescue teams on their way to you soon."

Twenty five minutes later, in the parking lot two thousand feet below, MRT Sergeant Bruce R. and I stood ready and waiting. A Life Flight helicopter had landed nearby, awaiting a break in the clouds that would allow it to transport us to a landing zone above our victim.

Our mission would be to evaluate avalanche conditions, and if safety permitted, lead the survivor back to the helicopter. If weather didn't allow the helicopter to wait around and fly us out, we would guide the man up to the hut at Emerald Lake and keep him comfortable while awaiting transport after the storm passed.

Jake was in no mood to cooperate. He was freaking out and had no desire to spend any more time in the freezing morgue. He jammed his snowshoes into the snow to mark the spot and began sliding his way down the mountain.

Lucky for him, no further avalanches broke loose and a DPS helicopter picked him up a mile from the parking lot, well below the cloud ceiling.

The clouds never broke, and even if they had, ICS wouldn't have sent teams up the mountain in such dangerous conditions to search a thousand-acre avalanche for what would certainly be a fatality by now. For the moment, our work was over. There was nothing else we could do. We went home, back to our families and friends and New Years Eve celebrations.

For the rest of us, New Years merely marked the close of another year; just another tick on the endless odometer of time. For one avalanche victim in the Timpanogos backcountry, the time for resolutions had passed.

A SAR member heads for an anchoring bush after setting off a small slab avalanche above Sundance

39 GHOST WHISPERER

Lieutenant Bennett and a team member were flying the Cessna over Mount Timpanogos on June 30 when they spotted a red mark in the snow around 9,000' up the Primrose Cirque.

When teams hiked up the trail and across a small rock and dirt ridge to the snowfield, they verified what Bennett suspected - the red mark was a coat sleeve, buried since a massive New Years Eve avalanche swept a snowshoer down the mountain - six months ago to the day.

By the time I strapped on my crampons and stepped onto the steep snow not far from the trail, the victim had been mostly dug out. He sat slumped forward in the position he must have held when the snowpack stopped sliding and turned to cement around him.

He looked worse than the other long-term avalanche victim I saw a year or two earlier - buried the day after Christmas and located on Easter afternoon. His eyes had begun to sink back into their sockets, and his skin looked a little leathery and sagged slightly around his face. The rest of his body was covered by his coat, gloves, pant shells and boots.

I turned away to help get the body bag and litter ready to transport him, when an eerie sensation filled the air. I looked around to see if anyone else noticed, but if they did, it didn't show.

Whatever it was, wherever it came from, it made me feel uneasy. As I continued to pay attention to the feeling, it seemed to grow clearer. I had the impression that Paul was still here, standing near us, and it was his tortured regret and anguish that caused the mild anxiety to churn my stomach.

I could almost hear him shouting, "This wasn't supposed to happen to me! I wasn't supposed to die!"

The impression caused goosebumps to break out on my arms, but I continued to pay attention to it anyway. As I listened, it seemed to calm and fade slowly away. I felt like the Ghost Whisperer watching some lost soul find its way to the light. After a minute or two, the sensation faded completely.

Whether Paul's ghost haunted these slopes for six months, I couldn't say. All I know is that the winter following the tragedy had continued to bring harsh weather and frequent storms. Snow piled deep, filling the cirque and blowing into massive drifts atop airy cliffs in every direction. Eventually, gravity overcame the snowpack's cohesive strength and broke loose all over again. Massive avalanches raged down the slope for months.

The Forest Service's Utah Avalanche center, with support from Wasatch Powder Birds' helicopter, surveyed the area and counted over 300 potential avalanche release zones above the impossibly massive search area. They bombed a few of the larger cornices, but could not hope to eradicate all danger. Such risky conditions precluded any search efforts until early spring.

Beginning in May, we flew up to Hidden Lakes several times and probed high probability areas like trees that may have caught the victim as the snow sifted over cliff bands. We used technologies like RECCO and dogs, but the search area covered so much terrain and the snow piled so deep that we may as well have been searching for a speck of dust in a barrel of flour.

Now, at long last, the search ended. We could return Paul to his family and, hopefully, they could find closure and gain a degree of peace about their loss.

We wore latex gloves and zipped Paul into the thick, protective bag, then strapped him into the litter. Someone set up an anchor around a tiny, beaten-down pine, and attached a brake rack and rope.

Two of us attached short lines to the litter and guided it down the snow slope, then carried it when the snow momentarily dried out near a small cliff band.

Someone hiked down the slope and set up another anchor for the next section of slope and we continued down the mountain. The decision was

made to fly him out, so we continued down for a thousand feet or more of elevation to the first available flat spot large enough for a landing zone.

Thunder rumbled through the cirque as a storm front blew over the horizon three thousand feet above.

"Let's spread 50' apart," advised one team member judiciously. "That way if any one gets struck by lightning, the others can revive him."

"And if lightning strikes *him*," I added, pointing to our package, "and he gets up... *run!*"

40 Utah Lake Monster

A killer lives beneath the waves of our county's enormous, shallow lake. This monster typically claims several lives every year, snatching its unsuspecting victims as they swim near the shore, near boats and rafts, or capsizing boats and sinking them in order to capture its next meal.

The monster is the lake itself.

In many areas, the lake bottom slopes slowly away from shore, allowing waders to walk for great distance on sand, rock, or mud without getting into trouble. Once the water rises above your chin, all bets are off.

When placid, the lake is dangerous enough, and swimmers sometimes panic and sink below the surface within a stone's throw from a marina jetty. When storm systems or weather fronts blow through, the lake grows agitated and even more deadly. Unlike deeper waters, Utah Lake wind waves stack up steep with brief intervals between them, making a three-foot wave more dangerous than a ten-foot ocean swell.

Such was the case one August afternoon when an east wind shoved two brothers on a float tube near Sandy Beach away from shore. They hopped off the tube to walk back, but the water had grown too deep and they couldn't touch bottom.

17-year-old Javier clung to a rope on the float tube and did a side stroke toward shore. Despite the contrary wind, they seemed to be making progress. Soon the lake bottom would rise up and touch the soles of their feet, and they could walk back to the picnic on shore with their family.

16-year-old Jorge swam fifteen or twenty feet ahead of his brother. He was getting tired. It was hard to suck in enough air to feed his oxygen-starved arms and legs. When he stopped swimming and turned back to look at his older brother, a look of desperation burned in his eyes.

And then he sank beneath the waves.

"Jorge!" his brother shouted and paddled frantically toward the spot where his brother went down. It was impossible to judge exactly the right spot as the waves rolled toward him and the wind continued to press against him and the tube. He knew better than to let go. Without flotation, he could easily drown himself.

When Javi judged himself to be at the right spot, he held the rope and dove under the murky water. He found the bottom and swam back and forth, reaching out into the inky depths in hopes of finding a wrist or an ankle, but all he found was mud and darkness.

The vacuum in his lungs forced him to the surface. He gulped down air, then dove again and again and again. Soon he could no longer ignore the fact that Jorge was gone. He had no idea how far he had blown from the spot where he went down.

The front passed and the winds died down, and Javi made it back to shore. As soon as his feet touched bottom, he let go of the float tube and raced up the beach shouting for someone to call 911.

By the time SAR arrived, there was no frantic searching. We knew better than to think we had any chance of saving the boy. We even knew our search patterns across the lake's surface were all but useless as the body probably wouldn't float for several days. We ran them anyway, on the off chance that we might find him, but more to save the family from the maddening anxiety of *nothing* being done about their lost brother and son.

Javi could not provide a specific enough description of the place last seen to make it practical to send divers, but we sent a boat dragging large hooks to comb the area.

CJ and I caught up with the float tube which had drifted far from shore and towed it back to the beach on watercraft.

Up to this point, I was enjoying the search. It was a gorgeous day to be out on the water. I felt sorry for the family, but couldn't afford to let myself think too much about their grief. That would only get in the way. It would weigh me down needlessly in coming days and turn SAR into a heavier burden than merely its time and money commitment created.

People die all the time. I came to terms with that fact long ago. SAR deals directly with as many as 15 deaths per year, though our average is about half that. I can only hope that I don't know them. Then it doesn't get personal. I can do my job, block out the rest, and move on.

Not all SAR members feel the same. Kevin, for example, loves to interact with victims' families. He keeps them informed, makes sure they stay hydrated, and attends funerals. He thrives on such connections and it motivates him to keep doing what he does.

I suspect that most of us are more like Susie. Her enthusiasm lights up a room and her friendly humor cheers up even the most discouraged victim. She naturally connects with those we serve but when we lose one, she takes it hard. Lucky for us, that has only happened once.

As CJ and I dragged our watercraft through the shallow water near shore, having shut off the engines to avoid sucking sand and rocks through the impellers, I saw Jorge's sister run down the beach toward her mother. She looked about eighteen years old and had the same olive skin, dark eyes, and jet-black hair.

A few brief words were exchanged, inaudible at this distance, and the sister doubled over and covered her face with her hands. She wrapped one arm around her stomach, collapsed onto the sand, and sobbed.

I looked away, but too late. The image was already burned into my mind and I could no longer escape her grief.

We would find Jorge a day or two later with the hooks dragging behind a boat, but for me, this story never quite ends. A tiny shred of that girl's loss has become my own and it will not let me forget.

41 FRIENDS IN NEED

Two of my friends have been rescued by our team, and I missed them both.

Raquel fell while climbing in Hobble Creek Canyon one spring. When the pager went off, I was out running laps around the local high school track, expressly thinking about getting in shape to be ready for rescues.

By the time I got home and checked my pager, then turned on the radio to find out what was going on, the call was already winding down. I didn't even know it was Raquel until I saw her a week or two later and she told me the story.

She came out fine, by the way.

The second, I more deeply regret missing. Following a SAR monthly training in a far corner of the county, I met up with my dad and a brother to ride snowmobiles and do some target shooting with pistols. When the page came out, I opted to stick around with my family, who had traveled an hour or two to meet up with me, rather than respond.

It turns out that my friend April had been riding a snowmobile down the Alpine Loop when another sled came around the corner and they collided. A neighbor of mine came across the crash first and did what he could to stabilize the victims and get a call to 911.

April's injuries took months to heal, and partly because of that, I wish I could have been around to help. When my friends get hurt, it's personal whether I'm there to see it or not.

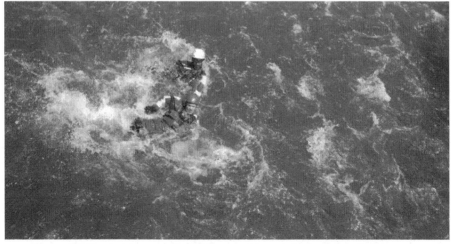

SAR members practice whitewater rescue in the Provo River

42 We Are Never Ready

I stopped my 4Runner on the River Trail above Canyon Glen Park and jumped out, pulling the last of my wetsuit on and zipping up my PFD. Tom's Sheriff truck had stopped in front of me and a dozen Provo and North Fork firefighters lined the trail and river's edge fifteen feet below.

"You ready?" Tom asked, quickly glancing over my gear. "Go!" he directed, and I scrambled down the bank.

My eyes swept over the scene as I took in what was going on. Kenny of North Fork Fire made his way up the river's edge, dressed in his dry suit and gasping for breath.

Firefighters lined the shore, some holding throw bags, none of them in water gear. Out in the middle of the river, pinned against a large rock, the pale legs of a nine-year-old girl showed through the clear water.

"You ready?" Kenny asked, between breaths. He had just gone into the river to retrieve the girl, but the current had been too strong and swept him downstream before he could pull her from the rock where the current had wedged her. He had already run a quarter mile up the trail in his dry suit when a passing biker had located her body only minutes earlier, then made a quick attempt to retrieve her, and he was now exhausted. "Go!" he directed.

Stephen, also of NFF, handed me a rope with a carabiner attached. His plan was to hold me in place long enough to retrieve the girl and bring her to shore. I wasn't wearing a type 5 PFD with a quick-release strap, however, and as a swiftwater rescue technician, I knew better than to clip myself to a rope that I wouldn't be able to escape if the river's laminar flow sucked me to the bottom.

I took the rope anyway and held on while I waded into the rushing white water.

Kimmie had spent the July afternoon with aunts, uncles and cousins. They stopped for a short visit to the small park below Bridal Veil Falls, about a mile upstream. Bikers and roller skaters cruised lazily along the River Trail, enjoying the breeze that their motion created. Mothers sat and kicked their feet through the placid reflecting pool below the falls. Children waded, splashed, and threw rocks into the shallow pond.

"Go get Carrie," Kimmie's aunt told her. "It's time to go." Kimmie nodded and walked away.

Carrie sat meditating on a large, flat boulder a few feet above the river's edge where Provo River spills down its steepest section over large boulders that whip the current white. Below her, the current licked the edges of sloped, mossy rocks .

The river's endless tumbling thunder created a relaxing cacophony that filled Carrie's ears and reverberated through her bones in a subtle inner massage. The sun beat down and warmed her skin. Her eyes drooped slowly closed as her body drank it all in.

Kimmie walked down the trail and called down to Carrie. "Time to go!" she shouted over the roaring whitewater. Carrie opened her eyes and stood up. She smiled at Kimmie and hiked up the riverbank. When she reached the trail, she found her niece's eyes glued to the flat rock. Kimmie looked up at her aunt with a question in her hopeful eyes. She wanted to climb down there.

"Sure," Carrie answered. "I'll take you."

Before Carrie could take her hand and lead her down the slope, Kimmie hopped off the trail and scooted her way to the rock. Kimmie's sudden eagerness, along with something about the river, all that power and energy, all that rushing and swirling, and all that cold, frothy water, made Carrie feel uncomfortable. Carrie scrambled down after her and was about to shout out a warning to stay away from the edge of the rock and not get any closer to the water. She was about to warn her about the slippery rocks below.

She didn't expect Kimmie to respond, but that would not be out of the ordinary. Kimmie always seemed to say more with her eyes than with her mouth. Even so, Carrie would watch Kimmie and make sure her eyes said "okay."

Before Carrie had time to utter a word, Kimmie jumped off the edge of the rock. The entire descent from trail to rock took only a few seconds. Her feet slipped and she slid into the current. The river grabbed her tiny body and swept her away.

"Kimmie's in the river!!!" Carrie screamed at the top of her lungs over the river's thunder. "Somebody help!!! Kimmie fell in the river!!!"

On the River Trail above, relatives looked toward Carrie then turned toward the river in shock to see Kimmie being swept by. They leapt into action, running down the trail with all their might.

Kimmie's Aunt April dove into the water, almost landing on her. With the current sweeping the pair around boulders and through pour-over troughs, April successfully pulled Kimmie toward her and held her against her chest, doing her best to keep her face above the surface. Just holding on took all her strength, and she couldn't swim against the current and back to shore.

April's brother Dan ran down trail to a break in the trees and waded into the river. Rocks and fallen logs created an eddy where the current wouldn't sweep him away. A thin tree branch hung over the water and Dan grabbed on for support while wading as far out as he could go and reaching for his sister and niece as they floated by. Unfortunately, they floated too far out in the current, just out of reach.

"Our little girl is in the river!" Dan's wife Crista shouted frantically as she ran. "Somebody call 911!" When she reached the next clearing and dashed to the river's edge, she saw April floating in the current, but Kimmie was nowhere to be seen.

Crista stood on shore and clung to two passing bikers and her teenage son

Keith who waded waist-high into the river and formed a human chain. Keith grabbed April's wrist and the whole chain got swept downriver. Luckily, they held on long enough to pull everyone toward the river's edge where they helped April onto shore.

Dan came running toward them and took in the situation. He saw April's panicked expression. He saw her arms. Kimmie was no longer there.

Crista stayed with April while all other family members again took off running. April didn't understand what had happened. "Where's the baby?" she asking in a shaky voice as her eyes filled with tears. "Where's the baby? I had her, I had her in my arms. I don't know what happened, how I lost her."

Downstream, Kimmie had one more chance. A woman sitting by the river in the Nunn's Park Campground was frantic. "Somebody help!" she screamed. "A little girl just floated by face down in the river!"

April's boyfriend Jack took off as fast as he could go, glancing again and again toward the river. And then he saw her not far away. He crashed through trees and brush to the nearest opening to the river. Stepping into the current up to his beltline, he clung to a tree branch for support. As Kimmie floated by, he reached out and grabbed her wrist.

Adrenaline surged and turned momentarily to elation, but in seconds the tug of war ended. With Kimmie now just downstream, water pressure built and ripped her from Jack's grip. His tenuous hold on her slippery skin proved no match for 440 cubic feet of water per second – weighing 27,500 pounds – rushing past.

Jack scrambled back to shore and ran downstream again but the trees blocked his path, the swift current outpaced him, and Kimmie got away.

The River Trail is sometimes separated from the river by as much as fifty feet, with thick stands of trees growing in the margin. Aunts, uncles and strangers did their best to find Kimmie's body in the river again, but many times along the way she got lost.

When a SAR page went out marked "River, Bridal Veil Falls, Urgent," I quickly changed and drove toward the canyon. Team members asked where exactly to respond to and ICS did not know an exact location, so assignments were made to search various spots of the river. I stopped at Canyon Glen Park and had half-changed into my wet suit when word came that the body had been located half a mile up-river. I jumped back into my truck and sped up the river trail to where I found a crowd of fire fighters and deputies.

A biker riding the trail had spotted the body, caught up in the middle of the river between Canyon Glen and Nunn's Park. I finished zipping up my wet suit and PFD and clambered down to the river.

Stephen fed out the rope and it steadied me as I waded into the current which tried its best to push me around and knock me off my unsteady footing of rounded, slippery rocks. When the water grew too deep for me to safely walk in and risk foot entrapment, I fell forward and the river swallowed me as the current carried me along. I swam hard for a moment, then let the current sweep me right up atop the glassy-smooth pour-over where I stopped, facing upstream. A few inches of water covered the rock, but I got my body out of the current enough that it let me stay in place.

I let go of Stephen's line then and looked down to my left. Kimmie lay there, submerged and face down, her legs only a few inches below the clear, glassy surface. I grabbed her legs and held on tight, determined not to let her wash away from my grip, and expecting to find her wedged in tightly based on Kenny's experience of having difficulty dislodging her.

Instead, she came right out. I lifted her limp body into my arms and cradled her against my chest. She felt small and light. She was not breathing. I didn't take the time to check for a pulse as there was nothing I could do about it perched precariously midstream.

I spun my legs sideways and the current swept us back into the river. My feet touched bottom and I took several steps through the boulder's eddy, then swam when the current knocked me down.

I kicked hard toward shore, holding the child up in front of me, then shouted "Take her!" to a fireman waiting with a throw bag as I swept past. He lifted her from my arms and I washed another fifty feet downstream before I could stop and climb onto the bank.

By the time I ran back up the trail, the girl was lying on the pavement, surrounded by paramedics. They pumped oxygen into her lungs through a bag mask and were busy administering CPR while an AED was readied.

They were able to get her heart beating, but it wouldn't keep going for long. We finally loaded her into a waiting helicopter and she flew to a Salt Lake hospital to undergo a slow rewarming process.

At last the flurry of activity ebbed. I checked onto the radio and was assigned to search the river for the aunt who had reportedly gone into the river, but the rumors didn't tell whether she got out safely or not.

Two firemen stood on my truck's running boards and we drove up river to Nunn's Park, watching for another body in the river. We saw nothing and eventually CP called everyone back to the Command Post.

As I pulled up next to half a dozen fire trucks and parked, I saw my friend Keith. I got out of the truck and walked toward him. "I just carried a little girl out of the river," I told him excitedly, and then came his shocking reply.

"That was *my cousin!*"

Oh, no. Oh, no! That changed everything.

Suddenly this was more than just another exciting rescue where we simply did our best and then hoped for a happy ending. Suddenly this became personal. Keith led me to a tree where his sister and father – also my friends – sat in the shade. I hugged Carrie and sat down next to Dan and put an arm around his shoulders.

Dan told me about wading into the river and reaching out for his sister's wrist as she had hold of Kimmie. He told me about Jack getting a hold on Kimmie but the current wrenching her from his grasp, then began to sob. "I felt so helpless!" he choked out through his tears, his face wrinkling together in grief.

"There's nothing you could have done," I assured him. I told him about the danger of diving in after her without a PFD and force of the water, how we carefully trained every spring just to remind us how powerful and dangerous it can be. I told him about the firefighter who washed past her, unable to stop and remove her from the river. He seemed somewhat comforted then - I certainly hoped so.

April was taken to the ER. The rocks in the river had beat her up and she had taken in enough water to make her nauseous, but with no more serious injuries she was soon released. The family grieved together and called Kimmie's mother in Colorado who drove all night to reach the hospital the next morning.

With the frantic rescue efforts over, the terrible waiting began. We hoped and prayed and counted the hours, waiting to hear the outcome. I desperately wanted a happy ending to this story. I longed to meet Kimmie under happier circumstances, to hug her again and this time, get hugged in return. I wanted to see her smile and laugh and grow up, and I wanted to become an even bigger part of this family who I already loved.

The hospital cautiously warmed the girl's blood at a single degree per hour. We didn't know what to expect. She had spent at least 20 minutes under water. Maybe 30. Just four minutes without oxygen can leaving irreversible brain damage, but we hoped that the cold water slowed the damage and gave her a chance.

By the following morning, it grew clear that our hopes were in vain. Kimmie would not live. Surrounded by her loving family, she passed away early that afternoon.

We're never ready. We are NEVER ready for what will happen next. I know some people involved are blaming themselves for not doing more, but what more could they have done? I imagine they're making lists of things they could have done differently, but that's not fair!!!

They ran. They reached. They swam. They tried their best, but they were simply outmatched.

We are never ready for our challenges, we don't get a trial run before the real thing, and all we can do is try our best. All we can do in hindsight is accept what has happened, grieve our irreplaceable losses, then let them go and carry on.

43 STRANDED

A boat's motor broke down one Sunday night out on 100,000-acre Utah Lake. No matter what they tried, it wouldn't slip into gear and the prop wouldn't spin. They called 911 and described their general location as a little ways north of Pelican Point, which reduced the search area to ten or twenty square miles.

ICS dispatched search teams to the general area while those of us not lucky enough to get sent out on personal watercraft stood around the command post hoping for another assignment.

Tom's phone rang and he answered. "Okay," he said, then added "Thank you" a moment later, and hung up. "They're directly below the moon," he reported while shaking his head. Apparently the stranded boaters had called to help us zero in on their location. "That narrows things down a bit."

The phone rang again and he turned toward the dark lake after picking up. "I see three airplanes," he said after listening for a moment, "which one is it?" He listened for a moment more, then said "Okay, thank you."

He hung up the phone, then turned it off, shaking his head again and expelling a heavy sigh from his lungs. "The first one," he relayed. "They're below the first airplane. Whichever one that is."

I got assigned to someone's personal ski boat and we struck out across the lake, the bow plunging smoothly through two-foot swells, the moon and city lights dancing over the glassy waves, turning the surface to glistening silver.

"Who's stupid enough to be out on a night like this?" the boat driver asked rhetorically.

I think it's beautiful, I thought in reply.

We soon found the boat and towed them to a nearby harbor.

A sailboat sits near the beach with a glorious sunset in the background

44 CAPSIZED

A storm front blew through the valley and kicked up steep four-foot waves on the lake that capsized a ski boat. Eight children and two adults were tossed into the lake and came up coughing, sputtering, and blinking the water from their eyes. Luckily, all the children wore PFDs and one of the adults had a cell phone in a waterproof container and managed to keep it dry long enough to place an urgent call to 911.

The mention of children in the water brought the team rushing away from work or whatever we happened to be doing possibly even faster than we'd have done otherwise.

State Parks provided approximate GPS coordinates five miles northwest of the Provo marina, and Olin and I were assigned as the first watercraft team.

We maintained a more or less wakeless speed along the inside of the jetties, and when we turned to exit the marina, immediately encountered the large waves. With any speed at all, our watercraft launched from wave crest to wave face, a jarring experience that made me wonder how long the hulls could stand it before smashing to pieces.

We adjusted our speed up and down for a minute, seeking the ideal speed to cross the wave intervals more smoothly, but only slowing down to a few miles per hour could reduce the pounding.

I turned toward Olin and pointed west. He nodded. The plan was to cross the lake nearly perpendicular to the waves rather than trying to drive directly toward our destination. I squeezed the throttle and felt the satisfying power of the 1.8 liter engine thrust the craft forward.

By changing our trajectory, we were able to ride around 60 mph. We still spent roughly half the time airborne, but we landed smoothly in the next trough rather than slamming hard against each wave face.

The speed felt good, as did the jumping, the smooth landings as the wedged hull sliced apart the water surface, and the combination of sun, wind, and occasional spray of water on my face. Having a destination and an important purpose made it all the more rewarding. No wonder everybody on the team likes lake rescues.

We crossed the lake in less than ten minutes, and turned north through the smoother water in the wind-protected lee of Pelican Point, then began scanning the lake for the capsized boat.

State Parks had successfully rescued the passengers and transported them to a nearby marina. Our job became recovery.

Once we located the boat – its upside-down white hull showing only a few square feet above the water – we got to work. I drove past the boat and jumped off my watercraft with a buoy to tie to the boat to make it easier to find, especially if it later sank completely. With the current weather and waves, State Parks wouldn't recover the boat any time soon.

I swam toward the boat hull and let a wave wash me into a sitting position straddling its smooth surface. I felt like a whale rider. Tying the buoy to the bow eye turned out more challenging than expected when the next wave nearly washed me off. I scooted back and braced myself more carefully for each wave until completing the task.

Olin called in the exact GPS coordinates for other teams to find us, then picked me up and gave me a lift to my watercraft, now blown a hundred and fifty feet across the lake.

Other watercraft soon arrived and we began running search patterns, collecting the wide-spread debris – seat cushions, bags, flip flops, lip balm, sunscreen, and anything else that floats – then relaying them to a larger boat when our hands and foot troughs filled up.

Once the task was finished, we raced back across the lake and reluctantly entered the harbor for a wakeless-speed-only cruise to the boat ramps.

Sitting atop the capsized ski boat

45 SCOUTING FOR DOLLARS

One of my favorite things about rescues is that they take me to memorable places I wouldn't otherwise go.

Grove Creek Canyon, for example, has a perfectly good trail switchbacking up its north side and crossing above the waterfalls that fall hundreds of feet down a narrow canyon bottom. Yet when two boy scouts got lost on the way down the trail, my team was assigned to search the river in case they slipped off the trail and tumbled all the way down.

The canyon bottom was so narrow that it felt more like a ravine. We jumped back and forth over the stream repeatedly when whichever side we were walking on turned into a steep drop of loose dirt into the water, or thick brush blocked our way.

The call came out around midnight, and two helicopters hovered over us, sometimes hitting us with their spot light and making it feel like a military operation back in 'Nam.

Once we reached the falls where the river plunges a thousand feet in less than a quarter mile, there was no way to continue safely up the river. And there really was no point in continuing to search it, because the helicopter spotlights and full moon would show us if a boy happened to miraculously get stuck there and not wash all the way down.

Rather than hike back down the river, we chose to search the steep hillside up to the trail now at least eight hundred feet above us. The steep scree and dirt never felt quite stable except for one or two relatively flat spots less than ten feet wide. When we reached small ten- or fifteen-foot cliff bands, I would try to climb over, but had to back off due to the rotten, broken nature of the only available hand holds. Instead, we worked our way around to passable places. Two members of our team had less experience in such loose terrain, and we often trailed ropes and used body belays - wrapping the rope around our back - to lend them a little extra security.

I never expected to find the scouts in our search area. In fact, I had a pretty good guess where they'd be. The trail splits after a long switchback up the side of the canyon and one path continues out across the face of the mountain. If the boys missed the turn, that's where they'd end up.

Sure enough, around 3:00 a.m., just as my team finished its climb up to the trail and radioed in for our next assignment, that's where another team found them, sitting in a little shelter they built above the valley, looking down at the lights of their neighborhood and staying put just like they had been taught to do when lost.

We hiked down the trail and reached the parking lot within half an hour to find a Pleasant Grove police officer standing there in the moonlight. He could hardly believe our selfless dedication and good attitudes as we showed up, laughing and enjoying our spontaneous midnight excursion.

"You guys are...*incredible!*" he said, "If I had a million dollars right now, I'd give it to all of you!"

With all my heart, I returned the favor by wishing that such a selfless person had a million dollars right then.

A SAR member ice climbs the first pitch of Stairway to Heaven

A bird's eye view of Upper Falls and The Fang in Provo Canyon

46 FAMOUS

The 12 year old boy dressed in his blue Cub Scout uniform stood at the front of the room. His eyes were closed, arms folded, and head bowed.

"And please bless us," he prayed, "that we won't get famous."

I had been asked to give a presentation on Search and Rescue to the troop in a friend's neighborhood. It's a common request for SAR members to present to scouts and at emergency preparedness fairs.

Among the exciting stories of high adventure and lives saved that I shared, between the survival tips taught, and nestled among the thought-provoking questions asked, I told the boys a sure-fire way to get famous very quickly: get lost.

I told them how to get lost – by doing the opposite of sage advice like to hug a tree, bring a map, know how to use a compass and such. I told them the down sides to getting lost – the dangers, discomforts, fears, and possible death. I begged them to hike carefully, stay in groups, not get lost, and not get famous.

As I listened to the boy's prayer that concluded the pack meeting, I smiled and knew that my message got through.

A hiker stranded between dangerous cliffs is lowered to safety near Bridal Veil Falls

47 IRON MAN

I sat in the Achilles raft with my team of four and waited. If all went according to plan, 2,000 swimmers would churn through the lake's murky water and pass us by without incident.

The racers and race organizers, however, were not the only ones making plans. Mother Nature had her own schedule to keep, and a strong front swept into the valley right on time - just as the starting gun fired around 7:00 a.m. Barometric pressure plummeted momentarily, and a stout wind rushed in to fill the vacuum.

Hordes of uber athletes plunged into the water, reaching out with muscular arms and pulling against the lake, then raised their arms above the water, fingers sliding up their lats and past bulging shoulders sporting a number written with permanent marker, and reaching ahead once more to punch the water, break the surface tension, and open a passage for head, shoulders, and body to slip through.

Legs kicked hard, bodies rolling elegantly back and forth from side to side as they charged fluidly forward; left, right, left, right, left, right.

Mouths blew bubbles underwater, releasing spent air whose oxygen had been sucked out by muscle cells now burning fuel like coal heaped into a locomotive's furnace. Now and then a racer twisted his or her neck to one side or the other to gulp down a fresh lung-full of air. The swimmers's lips resembled the blowholes of an enormous pod of very slow dolphins.

Against the racers blew the wind. At first it only kicked up large ripples and tiny white caps, but within fifteen minutes, swells built up to three feet tall.

The giant race markers - four-foot-tall, blaze-orange floating spheres - were anchored without enough rode - heavy chain designed to keep anchors flat and their spades digging in. Each passing wave lifted the buoys' anchor free from the clay lake bottom and the wind scooted the marker downwind a foot or two at a time. We sat and watched the markers blow past our boat and wondered what race officials would do about it.

What they did was cancel the swim portion of the race. Not only did the race markers' flight make a timed event impossible to fairly measure, but some swimmers could get in big trouble in the growing swells.

The radio relayed our assignment to send all swimmers back to shore. We started the outboard motor, hauled in our anchor, and got to work.

As we approached a swimmer, we blew a sharp blast on our whistle to get his or her attention. When they stopped and looked up, we shouted, "The swim is canceled! Swim toward the sun!"

We gave the morning sun as the navigation point, pointing east toward the brilliant globe rising over the mountains, because the racers' low vantage point amid the wave crests made the marina impossible to see, and even the mountain ridges to the east provided ambiguous direction since they ran the entire length of the valley.

Many swimmers were doing an impressive job, cruising along comfortably, rhythmically stroking and breathing as if the four-foot swells didn't exist. Others were tired or confused, disoriented and swimming toward every point of the compass, and a few on the verge of panic. These we helped into the raft and, once we filled the boat, transported them to a larger Sheriff or State Parks boat.

The bow air chamber of our motorized raft was slightly underinflated and once we filled up with eight or ten people, it would sometimes fold against the steep wave faces.

One swimmer seemed particularly confused. When I directed him to "Swim toward the sun!" he responded by asking, "Which sun?"

Unaware that the race was canceled, he must have assumed I was referring to one of the large orange race buoys which had long since absconded.

Elsewhere, watercraft performed the same work. CJ and others reached out to troubled swimmers and grasped left hands. Then, with a light touch on the throttle, let the water lift and set them gently on the back of the craft from where they could climb onto the seat for a quick ride to shore.

As the lake emptied of racers, news and medical helicopters hovered over the water and pointed us in the direction of any remaining bright green swim caps.

When we could find no more, we got word that six racers were still missing. We began running wide search patterns along the race course, hoping to find them.

We also received the news that one racer was dead. He drown near the starting line. I never heard a conclusive cause of death, and wonder whether he suffered a heart attack or if he got kicked in the face in the initial chaos, aspirated water, choked and drown.

As we plied the lake, a land search discovered that all missing racers had never entered the water.

Due to the uncooperative weather, the rest of the race was cut down to a half Iron Man. Future efforts to challenge the Utah Lake Monster were planned in shallower and more sheltered waters.

Later that year, all SAR members who participated in the rescue on the water were awarded the prestigious Exceptional Service Award at the Sheriff's annual awards banquet.

For my part, I gave up on the goal I set when I joined SAR of keeping track of how many lives we saved. There was simply no way of knowing.

EXCEPTIONAL SERVICE AWARD
2002

SHAUN ROUNDY

Presented in recognition of performance by a unit or team significantly above what is normally expected while serving on the U.C.S.O. Search and Rescue Team on June 8, 2002 in support of the 2002 Ironman search and rescue at Utah Lake.

48 THE BODY

I was working from home when the pager went off at 11:30 on a Thursday morning in April. 02-02-69 - code for River-Provo-Missing Person. I changed quickly and jumped in the car.

A motorized wheelchair had been found tipped over near the river's edge. We didn't know if someone had fallen – either accidentally or intentionally – into the river. While Provo PD and Tom followed up on clues and leads, we began a thorough search of the river.

Lookouts were stationed on bridges to peer through the turbid water. Fishermen lining the shore were told about the search and asked to let us know if they saw anything. One of them had just been rescued from Utah Lake the weekend before and voiced his strong support for our efforts.

My team started at the lake and searched the shoreline for a body caught up in branches. Once we finished our area, we jumped into the river and floated down in case a different view would reveal something we missed.

The Provo ran as high and fast as I had ever seen it. A long, wet winter piled some stations above the Provo River drainage with over 150% of normal precipitation and climbing. Water managers emptied mountain dams as quickly as possible to make room for the anticipated spring run off.

Boats and watercraft passed us as they made their way up river on their search.

After completing our assignment and checking the jetty protruding a hundred yards into the lake, Darin drove us a mile up river and had just dropped us off for another floating search when a request came over the radio.

"We need more people in dry suits up here," Tom said. "We may have something."

Our ride turned around and we climbed back into the pickup for a quick lift up the river trail. We grabbed ropes, webbing and 'biners from deputies to build a rope system across the river if needed.

The current upstream ran much faster than what we had searched near the river mouth. The lake began to dam up the river there and it ran deeper and slower. Here, it swept by dramatically, and floating down it would very likely wrap anything or anyone around a strainer – a log or stick in the current – that would prove next to impossible to escape.

Lucky for us, the white object – about the size of a t-shirt – that glowed eerily two or three feet below the water's cloudy surface had caught against a log that divided the swift current from a shallow eddy. Four of us waded carefully to the protected side of the log and peered down.

"What do you think?" asked Swiftwater Sergeant David Lynton.

"It feels like a body," assured Chris, one of the two team members who had already investigated, poking the body with a stick like an avalanche probe. Curiosity then got the best of him and he leaned over the log and down into the water. His eyes widened and he exclaimed, "I think I've got a hand!"

With a grip on the body, Chris didn't want to let go and risk losing it. At the same time, we knew better than to simply pull. We stood no chance of winning a tug of war with the river once the body was dislodged from whatever hung it up. The river would rip it from our grip and we'd have to begin the search all over again.

Having already searched for three hours, there was no urgency to extract the body. This would not be a rescue but a recovery, and caution and safety was the name of the game.

Someone on shore tossed us the end of a throw bag rope and David reached down to attach it to the body. As soon as he bent into the river, however, the water pressure against his arms threatened to knock him over.

"Hurry," Chris admonished, "my hand's going numb."

"Steady me," David requested. "The current keeps shoving me too close to Chris' whining."

We grabbed onto his PFD and held him in place while he wrapped the rope several times around the body - what must have been the wrist - to hold it fast. At last we were ready to pull it free. Even if the current caught it now, we had fifteen feet to pull it into the eddy before the current swept around the next set of strainers.

Chris and David tugged on the rope and up came not a body, but *half* a body.

By the look of it, it had spent several months in the river. Its skin was bleached white, and large eyeballs protruded from their sockets.

Also, it was a goat.

The hand Chris thought he felt turned out to be the roof of its mouth. We joked about notifying next of kin and dragged it from the river.

We soon got word that the wheelchair's serial number had led to the owner, who informed us that it was stolen the previous weekend. The thief had probably gotten tired of it (or the batteries wore down) and abandoned it near the river. The entire search had been a wild goat chase.

49 THANKSGIVING DAY

Nothing beats Thanksgiving dinner with all the trimmings. I sat at the table with a dozen friends, eagerly waiting to fill up my plate and dig in. Our friend Jenn was not only a superb chef, but extremely generous, and this made the third year in a row that she invited a dozen of us over to put on a few pounds.

Someone said grace and I lifted a large spoonful of stuffing onto my plate. Next came a healthy serving of candied yams. The rich smell of brown sugar filled my nostrils and I'm sure I smiled as I passed the pan down the table to make room for the next delicious dish.

Suddenly a loud chirping sound erupted from my belt. I set the pan down and pulled out my pager. I read the message text and continued to stare at it, my eyes darting briefly between the screen and the plate of steaming food just beyond it. Of all the rotten timing.

I thought of the rest of the team, probably sitting down with their families right now. Perhaps relatives had traveled to bring extended family together. If they left home now, they'd be missed. If I responded to the call, it would leave that much less need for them to leave home and family.

"I'd better go," I said glumly.

I snarfed down what had already been dished up, then began my goodbyes and stood up to get my coat.

Jenn was already a step ahead of me. As I turned toward the door, she handed me a ziplock bag with a couple fluffy white dinner rolls - my favorite - and a paper plate folded around a slice of pumpkin pie - another favorite.

"Thanks," I said with a grateful smile.

"Be safe," she advised as she wrapped her arms around my waist and gave me a goodbye hug.

From the Provo Canyon pull out above Nunn's park, a fire was visible high on a cliff, two or three thousand feet above us to the southeast. Hikers from out of state had seen Cascade's stunning cliffs and decided on the spur of the moment to climb over it. They found their way through multiple cliff bands, then climbed hundreds of feet of near-vertical cracks in the rock only to find their passage blocked by sheer vertical limestone. They couldn't go forward and didn't dare retreat back the way they came.

Night had already fallen and the darkness made it impossible to see the exact route to their location, but we had done several rescues in the general area and I knew most of the way.

ICS put Kevin and I on a hasty team to scout out a route to the stranded hikers and possibly bring them down. We packed up the gear we thought we'd need and started up the mountain. A rocky dirt road led past a gate and to a steep, abandoned four-wheel drive road. From there, we caught the Great Western Trail and hiked up canyon to a rocky ridge where the scrub oak grew a little less thickly than the rest of the slope. Eventually we gained a large ravine and tall cliffs engulfed us.

Near the top of the ravine, a fifteen-foot cliff provided access to a steep dirt slope extending a few hundred feet above us. We clung to branches for support and dug our hard boot soles into the loose earth to keep from tumbling back down to our deaths. After reaching a knob where the ground flattened out for ten or fifteen feet, we crossed a washed out slope and turned left up a steep rock ramp.

Now all we had to do was find our way through small cliff bands for half a mile up-canyon, and a broad slope would lead us to the base of the cliff where the hikers stood around their fire and waited.

I had come this far earlier this year for a pair of hikers, and it seemed a miracle that we had found the passage so quickly in the dark. From here on, the terrain was new and unknown and I wasn't sure what we'd find in the final two hundred yards before reaching the open slope.

Kevin took off ahead of me, and we ended up taking slightly different routes. He took the high road, I took the low. In such precarious terrain, I judged it prudent to stick together in case one of us got into trouble, so I climbed straight upward to close the gap between us.

As I climbed through the dark, a doable route appeared in my headlamp beam, but when I reached the final fifteen foot cliff, it looked a little sketchy. I couldn't be sure exactly how strong the rock and dirt would prove once I applied my weight to it. Had it begun on flat ground, I'd have scrambled up it without a second thought, but such was not the case. Below me lay hundreds of feet of steep mountainside. If I slipped, I probably would not stop. That didn't sound like fun.

Luckily, Kevin had waited for me there and dropped down the end of a 20' strand of webbing. I grabbed on and felt sure I wouldn't fall with the added support. I grabbed onto thin branches and kicked my boots into soft dirt and climbed easily upward. Once I gained the top, I brushed the dirt from the climb off my legs and we continued our ascent.

When we encountered cliff bands, we climbed over or found our way around them. Team members down on the highway watched our headlights and gave their opinion on which direction might lead us through the cliffs, dimly lit by city lights reflecting from high clouds.

We arrived within a hundred yards of our passage to the open slope below the hikers when a team behind us knocked a pile of large rocks loose. The small boulders went crashing down the steep mountainside and someone shouted "Rock! Rock! Rock!" into the radio to warn teams below to take cover.

This event made Tom reconsider the current plan. The hikers were safe and comfortable with a warm fire burning. They had a wide, safe ledge and even a shallow cave nearby for shelter. They could wait till morning for rescue. Sending teams up through the dark simply did not merit the risk of treating them like bowling pins for a mountain full of loose rock.

"All mountain teams," he radioed up, "let's stay put for the night. I don't want anyone to get killed."

The order caught Kevin and I on a steep but stable hillside. If we stopped in

A team member makes his way across Cascade's rugged NW corner

our tracks, we would not sleep. If we slept, we'd wake abruptly from a falling dream that didn't end when we opened our eyes.

We advised CP that we would continue until we found a safe place to stop, which happened to be a six-foot-wide ledge surrounded by a few ancient pines growing through cracks in the rock.

After spending ten minutes scraping away rocks and leveling the dirt, we settled in. Kevin unrolled his bivy sack and I opened the emergency foil bivy the team bought for all members a year before. Nights like tonight are why we always carry enough gear - food, water, clothing and shelter - to spend 24 hours on the mountain. Enough gear to survive, that is, which is not the same thing as being comfortable.

My bivy didn't breathe, and when the moisture from my body built up in raindrop-size beads of water, I occasionally woke up and turned the bag inside out. During one of these noisy adjustments (sorry, Kev!), I remembered the rolls and retrieved them from the top pouch of my back pack. Mmm. My favorite. Thank you, Jenn! Happy Thanksgiving.

As we slept fitfully through the night, I sometimes awoke and heard sounds of something walking around our camp in the dark. In the morning, we found mountain lion tracks in the soft dirt not far from our ledge.

Kevin and I awoke early and, by daylight, found an easy passage down a steep slope and onto the open slope leading to our stranded victims. We traversed across to the base of the cliff that held our victims trapped and looked up. The crack looked like an easy climb, maybe 5.5 in the Yosemite Decimal System, though the exposure of a hundred feet just up the first of two or three pitches got us talking about how to protect it. Kevin felt comfortable going for it, while I wanted to jam at least an occasional improvised chock stone into the cracks, the way mountaineers did before the advent of wired aluminum chocks and mechanical camming devices.

Sure, the climb would be easy, but this rescue wasn't worth risking our lives for.

That's when the arrival of a Life Flight helicopter ended the debate for us. They landed in the parking lot near CP and secured a paramedic to the hoist cable. The chopper then flew him up the mountain, hovered over the hikers and lowered him down. They flew away while the medic put a hiker into a harness to be flown down to the parking lot with the medic, and repeated the trip five times until all our victims were safe on the ground.

I could tell Kevin was disappointed. He wanted to reach the victims first. He wanted to be the hero. It certainly would have been memorable and exciting. It would have made it worth missing Thanksgiving dinner.

We scrambled our way directly down the slope and rappelled over the large cliff bands that made an approach by this route impossible. Then retraced our steps down the rough scree back to the trail and the parking lot.

Far below, waiting patiently for me the whole time, sitting on my car's dashboard, sat a thick, sweet slice of pumpkin pie. Mmm. My favorite.

Climbing over one of several barriers in Cascade's NW cliffs

The first Rappel with the highway far below

50 Quick Change

Lindsey arrived at Utah Lake State Park and pulled her wetsuit from the back of her SUV. A boat had sunk across the lake and its passengers were treading water in two-foot waves. South-end team members had picked up watercraft from the S.O. and were now backing their trailers down the boat ramps. If Lindsey wanted to get an assignment to ride one to the scene, she had to get ready quickly.

By opening the driver's door, her car and the truck parked next to her made an enclosed dressing room where she stripped down and put on her swimming suit before stepping into the tight-fitting neoprene wetsuit and slipping her arms into her PFD. She stuffed a waterproof radio into one of the pockets and took one last look over herself to make sure she had everything she needed.

Now ready for action, she slammed her car door shut and started toward CP for an assignment when a face caught her attention. A face through a windshield. The man in the truck parked next to her with a front row seat to her private dressing room wore a wide, happy grin.

Climbing Ed & Terry Wall in Rock Canyon

5 1 Good Intentions

Good intentions don't always result in good ideas. Some people would say the bad ideas began a long time before Danny's friends got him stuck between a rock and a hard place.

They would say it was a bad idea to drive seven miles into the West Desert and up a rocky road that would happily rip out your transmission or puncture your oil pan if you didn't drive very carefully.

They would say it was a bad idea to clamber down a fifteen-foot hole in the ground and crawl through a long, tight, wet squeeze into a subterranean labyrinth of narrow winding passages through solid rock.

In hindsight, even well-intentioned friends would admit that it wasn't such a good idea to give Danny's arms a tug when his body couldn't quite fit through the narrow, awkward slot they had just squirmed between.

"Breathe out!" Mindy directed, "empty your lungs to collapse your rib cage and then we'll pull you right through."

Mindy and Thomas succeeded in getting Danny's rib cage past the tight spot, but then came the pelvis. No amount of breathing out would collapse his hip bones.

Backing up didn't work, either. Not just because body's don't pull backward as well as forward. There was hardly any room near Danny's feet to pull from.

Eventually, they began to make up for their error in judgment by returning to the surface and dialing a three-digit phone number.

Search and rescue made their way to Nutty Putty Cave and clambered, crawled, or walked - usually hunched over or leaning against a slanted rock slab - to the passage where Danny lay lodged half way through a narrow passage.

Derk and others went to Danny's head while I found my way to his feet. A giant square block formed one wall of the chamber and rescuers could squeeze their arms over and under it. I had just enough room to sit up and, if I took off my helmet and slid my head into a narrow slot in the chamber's roof, I had enough room to avoid getting kicked in the face by the pair of white sneakers I would stare at for the next few hours.

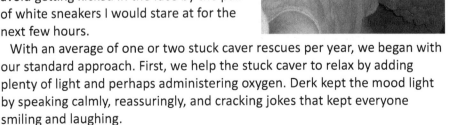

With an average of one or two stuck caver rescues per year, we began with our standard approach. First, we help the stuck caver to relax by adding plenty of light and perhaps administering oxygen. Derk kept the mood light by speaking calmly, reassuringly, and cracking jokes that kept everyone smiling and laughing.

Most stuck cavers aren't as stuck as they think they are. They get into a tight spot and they panic. They want to get out NOW. They want yards. We talk them into inches, locking fingers or hands and pulling while they push forward with their toes. "Fantastic!" we say encouragingly as they scoot half an inch forward. "Ten more like that and you'll break free!"

If all that fails, then we consider more extreme measures like greasing up the rock with vegetable oil, removing clothing, or chipping away at the rock.

Our first tactic with Danny was to treat him like one of those mind-bender puzzles that you have to twist just right to get apart or reassemble. Seemingly disembodied arms reached over the block and down to grab onto the hammer strap on Danny's jeans. I lifted his feet and others worked his torso. We lifted and twisted, pushed back and forth, looking for the magic angle that would let his frame slip through.

We dropped webbing into the tiny chamber and tied them around Danny's legs to facilitate our efforts, but after half an hour or more of trying, we still couldn't slide him free.

I could see the spot that made extrication impossible. A two-inch projection of rock prevented Danny's hips from falling into the widest section of the passage. If we could remove even half of that, he might slip right through.

We brought in a pneumatic drill that someone had in their truck and powered it with a SCUBA tank. I chipped away at the rock while others hoisted Danny out of the way, and then another team member reached below the block and worked from the side. Bit by bit, the pointy obstruction chipped away.

At one point while I sat at Danny's feet in my tiny cubby hole, I experienced a moment of the claustrophobia that some people feel in just reading this story. A sense of panic welled up in my chest and began to climb its way into my throat, threatening to clamp it down tight and make it difficult to suck in a breath of air.

*That's **not** going to happen!* I told myself. I took a deep breath and forced my body to relax. The panic hesitated and stopped rising toward my face. I took another breath and it began to retreat. A third and a fourth breath, and the battle was over. The panic faded completely away.

After shaving away an inch of the tiny projection, we tried again. Webbing fastened to Danny's waist and legs lifted and twisted. Derk pulled, I pushed, and suddenly my little room grew larger as Danny's body slid forward and out. Free at last, he scampered out of the cave in good spirits.

Free at last, Danny heads for the cave exit

*Approaching the summit ridge on Mount Nebo
searching for an injured boy scout*

*SST members use a 3-to-1 mechanical advantage system
to raise a motorcyclist's bike back onto the trail*

52 The Boy Who Cried Lost

The first time we rescued Johnny, a 23-year-old slightly autistic man, we found him on a steep scree slope just up-canyon from Bridal Veil Falls. The sun had set and the sky turned a beautiful dusky blue as daylight drained slowly westward.

Summer had arrived and Johnny liked nothing better than getting out for a good hike in the mountains. His blond hair blew lightly in the late-evening canyon wind and he sat glued to the loose slope while we commended him for calling us rather than risking a fall, and strapped on a harness to support him in walking back to the trail.

We met again a few weeks later in Dry Canyon above Lindon. Once again, nightfall caught him on a steep slope far from any trail. Johnny was a sweet, friendly kid, and Tom gave him a headlamp and advised him to carry it with him to help out if he got caught out after dark again.

Perhaps we shouldn't have been surprised when Johnny called us once more, this time near the top of the front-range peak between Slide and Slate Canyons above South Provo.

He had his headlight with him (some team members made *tsk, tsk* sounds with their tongues and jokingly chided Tom for enabling Johnny's risky behavior) but evening caught him crossing a steep summer snowfield. The snow was hard-packed by warm weather, rain, and refreezes, and a slip on the hard surface would be difficult to arrest.

Terrain along the front range of Provo's mountains belongs not to County SAR, but to the Provo Mountain Rescue team made up of police officers and firefighters. They call us anyway for some of the more technical rescues or when additional manpower is needed.

Thus I flew up in the second helicopter shuttle with Sam Hunter, a Provo police officer and PMR member. I enjoyed the exhilarating sensation of rising straight up into the sky while the ground fell away. The criss-cross grid of street lamps and front porch lights swiveled as the helicopter rotated mid-air and headed south for Slide Canyon.

The nearest LZ was at least a mile away from Johnny's position, in a flat meadow not far from Camel Pass road between the front range and Provo Peak. Johnny shone his headlamp at us as we flew past overhead, a brilliant white gleam flashing near the crest of the dark mountain.

Two other PMR members had already struck out from the LZ and begun the traverse and climb toward our victim. Sam and I followed, cutting a gently upward route across and up the hillside, through tall mountain weeds and over hard, clumpy dirt shaped by deer and elk hooves during rainy periods when the earth turned to soft mud. Our gradual ascent would make for the best time and least effort.

Weeds turned to old pine forest, snow fields, then fields of wild roses growing across a thirty-degree slope. I donned my crampons to cross the snowfield and the spikes later caught on the roses as I tried to high step over them, pressing the stalks down to prevent the sharp thorns from tearing my pants. Before I could lift my other foot forward to catch me, I fell forward and did a pair of tumbling summersaults down the hill. Despite a series of scratches that brought beads of crimson blood to my bare forearms, I had to laugh as I got up and continued on.

When we reached a wide, snow-filled gully, I turned left to traverse around it without losing elevation, rather than dropping down and climbing back up the other side. Sam asked if we ought to just cut straight through, but endless miles of hiking through remote mountains had taught me that elevation comes harder than distance and we'd be better off adding another hundred feet to our route than climbing down and up fifty.

This played out perfectly when, not long after, Johnny saw our headlamps and called out to us. From over a mile around the mountain, we had hiked to within seventy five feet elevation of his position. Later on, down in the Slate Canyon parking lot, SAR members would overhear PMR talking and report to me that they thought SAR was made up of geniuses even though hitting Johnny that close on was as much chance as skill.

Sam and I passed up the first PMR team who wound up below us. They climbed a hundred yards or so to our position and we made our plan. Rather than guiding Johnny all the way back around the mountain the way we came, we elected to drop down the snowfield directly to the dirt road running up Slate Canyon.

The problem was that no one besides me had axes and crampons. Actually, Sam did, because I brought up an extra pair. Everyone put on their harness and clipped to Johnny with webbing loops. I went down first and kicked deep steps in the hard snow for others to walk in. I stayed close enough to catch anyone who slipped before they could gain much momentum. Sam went behind, ready to dig in and brace himself should the need arise.

But it never did. We picked the most gentle route down the mountain, taking advantage of trees for support and eventually running out of snow. Teams driving four wheelers and a side by side on the dirt road saw our headlamps and picked us up once we arrived and drove us to the parking lot.

Far from any danger, Johnny wasn't off the hook this time. While mountain teams treated him kindly, Tom and the police chief had a different duty.

"You have to stop hiking alone," Tom ordered him, but Johnny didn't get it.

"But nobody wants to hike with me," he whined. "Anyway," he reasoned further, "I want to be a police officer someday. Don't you like officers to be strong?"

"We like our officers to have good judgment," the chief countered. But try as they might, the message just wasn't getting through. After at least half an hour of trying to reason with him, the chief finally saw that it was pointless and got tough and crystal clear.

"Okay, listen," he said tersely, "I'm trespassing you. If we catch you hiking alone again on any trail in Utah County, you're going to jail and you're going to see a judge. Do you understand?"

Johnny paused. He couldn't refute or evade the direct statement. "Okay," he said glumly after a moment of contemplation, "but can you say it nicely?"

Team One on NPS motorcycles at TICA

Preparing to rappel to the stranded hikers

Jake prepares to lower the last hiker over a 200' cliff

5 3 National Search & Rescue Week

May 16-22, 2010 was declared the first ever National Search and Rescue Week by the US Senate to recognize the thousands of volunteers and professional rescuers across the country and all they accomplish.

Utah County SAR kicked off the week quickly Sunday night with an exciting rescue in American Fork Canyon.

Three men in their 20's hiked up the old trail near Timpanogos Cave National Monument. The old trail has been out of use for fifty years and for the most part is barely visible as it climbs the vertigo-inducing canyon walls.

TICA's current asphalt trail is not much better. It's about five feet wide and climbs over 1,000' elevation in 1.5 miles between the visitor's center and the cave entrance. Many sections of trail are marked with a thick red stripe down the center - this marks spots where hikers should not pause to catch their breath because rock fall could come cascading down at virtually any moment. Walking down the trail in the evening, you can often spot rocks along the pavement that weren't there in the morning. When the monsoon rains arrive in August, it's not uncommon to find several feet of gravel and broken limestone piled across the trail.

This speaks to the precipitously precarious geology of AF Canyon.

This particular evening, the three men decided to skip the trail on the way down. The trail wasn't much to begin with, so why not just bushwhack and make their own way?

Eventually, they encountered a cliff, and their inexperience and lack of judgment began to show. Rather than hike horizontally to seek a passage around the precipice, they chose to downclimb a nearly-vertical 250' drop. A large crack made the passage possible, but the exposure was frightening.

Once they all miraculously reached the bottom of the cliff safely, they encountered another hitch in their plan. Another 200' cliff separated them from the slope below, and this time no sloped crack offered access.

For once they employed better judgment and dialed 911 rather than attempt to climb back up the way they came. We appreciated their decision as it's much easier to walk people out than carry them in a stretcher.

Having worked as a park ranger the summer before, I was excited to see a rescue at the cave show up on my pager. I said goodbye to the friends I was spending the evening with and headed for the canyon, hoping to arrive in time to get a good assignment.

Greg was running CP and I pulled off the road and hopped out of my car to talk with him. He pointed to a cliff high on the canyon wall where our victims were ledged out and had lit a fire, and I shared my opinion about the best way to approach it. Greg then expressed his doubts that we would be able to reach them tonight. There were simply too many cliffs, and in the dark and from the highway, it was impossible to tell for sure how to get there.

Greg assigned me as team leader for Team One and asked me who I wanted on my team. I wanted people I knew I could trust in steep terrain and chose Olin first, but CP wanted to keep him around for Team Two. Instead I chose David, Bryan, and Jake, and from that moment on, everything seemed to go our way. Even things that turned against us, we managed to twist again to our favor.

For starters, Jake was a new resource ranger at TICA. He had read the manual the week before and discovered that National Parks could allow certified motorcycle riders from other government agencies to operate their motorcycles in an emergency. All four of my team members were approved SST members and fit the specs. Jake mentioned this regulation to his boss and before we knew it, we each sat astride a tiny motorcycle, ready to head up the trail.

Time is of the essence, we all said, and the bikes would shave half an hour of hiking off our approach time and spare our energy for the dangerous route finding that would come once we left the pavement behind and struck out into the cliffs and scree.

All last summer, I dreamed of riding a bike up this trail. Every morning, I would hike the path in the cool air, taking at least twenty minutes to reach the cave entrance where I would begin my tours. I always enjoyed the fresh air, friendly conversations with visitors and other rangers, and magnificent views; but watching the maintenance crew zip by on their way to some task still made me a bit envious.

Now it was my turn and I enjoyed every moment. The little bikes with 110cc engines didn't have much power and we rarely got into third gear, but that was just as well. Riding off the edge of the trail would pretty well guarantee a long tumble down the steep canyon wall before being able to stop. Besides, the little bikes could maneuver well, which meant that a small tug on the handlebars sent the front wheel veering a foot or two to one side. Going too fast was not a good idea.

We rode around corners, through brief cave-like passages, through the gate which Jake unlocked, past Kodachrome, Lightning Point, Soda Pop, up through the W's, and eventually arrived at Dead Dog point, our jumping off place four turns before the cave entrance. We parked the bikes and traded motorcycle helmets for climbing ones.

Olin appeared then, hovering nearby in a Life Flight helicopter. He had been sent up to scout a route through the cliffs. It was difficult to see in the failing light, but he told us by radio that it looked like we may be able to cut more or less straight across, then drop down right on top of them. We thanked him for the information and started on our way.

It felt strange, after so many months of making kids walk and not run, ordering them not to throw rocks, and keeping them on the pavement, to hike off it myself. Strange, but good. Exciting. Purposeful and important.

We walked down a steep dirt slope and reached a snowfield. The snow was soft enough and we walked through it rather than dropping down and passing its lower edge which would place us within ten feet of a sixty foot drop. We made our way through thick trees and bushes, and found passages through cliffs running down precarious ridgelines. We climbed up and down steep dirt and scree, up and down cliff bands, and finally, guided by teams on the road and across the canyon who could see our lights and our victim's firelight, we passed by above our victims.

We nearly downclimbed too far as we found a better route down than they had, but spotting teams across the canyon stopped us and sent us back up. This played to our advantage when we backtracked and found an ideal spot to rappel from. A slot divided the cliff and by downclimbing the crevice and a ten foot cliff below that and tying a webbing anchor with a rappel ring to a large pine, we got within 200 feet of the hikers. This allowed us to rappel and pull our ropes more easily than if we had rappelled their same route, which would have forced us to rappel past a knot and pull that knot through our anchor in order to retrieve the ropes after rappelling because a single rope wouldn't have been long enough.

As I made my way over twenty feet from the anchor before dropping down the best spot, however, I found several large boulders - one four feet wide - that would crash down the cliff without much provocation. There was no way I dared to rappel below it. After shouting down to the victims and very carefully verifying that they had moved behind a series of hundred foot tall pine trees and would stay there until I told them otherwise, then checking the radio to ensure that no teams were exposed below, I reached a foot out and gave the rocks a shove.

One kick was all it took. The boulder rotated sideways and slid down the dirt, then went airborne for two hundred feet, smashing onto the ledge below. It didn't stop there, but continued downward, and judging from the crashing sounds that echoed throughout the canyon, it entrained additional rocks and logs along the way.

With the route clear, I fed the line through my rappel device and slid down the rope, bouncing away from the cliff and swinging back against it as I went. Dangling from my harness was another 75' rope, just in case the 200 footer ran out before the cliff did, but I didn't need it.

"How are you guys doing?" I asked as I approached the three men gathered around their fire. They were fine, though a bit chilled.

We experienced a minor hitch when I discovered that we had only brought one 200' rope. I had tied my 200'er to the pine tree to rappel down, but if we wanted to pull the ropes after us, the last one down would have to rappel on two lines doubled over at the top. When they reached knots tied in the 75'ers, they would have to stop, attach another rappel device below the knot, then detach the upper device and continue down.

Doing so wasn't a serious problem, but would take an additional five minutes or so, so someone had a brilliant idea to avoid the whole hassle. We tied one end of the rope to a tree at the base of the cliff - the side with the 75'ers. The 200'er then ran through the rappel ring and all the way down the cliff. The last one down would rappel on a single line and not need to deal with passing knots.

The rest of my team came down and we dug extra jackets, harnesses, helmets, and headlamps from our packs for our victims to wear. We passed around water and asked if they needed food, but they assured us they had enough and were fine.

The next hitch came when we tried to pull the ropes. Inexplicably, it had gotten stuck. We knew that all the knots were clear and the remaining rope simply ran through the steel rappel ring, but it must have gotten shoved into a narrow crevice, because no matter how hard we pulled, it wouldn't budge.

If we couldn't break the rope free, we'd be in big trouble. We'd probably end up waiting till morning for another team to trace our steps and drop in from above to fix the glitch. Without knowing what the rope was caught on, without knowing how dependably it was caught, we couldn't ascend back up to fix the situation. Without breaking it free, we wouldn't have the lines needed to continue down, or even drop a line for lower teams to attach more ropes that we could pull up to escape on.

Jake and I set up a quick three-to-one mechanical advantage system by putting two 180 degree bends in the rope. The first bend turned around a pulley attached to a tree and had a prusik to capture any progress we made. The second bend attached to the rope itself, the part running uphill, with another prussik, then turned back downhill for us to pull against. Every foot of rope we pulled was divided by the three moving sections and translated into four inches of progress on the upper line. In effect, this tripled our strength.

We pulled several feet of rope through the system as the rope tightened, then let the first prussik hold the tension while resetting the second one farther up the rope to try again. We gave the system another tug and the line suddenly broke free of whatever had held it.

My team didn't think much of it. Of course we would solve any problem that came up! Unbeknownst to us, everyone on the ground breathed a collective

sigh of relief when we reported our success.

"That was cool," one of the hikers said, and began to ask about various pieces of gear dangling from our harnesses. We explained their various uses and emphasized having the right gear for the job and knowing how to use it.

"We should probably get that stuff before we come back here," one said.

"Actually," I explained further, "you shouldn't come back here. Real climbers don't come places like this." I explained that not only was this type of terrain uncontrollably dangerous, but that other areas had far superior climbing.

When Tom later interviewed the men, he discovered that they had gone to a hardware store before their hike and purchased a hundred feet of rope. Not only was it not climbing rope, but they cut it into three pieces, dividing it amongst themselves. It's unclear what purpose three short rope lengths would serve, or what advantage it held over a single longer line. Tom managed to relay this information while standing in front of a news camera, and I admired his composure as he did so matter-of-factly without a trace of a smile on his lips.

A humorous comment on the news station's web site thanked heaven that the three hadn't gone skydiving instead. "Imagine what would happen if they each had 1/3 of a parachute!" it read.

David and Bryan set up our last anchor and Bryan rappelled over the edge to make sure the route was clear and safe. We then lowered our victims, one by one, over the cliff, where waiting teams picked them up and escorted them past cliff bands and down a long scree field to the highway.

The last of us got back down to the highway by 2:15 a.m. and received many compliments for a job well done.

"Was it hard?" Greg asked.

"No," I replied. "Not really. We just got the job done one step at a time."

"I think it went so well because of who we had up there," he confided.

I thought through the terrain we crossed, my team's stamina and speed, the outstanding teamwork in our route finding, the appropriate caution and problem solving that led to a perfect outcome, and had to agree.

54 RETURN TO TICA

On Wednesday of National Search and Rescue Week, the pager went off again, again calling us to Timp Cave. Many team members wondered if it was a mistake, an accidental echo of Sunday's page, but it wasn't. An 11-year-old girl on a school trip to the cave had turned around to talk to friends while walking down the trail and accidentally stepped off the edge and fallen about fifty feet, then tumbled down steep scree for another fifty.

A ranger friend texted me with additional information. "Conscious breathing left shoulder and back hurt. Blood coming out of mouth. Need ropes litter."

I hurried up the trail and found Tom and other SAR members rigging a raising system back up to the trail. We were lucky to have a convenient gully nearby where the initial drop from the trail fell only three or four feet.

Tom asked me to take charge of the lower end of the system and someone handed me the end of the main line to pull down to the rangers and Alpine fire fighters already gathered around the girl and assessing her condition. For the most part, I stayed out of their way, but she seemed to be in surprisingly good condition considering the height of her fall.

Alpine Fire attached her to a backboard and we lifted her into our litter. We attached the rope, carried her across a fallen log and through a few thin trees, and the raising system made our job easy as we walked the litter a hundred feet up the slope to the trail. We handed the litter up to the trail where a waiting cart rushed her down the trail to the helicopter parked in the middle of the highway.

So far, National SAR Week was going great. People were alive and we were doing a great job.

Thursday, the pager went off again, and again called us back to the cave. Some SAR members didn't even check the radio, assuming this time it *had* to be a mistake.

No such luck.

SAR, NPS, and Alpine Fire prepare to raise a fallen girl back up to the cave trail

55 RANGER DOWN

On Thursday of National Search and Rescue Week, a resource ranger drove a motorcycle off a 40' cliff near the cave exit. Judging by the scrape mark from his boot heel that we found on the paved trail the next day, the bike had tipped, he put his foot down to catch himself, but was unable to stop in time.

He landed on a scree and dirt slope and though we'll never know for sure, I hope the initial fall killed him. The green motorcycle stopped against a stand of small trees 50' farther downslope, but the ranger did not. He sailed over another 80' cliff, then tumbled for 250' to the same steep, narrow, rock-filled chute where the Russian died several years earlier.

Again, I was put in charge of the advance team, and we left the lower trail and climbed a steep snowfield, bringing helmets, water, jackets and harnesses to the rangers who had rushed up the ravine in case their fellow ranger was still alive. The operation slowed considerably once they verified that he was not. Now the priority was to make no more mistakes and suffer no more losses.

The next SAR team brought up a litter and pickets to build snow anchors for lowering stations. Most remained around the corner from the narrow chute where they would stay safe from rock fall, and two of them carried the litter up to the spot where the ranger had come to rest.

We waited there with the two rangers who climbed all the way up. We gave them helmets, water, and our extra jackets, and lowered them down to the station below as soon as we fixed lines. We waited, unmoving, until all rangers had been lowered down three stations and beyond the risk of rock fall, then got to work preparing the fallen ranger for transport.

We zipped him into a protective body bag and strapped him into the litter. We carefully lowered him over the first fifteen foot cliff, and two team members accompanied him the rest of the way down the chute, pulling the litter along when gravity didn't do the job on its own.

Once the next station picked up the package, we again sat tight, barely moving to avoid sending rocks careening down the chute toward team members below.

Near the bottom of the trail, the ranger's family had gathered. Team members managing the cart carrying him down backed away respectfully and allowed them all the time they needed to say their goodbyes.

This ranger had a reputation for making you feel like you were his best friend every time he spoke with you. I got the impression that he had lived a high quality life and filled it with more love than most people would comprehend.

He sounded worth meeting, worth knowing, but in this case, I'm glad I never did. I'm glad I could shift into rescue mode, get the job done, and not think too much about the terrible loss and grief that everyone around us felt so acutely.

National Search and Rescue Week ended as six of us returned on Friday morning to retrieve the motorcycle and gather any additional photos and clues for the sheriff's report.

Examining the motorcycle where it stopped against a tree

We hiked up the trail in the cool morning breeze and finished the job before the day's first tour exited the cave, mercifully oblivious to our task. I rappelled from the trail near where the tragedy began, tied off the motorcycle - the same one I rode Sunday night, and steered as the others pulled us up the ravine and back onto the trail.

Here's the part, at the end of this set of stories from National Search and Rescue Week, where I say something about how great SAR is, about the difference our volunteer efforts make in thousands of lives every year, but anything I come up with sounds trite compared to the actual stories I've participated in over the past eleven and a half years. It sounds meaningless in comparison to the suffering, relief, and joy experienced by those who are lost and found, broken and healed, those who depart this world and those who remain.

I'll simply say this: it matters, and I'm lucky to play a part in it.

SAR members lift the bike back to the cave trail

56 TIB/FIB

Holidays are popular times for accidents and emergencies. With so many people off work and recreating in the great outdoors, something somewhere is bound to go wrong.

Such was the case with a group of mountaineers climbing Timpanogos over the 4th of July weekend. A long and wet winter left the mountain still half covered in deep snow despite occasional hundred-degree days in the valley.

The mountaineers went equipped with crampons and axes and summitted without incident. They traversed across the knife-blade summit ridge and dropped down the glacier to Emerald Lake, still frozen below the snowpack. They hiked past Hidden Lakes and looked down the Primrose Cirque toward Aspen Grove.

"Last one down's a rotten marmot!" Jed shouted to his friends. He grinned at them, then sat down on the brink, holding his axe to one side, one hand on the shaft and one wrapped over the head, lifted his heels, and began glissading down the slope. One by one, his three friends followed suit.

Sliding down the slope made the going so much easier than the slow ascent. Warm rays from the morning sun had softened the top layer of the frozen snowpack and made the ride comfortable despite the cold working its way through their pant shells.

"I think I'm getting frost butt," Jed quipped as his friends caught up to where he had paused, digging in his axe pick to stop.

Below them stretched a wide open snowfield with five hundred feet of elevation without a single cliff band to traverse around. "Anybody wanna race?" Jed asked, shooting a challenging glance toward his friends.

"Sure," Dave answered. "I'll take you on."

"Last one to the flat," Jed explained, indicating a spot where the slope leveled out five hundred feet below, "buys lunch."

"On three," Dave replied, then began counting. "One...three!"

Both climbers sat quickly, raised their heels, and began to slide. Within seconds, both were scooting along over thirty miles per hour.

The snowpack was harder here than the higher slopes. More exposed to sunlight, it had melted more thoroughly before freezing up again overnight. Thousand-foot cliffs behind them had spent the winter avalanching, further packing the snow.

Jed had the lead, but bouncing over the snow grew uncomfortable - not just on his rear end, but his courage began to ebb as well. "Screw it," he muttered to himself, and dug in his axe blade.

The blade caught hard and nearly ripped out of his hands. Jed felt the first surge of concern bordering on fear. He let the axe pull him over onto his stomach so he could get a better hold on it, just like he had practiced in training. Glancing uphill, he saw that Dave had stopped himself fifty feet earlier.

Unfortunately, in Jed's light-hearted approach to mountaineering, he had neglected one other detail of his training. He was glissading without first taking off his crampons.

Eager to slow his rapid descent, Jed kicked his steel-spiked toes into the snow surface. Everything happened very quickly then. First, his crampons stopped, but the rest of Jed's body did not. His right shin broke in half. Both the tibia and fibula snapped under the sudden pressure. The abrupt traction flipped Jed up and over through the air.

Through pain and confusion, he managed to maintain enough presence of mind to keep his grip on the axe, and when he landed, he jammed the blade down again, this time lifting his toes away from the snow.

He stopped and let his toes fall to the snow again. His shin hurt too intensely to breathe, much less scream, and he pressed his pain-contorted face against snow, his mouth wide open and waiting for his voice to return.

After what seemed like a long time, Jed finally took a breath. The air came rushing in fast and deep, and his diaphragm quickly expelled it again in an anguished shout.

His friends ran down the hill toward him. When they saw Jed's mangled leg, they did what they could to make him comfortable and one took out a phone and dialed 911.

By the time Olin and I reached the accident scene, North Fork Fire and other SAR members were already attending to Jed's injuries. They splinted his leg, monitored vital signs, and ran an IV into his brachial artery to keep him hydrated.

SAR and NFF package the climber

They built a four-point snow anchor from axes buried in the snow with a collection point to attach a rope to which ensured that each anchor held an equal portion of the load's weight.

Olin and I measured 200' down the mountain and set another anchor with a pair of pickets. The snowpack was so hard that we had to pound the pickets in with a rock that had rolled down the slope from the cliffs above.

We again used a 200'er to measure the distance for the next anchor and, when the litter arrived below, used our anchor to get the litter up the slope more quickly. With the rope running through a biner at the anchor and

the far end tied to the litter, Olin ran down the hill, dragging the litter in the opposite direction as he went.

Before long, we had Jed packaged in the litter and the lowering began. When the package arrived at each subsequent station, we attached the line through the new brake rack and continued with barely a pause.

Once the snow ran out another thousand feet down the mountain, we attached the litter's wheel and carried Jed the rest of the way down to the waiting ambulance.

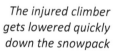

We had to use rocks to pound the pickets into the hard snow for an anchor

The injured climber gets lowered quickly down the snowpack

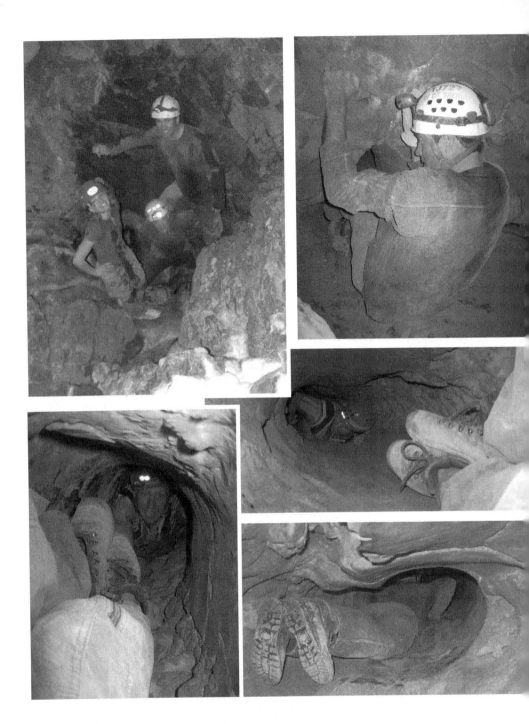

Photos from a 2009 trip to Nutty Putty Cave

Top Left: Cave entrance
Top Right: Entering the Atrium following the Aorta Crawl
Lower three photos: Aorta Crawl, commonly called the Birth Canal

57 NUTTY PUTTY

Thanksgiving is a time for family togetherness and expression of gratitude for whatever degree of abundance we enjoy. But just because we're celebrating doesn't make the circle of life stop spinning.

On November 25, the day before Thanksgiving, the eyes of the nation focused on a rounded hilltop in Utah County's West Desert. A family was in trouble and a hundred million people watched nervously from their living rooms, hoping and praying for a happy holiday ending.

John and his brothers decided to visit Nutty Putty Cave late Tuesday night for some exploration and adventure. His 6' 3" frame weighed 210 pounds - not the kind of body that fit easily into tight, confined spaces, but a minor inconvenience like that could not dampen his adventurous spirit.

"We'd better get through that cave before filling up on Mom's turkey and stuffing or we'll never fit!" John joked. He kissed his wife and little girl goodbye, then climbed into the car with his brothers.

After driving along Highway 68 to the south end of Utah Lake, the car turned right onto a gravel road into the West Desert. Seven miles of gravel and dust led to another right turn and a rutted dirt road running north. After about a mile, the car passed through a gate and turned right once more, then climbed a steep, rocky hill until it could climb no farther without scraping off the exhaust pipe.

The brothers got out and hiked to the rugged, rounded hilltop. They found the cave entrance - a five-foot by ten-foot gap in the rock that dropped fifteen feet and narrowed to two feet wide by the time it hit bottom.

Next came the ninety-degree corner and awkward squeeze through a shallow puddle of warm water. If the water could freeze, it would help. It would make sliding into the cave easier and it wouldn't soak everyone's chest and legs in the process; but warm, humid air spewing non-stop from the cave's throat made sure that winter never crawled inside with the hordes of boy scouts, university students, and a few mice.

Once inside, the cavern roof rose and the room widened until everyone could sit comfortably without leaning over. They now had two possible directions to explore.

John ignored the maze - a series of long parallel passages following a fault line's multi-layered strata to the left - and led his brothers down the slide - a long, downward-sloping tunnel - to the more exciting adventures to be found there. That's where long, narrow, claustrophobia-inducing passages through solid rock awaited, like the birth canal, aorta crawl, and scout trap.

"You guys, check this out!" John exclaimed. He had discovered the bunny holes by sliding below a sloping roof of rock not commonly explored by the amateur cavers who frequented Nutty Putty.

Diving down the hole on the right, John followed the two- or three-foot wide passage down eight feet, then up at a 45 degree angle and flat for 12 feet. At that point, the hole dove almost straight down ten feet. John tried to bunch his body up enough to slide his feet forward to go feet-first down the hole, but there was not quite enough room for his large frame to turn around.

"Hold my feet!" he directed his brother, crawling right behind him through the narrow tube. With the added support and a few good hand holds on the walls, John managed to reach the bottom of the drop, where the tube turned into a narrow slot where he could nearly stand up. "This is awesome!" he exclaimed enthusiastically as his brothers followed.

From there, the passage grew increasingly narrow. 90-degree corners made squeezing through more difficult, and the roof dropped to just over a foot high in one spot. At last, the passage doubled back in a sharp bend and began to slope downward again.

Finally, John paused. *Maybe this isn't such a good idea,* he thought. The yellow beam of his flashlight cast a soft light against the calcite walls folded narrowly around him and the thought of sliding down the steepening slope ahead gave him pause.

"We gotta turn around," he called back to his brothers. "We gotta get in here feet first."

The brothers backed off, but the smooth surface of the tube provided John with no handholds to push himself back up the slope. "Gimme a hand!" he called back, and one brother returned to pull him up by his feet. In the cramped space, it didn't help much.

"Maybe I should keep going forward," John finally reasoned after struggling for a while without success, "and find a wider spot to turn around."

Sliding downward came easier, but the wider turn-around spot never materialized. Instead, the situation grew serious. The slope steepened and now John was definitely trapped.

With that thought, the first faint surge of panic welled up in his mind. Adrenaline pumped into his veins, quickening his heart rate and raising his blood pressure. John blinked his eyes and drew in several deep, rapid breaths to expel any thoughts of being permanently stuck here. *We'll figure this out,* he told himself with all the confidence he could muster, *of course we'll figure this out.*

Once satisfied that they couldn't get John out of the tiny crawl space, his brothers backed out of the tubes and climbed back up through the cave to the surface.

It felt strange to clamber back into the wide-open space of the open hilltop, and the billion tiny points of light dotting the early-morning sky looked farther away than ever. The night had grown cold and black, and they stumbled a bit as they retraced their steps down to the car. One brother turned on his phone and was relieved to see two bars. He dialed 911 and explained their situation.

The pager woke me up and I rolled over in bed and pressed the button to silence its loud chirping. Nutty Putty. Stuck caver. Comprehension seeped slowly into my groggy mind as I considered whether or not to respond.

On one hand, cave calls could be fun. At the very least, we'd get to go caving, and I rarely went to Nutty Putty without an emergency as motivation.

On the other hand, it was a 60 mile drive around the lake just to get there, and people usually aren't as stuck as they think. They sometimes free themselves before we arrive, which could mean two hours of lost sleep and twenty dollars of gas burned all for nothing.

Also, I had important deadlines to meet the next day. If I didn't polish up a few documents and get the files to the printer in the morning, the holiday would delay the project by a week, and I needed to start shipping books immediately. The Christmas selling season wouldn't last much longer.

Besides, we had plenty of team members capable of helping in a cave. Whatever needed doing, other team members could manage without me. I wouldn't be missed.

All these thoughts rolled around in my mind for several minutes, and I eventually decided to skip this one. I closed my eyes and instantly fell back asleep. I slept soundly until six a.m. when my phone rang.

"Hey, buddy, we need you out here," Olin said when I answered.

"You're still not finished?" I asked, surprised. Even with an hour drive and accounting for time to reach any spot in the cave, that still left two or three hours to work already. "What's up?" I asked.

"We need more skinny people," Olin explained, and related the basic situation. If I was really needed, that changed my calculations. Maybe we could finish up quickly and I could still get back in time for the printers. I got dressed and headed south around the lake.

Atop the hill near the cave entrance, someone had sent up breakfast boxes and I downed a few slices of French toast before escorting four ranger friends from Timp Cave down the hole with the team assigned to me. One was an interp - a tour guide ranger who I worked with the year before and with whom I had crawled through Nutty Putty earlier this year, and two were professional cavers with extensive experience, at least one of whom had spent weeks on end below the earth's surface without a single glimpse of daylight.

In the bottom of the cave, teams had tied webbing around John's ankles in a relatively comfortable lover's knot and run ropes back and forth, up and down, through over fifty feet of narrow tubes before reaching a chamber large enough to get enough space to pull effectively from.

Rescuers present came from a mix of several agencies. SAR, Utah Cave SAR, National Park rangers, local expert cavers, and medics all seemed busy with their tasks. Two 3-to-1 mechanical advantage systems had been set up and we pulled as hard as we could on them, but the winding passages and awkward doubled-back angle we needed to pull John back up the passage prevented any progress.

Work ceased for a while while a medic tried to get close enough to insert a hydrating IV into John's ankle and a thin, experienced caver, one of the few able to fit as far as John's waist, attempted to deliver a the tube from

a hydration bag through a tiny hole in the rock where she hoped that John would be able to catch it in his mouth and take a drink.

"Can you give me a little help?" she asked John. "See if you can lift yourself up just a bit."

"I can't," John said in a hoarse whisper. "I'm spent. I've been here for three days."

So many hours in the dark made John's mind play tricks on him, which is not uncommon. Ten hours in the dark typically induces such hallucinations. Earlier, John had been convinced that all we needed to do was break through the solid rock to his right. "There's sunshine right through this wall!" he insisted. I took two SAR members and we went exploring all nearby passages, just to make sure no passages came anywhere near him. They didn't.

"You haven't been here for three days," she corrected him. "It's only been about eight hours." The truth fell somewhere in between. The caver knew that John had been stuck for twelve hours by that time, but she also knew that her encouraging deception could save his life.

John instantly brightened and discovered renewed vitality. His arms suddenly found the strength to strain against gravity pinning him head down on a seventy-degree slope and he lifted himself up a few inches.

A few hours passed and those who had spent all night in the cave were called to the surface for a break. Some had a heavy emotional investment in the mission and were reluctant to go. Susie, for example, one of our smallest team members, spent hours near John, talking to him, comforting him, singing to calm his nerves and lighten the mood.

With a sudden vacuum of leadership, the rangers and I moved forward into the tube to assess the situation.

Within forty feet, I felt glad I came. I found a five foot section where the rope we were trying to drag John out with ran across bare rock as the passageway made a pair of sharp corners. Especially when the rope was weighted by John as anchor on one end and everyone pulling on the other,

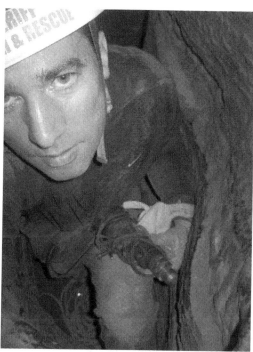

the rope drag created by this section alone would prevent practically all progress.

Someone mentioned that a slick fabric had previously been laid there to help the rope slide, but I wanted better. I called back for a drill, and soon two climbing bolts and hangers drilled into the walls had rerouted the rope through pulleys that eliminated all drag through the section.

Most of us crawled back to the main chamber then, leaving a medic and a few attendants forward in the tube.

I found a group of burly fire fighters from the urban search and rescue team in the room now, and they had brought a squawk box - a wired communicator for areas where radio signals could not penetrate. I overheard that John's wife and parents had arrived on the surface and hoped to speak with him, but the box was malfunctioning.

It so happened that Nutty Putty allowed for surprisingly good radio traffic straight down the main slide, but no signal continued into any of the smaller side passages. While the fire fighters worked on their box, I got another idea.

I instructed the surface to speak on our main SAR channel while I played that into a radio transmitting on our tactical channel. This nearby

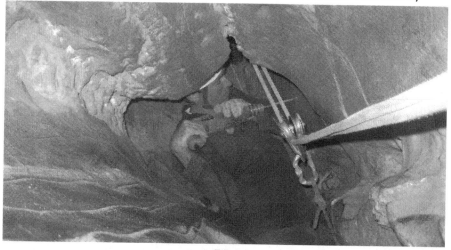

signal made it through the winding passages to a radio where John could hear his wife's and parents' voices. When they finished speaking, we reversed the radios and John spoke back to the surface. Words of love and encouragement cheered him considerably.

For me, this was one of two bright spots in a dark afternoon. Finally, we had accomplished something that made the situation a tiny bit better.

Soon the medics finished with whatever efforts they were making and with the raising system rerigged more efficiently, we tried again. This time, we also had half a dozen burly firefighters pulling on the rope. This time, the system worked.

With a good effort, we pulled the rope three feet at a time. After passing through the 3-to-1 mechanical advantage system, this translated into twelve inches of progress on John's end.

"It's going to work!" I said ecstatically while exchanging congratulatory high fives with rangers and team members whose concerned expressions revealed how invested they had each been in the outcome of this mission for many hours.

Soon we sucked up all the rope space between our anchor and the pulleys creating our mechanical advantage and paused to reset the system and continue. I stuck around and helped pull another fifteen feet of rope - or five feet on John's end - before I had to go.

It's not that I wanted to leave, and I certainly didn't need a break, but I now had spent eight hours in the cave and CP had been calling me to the surface for over an hour now for a break. Finally, I felt expendable. Finally, everything would turn out fine. A few more feet of progress would bring John through the narrowest gap, around the most awkward corner, and for all practical purposes, John would be free.

Over the radio came another request from John's wife to speak to him again on the radio.

"Standby," I replied. "We'll have him out soon and then they can talk all they want."

For me, this is one of the darkest spots in a very dark afternoon. I wish I could take it back. I wish we had paused for a few more minutes and set up our manual radio patch. In the grand scheme of things, it may not matter much, but I'll probably never fully break free of the regret.

I gathered up my things and climbed to the surface with a few others, hauling out some of the bags of gear that would no longer be needed below.

Once on the surface, Tom called me into a large tent full of agency leaders and I reported on our progress. I told them that we seemed to have overcome the friction problem and about the steady progress that had begun. Tom then sent me to share my report with the crowd of news cameras and reporters gathered near the cave entrance and the millions of Americans following the story by television, radio and internet.

As the sun dropped over the horizon, I stood in front of cameras and shared the good news - we were making considerable progress and it might not be long before we had our man back on the surface.

Never do that. Never, never predict an outcome until the chicks are hatched, grown, slaughtered, stuffed, baked, carved, served, chewed and swallowed. Then and only then can you pronounce that all is well.

What I did not yet know as I described the situation below and answered a few questions was that something had gone wrong underground and would continue to do so until the bitter end of the story.

I spent the next 45 minutes sitting in the back of an ambulance with John's family. I showed them pictures on my camera of the systems and rescuers. Someone had given them a radio and they listened to the operation as we spoke.

But something in the system had broken. John slid back down the slope to where he began and an attendant was struck violently in the face by flying rope or gear. A paramedic stitched up a gash in the side of his face while down in the cave.

I got conflicting reports about which piece blew. For a while I worried that one of the bolts that we placed had pulled out, which seemed unlikely, but then so did everything else. Soon those concerns were more or less laid to rest and I breathed easier.

Some said it was a prussik, a simple rope-grab, progress-capture device that prevented any progress from slipping backward, but that didn't make sense because we had two separate rope systems and prussiks on both systems would have to fail for John to slide back down.

Others blamed a cam, a spring-loaded mechanical unit jammed into a crack, then attached to the rope with a caribiner and, hopefully, a pulley, to direct the rope systems through the labyrinth. This makes more sense, perhaps when taking into consideration the relatively soft rock deep in the cave, though it would still come as a surprise.

I guess it doesn't really matter exactly which piece failed. What matters is that John's state of mind and health also began to collapse. He had been trapped, head down, for over 24 hours now, and the pressure to his head couldn't have been easy for his physiology to handle.

I don't know what happened underground after that, but within a few hours, John died. I had already gone home, still expecting the best, and I didn't find out otherwise for several more hours. I woke up at 4 a.m., turned on my computer to check the news, and my heart dropped when I read of our failure.

For the first time in my decade on the team, we failed. For the first time, we found someone alive and did not bring them back alive. Other victims had died, but never before on our watch. Extreme odds conspired against us and experts deemed the situation hopeless, but even that doesn't completely quiet the voice inside my head from asking "What if...?", erase my regrets, or satisfy my unanswered questions.

For weeks afterward, I replayed the entire mission in my head, as did many other team members, wishing we'd have done this tiny detail differently or done that a little sooner. But hindsight doesn't change anything. We did our best. There's no use second guessing.

A week later, I read a report that helped put my mind at ease. The highly respected expert caver who pronounced John dead provided additional details about the twists and turns in the cave beyond the point I saw for myself. Not only did it include more twists and turns than I knew of and tighter squeezes, but it described just how awkwardly John would have needed to be maneuvered, lifted and twisted, avoiding narrow slots, and managing other impediments in the tightly cramped quarters.

In the end, the Sheriff opted not to endanger rescuers further by exposing them to the biohazard of recovering the body, if it could be done at all, and land managers decided to close the cave, dynamiting the lower portion of the slide and pouring thousands of pounds of concrete to fill the cave entrance.

Friends and neighbors, along with citizens who sent notes through the SAR website, have shown their support and concern for the rescuers as well as the family, who praised our personal dedication and expressed deep gratitude for our efforts both publicly and privately, never casting so much as a shadow of blame or resentment on anyone involved.

A five-year old neighbor girl brought me a banana in a decorated sack with a pair of notes that read "You are loved" and "thank you for cherieing [trying] to save that man."

If the unhappy ending carried a Thanksgiving message after all, it would be found in the noble attitudes of John's family members, who proved to be

one of the most unfailingly supportive and grateful families we have ever worked with.

And it's nice to consider, as several friends have pointed out, that as far as the score card goes, any failure is far outweighed by the many, many, many successful rescues when we intervened in challenging circumstances and triumphed.

As always, at least we showed up. We tried our best and we never gave up. Even so, we will always deeply regret that we didn't win again this time.

A SAR member accompanies the sked out of Blowhole Cave during a training exercise

58 In The Arms of the Avalanche

Eight snowmobiles paused and shut off their engines in a New Year's Eve snowstorm. A full-blown blizzard howled across the Rocky Mountains, dropping as much as three inches of wet powder per hour in its wake. Even if the night wasn't already pitch black below the thick, heavy clouds, falling, swirling snow would have hidden everything from view - a pine forest climbing the surrounding mountains, 400' cliffs half a mile away across the canyon, and the ski lift another mile up the drainage.

The thick sound of falling snowflakes - which both dampens all distant sound and fills the air with its crystal tinkling as it lands on crisp gore-tex coats and pant shells - was shattered as the air was rent by the unmistakable sound of a 747 jet airplane roaring its way, flying blind, all engines spinning on full throttle, down into the canyon.

Avalanche. A big one!

"We don't belong here," I said to the group who nodded in agreement. We could have been home with our families. We could have been at parties with friends. We could be warm and laughing, standing near bright, crackling fires lit in fireplaces, sipping hot cocoa and counting down the final seconds as the year slipped away forever, blowing away with the howling wind and snow.

Instead, my nose is numb and I adjust my balaclava under my helmet to protect it from frostbite. An inch of snow has piled against my jacket during the ride and I brush it away with a gloved hand.

Rescuing a lost child and guaranteeing that he would see the new year seemed more important than the party it took me from. I may as well ring in the year with my SAR friends anyway.

Three teams had been dispatched from Tibble Fork to search for a teenage snowboarder who rode out of bounds in Snowbird's Mineral Basin and got lost in the storm. The majority of the resort lays on the Salt Lake County's Little Cottonwood side of the 10,000'+ ridgeline, but Mineral Basin is ours. Where the resort ends, there is no parking lot, no shops or restaurants, nothing but ten miles of mountain wilderness. Nothing but a long-abandoned mining town, snow, aspen, pine, deer, lions, elk, and a groomed snowmobile trail.

Olin and Chris reached the parking lot first and were sent up as the hasty team. Their job was to clear the road all the way to Snowbird. If the boy was walking, he would find the road and surely prefer it to the difficulty of hiking through unpacked snow where he would sink up to his waist with every step.

They made their way fast, headlights blurring the giant snowflakes as they sped along. They stopped periodically to shout the missing boy's name just in case, especially once they reached Mineral Basin, right below Snowbird's lift, where the boy could be off the road and injured.

Most of the snow-covered road was flat and far enough away from steep slopes to make it relatively safe from avalanche danger. Once it reached Mineral Basin, however, the road and surrounding terrain grew steeper. Teams Two and Three stopped after the first steep climb into avalanche territory. We heard an avalanche roar down the far side of the canyon and wisely decided to turn around.

About the same time, we got word that Olin and Chris had reached Snowbird and found nothing. They were heading back in our direction as well.

As much as we wanted to find the missing boy, the lack of visibility and such dangerous avalanche conditions - three inches of snowfall per hour is never stable - made searching further pointless. We had done everything we could safely do, and more. There was little chance we'd find him off the road in the long stretch of flat terrain we already covered along the road, and we couldn't safely search the steeper areas in Mineral Basin. Even without the thick curtain of snow limiting visibility, it was too dark to see anything.

If he was out in the snow and alive, he'd have heard our shouting and answered. If an avalanche had buried him, then he'd be just as alive tomorrow or next week or next month. We would have to wait until morning to find out.

After riding all the way to Snowbird, Olin and Chris turned around. Before leaving the Mineral Basin area, they encountered a ten-foot high debris pile blocking their path. A large avalanche had crossed the road since they drove past.

"Whoa!" Chris exclaimed as his headlight illuminated the towering pile of now-hardpacked snow.

"Let's turn around," Olin suggested. "We can get a ride back home from Little Cottonwood."

"Yeah," Chris agreed. "Let's play it safe." They turned their sleds around on the narrow road and hit the gas.

Fifty yards later, they found their way blocked again by yet another ten foot pile of snow. Another slide had barely missed them - or perhaps the same one split around a ridge and surrounded them from both sides.

This is a good place in the story to stop and thank everyone who prays for our safety while we're out rescuing others. I believe in guardian angels.

The hasty team made their way back to the resort and a snowcat brought them down the far side of the mountain.

Teams Two and Three made their way safely back and reached the parking lot a little before midnight. After loading the sleds onto trailers, there wasn't enough time for the last of us to get back to our parties before the ball dropped. Someone passed around sparklers and we lit them while while standing in an inch and a half of slush. Tom turned on his overhead red and blue lights which turned every giant, wet ticker-tape flake in the sky to a brilliant, tiny, colorful mirror. Time Square couldn't have decorated the sky any better. Sirens ripped through the air at midnight, we shouted, "Happy New Year!" and then we went home.

Driving down canyon, many small avalanches reached the road, mostly loose sluffs, some still slowly spilling powder as we drove nervously past.

The next morning, with the storm gone, a helicopter overflew the area and the boy appeared. He had dug himself a snow cave, citing learning that from one of the most-despised-by-climbers climbing movies ever made due to its abundant absurdity and preposterously erroneous information.

When he told his survival story, he reported hearing searchers calling his name, but he was too tired to climb out of his snow cave. We didn't much appreciate that part of his tale.

He got lucky. Lucky he didn't get buried by a massive avalanche and remain buried until spring, and lucky two rescuers didn't die because of his failure to respond to their calls.

Back at the parking lot on New Years Eve
after brushing away an inch of snow from my coat

59 In the Neighborhood

If you happen to have a potentially-fatal accident, it's a pretty good idea to do so while an entire search and rescue team is training nearby.

On the first Saturday in February, we towed our snowmobiles to Tibble Fork for practice and training on towing our new snow ambulance trailer bought with a generous donation from a local manufacturing company.

Because Wasatch Backcountry Rescue - a team packed with experienced snow riders - already had a snow ambulance, we invited them to attend and acquaint us with how to tow it without getting it stuck, what type of snow it can pull through, and how it feels to ride in back.

We had nearly finished cycling members through various training stations when a frantic snowmobiler rode into the middle of the group. "My friend just had an accident!" he shouted, then immediately turned around and started to race back up the mountain.

"Hold on!" someone shouted, raising both palms toward him, slowing him down enough to wait for us to hop on our sleds and follow.

The track led a mile or more up canyon, its sides growing ever steeper and narrower. The friend then turned his sled straight up a steep hill and climbed hundreds of feet. WBR had no trouble following, but some of our sleds were several years older and not built for attacking that sort of grade.

My sled was one of those. I made it about half way, then had to turn back down hill before digging in and getting stuck. I rode down through the bottom of the narrow gully, braking constantly to avoid getting out of control, and up the other side to get a run and try again.

The bottom of the gully was so narrow and abrupt that it didn't allow for much of a run, and I only made it a hundred feet past my first attempt.

As I turned and rode back downhill for yet another attempt, a new member waved me over. "Do you want to trade machines?" he asked. I gratefully accepted his offer and climbed on to the newer machine he had brought. This time I climbed the hill with ease.

Beyond the initial steep climb came a few shorter hills before reaching a wide open bowl where I saw a group of people clumped together a few hundred feet up the far slope. I rode up near them and hit the kill switch.

A glance uphill from the group told the whole story. A snowmobile lay upside down and perpendicular to the fall line there, caught against a small pine tree. The sled was a new 900cc racing machine with nitrous and an extended track with 2" lugs. The tracks dug into the snow above it revealed the details of how it got there.

The rider was attempting to ride up the sixty-degree slope, but backed out when he feared he might not make it. He didn't have much room to decide as small trees and rocks constricted the passage above him.

Either when he tried to make a quick turn or just before, his powerful engine lifted the front end off the snow surface, and half way through the turn, it flipped over and rolled back down the hill, doing a complete rotation with nothing but the rider's helmet making an impression in between. The sled rolled a few more times and stopped against the tree.

The friend filled in what happened next. The rider was knocked unconscious, and his friend helped him slide down the steep slope to the small knob where we now gathered. Unable to do anything more, he jumped back on his sled and raced down canyon for help. Lucky for him, he found it.

I stepped toward the crowd of medics and waited for the chance to help out. The victim was decorticate posturing as we strapped him to a backboard - arms tense and curling up around his chest - a probable sign of serious brain or spinal damage. I grabbed a roll of medical tape from my pack to tape his wrists to the backboard to keep the IV in place.

Soon after we had him strapped down with a c-collar in place and vitals taken, an AirMed helicopter arrived and landed in the wide meadow a few hundred feet below.

Other sledders stood as avalanche watch from various points around the bowl. Their warning wouldn't do us much good if the snow above us broke loose, but at least they could zoom down and dig us out.

The first third of the way to the chopper was easy. We simply held the backboard and slid down the steep slope. After the slope leveled out came the hard part. Even with six people lifting the backboard, wading through thigh-deep powder exhausted us quickly. Even so, we did not slow down. Fresh hands stepped in and took over for those rescuers who fell to hands and knees, gasping for breath; and a pair of snowmobiles tracked and half tracked the snow before us, packing it down and making the going a little easier.

At last we loaded our victim into the helicopter, they spun up their rotors, and we backed off while they flew away.

Via radio, Tom asked me to document everything about the accident. I took photos of the snowmobile and it's tracks from every angle. I held a compass in front of the camera for orientation and recorded GPS coordinates. There's a good chance we had entered wilderness area where motorized travel is illegal, and I wondered if anyone would press charges. I don't think they did.

The next task was to get the crashed snowmobile down the hill. Half a dozen of us gathered around and lifted. "On three," someone called. "One, two, three!" We heaved and got the sled about 30% free. "Again!" they repeated, and we lifted and gave the sled another shove.

The radio broke the silence as we repositioned ourself for one more try. A storm front was moving in with the possibility of heavy snowfall, and CP wanted everyone back to the parking lot before it hit. The NYE near-miss with the avalanche that wrapped around Chris and Olin was still too near and they didn't want to take any chances with a repeat.

"Let's finish this," I told the group. That seemed wiser than making someone come back for the sled and risk another accident while we could complete the task right now. Someone counted to three again and we hoisted the sled free. Someone climbed aboard, started it up and rode it down the hill, and we all headed for home.

Later that night, a page from Tom informed us that our victim was conscious and doing fine with no known permanent damage. I kept that page on my pager for a long time to remind myself of the difference we make in the lives of strangers who we will probably, hopefully, never meet again.

A winter ascent of Timpanogos' North Summit

60 The Hand

Jeremy took his daughters - Molly, 9, and Latricia, 12 - hiking up the Primrose Cirque in early July. Jeremy couldn't be more proud as the young girls marched on for miles, climbing thousands of feet up the trail, without a note of complaint.

"Daddy, what's that?" Molly asked, pointing across a wide, steep snowfield.

"What's what, honey?" Jeremy asked in return, stopping and peering in the direction his daughter's finger indicated.

"There's a hand over there," she said, still pointing.

Jeremy gazed around, looking for a tree or rock in the shape of a hand.

A speck of movement caught his eye at the base of a cliff with a small waterfall pouring out from under the snow. He narrowed his eyes and looked more closely. His heart rate doubled when he realized that his daughter was right. A human hand was reaching out and waving from the ice moat - the space between cliff and snowpack where the waterfall and radiant heating had melted a gap in the snow.

Jeremy dialed 911 and began to explain. "I'm not sure, but I think someone's in trouble up here."

When the pager went off, six SST members were at the far end of the Kirkman/Pumphouse/Packard trail loop we often rode in Hobble Creek Canyon. It didn't tell any detail other than the fact that a hiker needed assistance near Aspen Grove.

"It'll be over before we get there," Olin opined.

"We might as well call in and head that direction and get it on our call-out stats," I shrugged.

Everyone on the team is expected to respond to at least 30% of missions. If not enough people check on the radio, CP may page the call again and those who didn't respond the first time then reconsider their availability. Our stats weren't in danger of dropping below 30%, but there was still an informal competition to get the best numbers.

The group split as some riders wanted to ride deeper into the mountains and Olin and I checked on the radio, then rode back up and out the same way we came in. We loaded the bikes at our vehicles and headed north toward Provo Canyon, Sundance, and Aspen Grove.

"How soon can you two be ready?" an ICS member asked as we arrived.

"What do we need?" we asked. When he told us "Light technical," we told him we could pack up in five minutes.

"Hustle," he ordered. "You're the last two going up in the helicopter."

Olin and I looked at each other and smiled. Responding to this call would be worth it after all. We had no idea just how glad we would soon become that we showed up.

After filling our packs with snow travel gear, clothing, the 14 essentials, some webbing, hardware, and 75' ropes, we climbed into the AirMed helicopter and took to the sky with a gentle jolt and momentary sensation of increased gravity that makes your stomach drop like when an elevator starts to rise up its shaft.

On the ride up, we got an overview of the mission. A hiker walking through the summer hard-packed snow had stepped over a log and his foot punched through the snow on the other side. The unexpected plunge sent his weight toppling forward hard enough to throw him down, and landing on a steep 60 degree slope meant he didn't stop for 600 feet.

A brief dry section of dirt and small rocks before a 25' cliff may have slowed his descent slightly before falling over the edge and landing in the moat. With an injured arm, he couldn't get himself out. If the little girl hiking by hadn't noticed his good hand waving over the edge, he would have died there like a scout that fell in the same place twenty years earlier, and it may have taken the team weeks to find him.

AirMed circled around again and again, looking for an LZ below the scene rather than dropping us off at Hidden Lakes and making us descend 700', but we saw nothing. That was just as well because it turned out we were needed much more on the top half of the slope than below the waterfall where half a dozen team members had already gathered to load the victim and prepare him to be raised back up.

In hind sight, we should have taken our victim down the mountain, not up, but in foresight, we didn't anticipate the challenges that would take the entire night to work out.

As Olin and I passed the stand of pine trees atop the last 500' of mountain above the falls, we found the probies dutifully setting up a raising system. Their choice of anchors was excellent, their knots impeccable, but we instantly saw a problem. The next station was 400' away and all they had was a pair of 75' ropes.

We dropped off our 75'ers to extend their system and continued on down, our crampons digging into the snow for traction and axes at the ready in case we slipped, to see where we could help.

Above the cliff, we found the first raising station. A pair of pickets had been driven into the hard snow and equalized to distribute the litter's weight. We added an axe as a backup just in case and helped hoist the litter up over the cliff with everyone lifting from below as well.

With the litter above the falls, we were ready to work out our next moves, but encountered several extra challenges to work out.

In the first place, the on-scene commander had been exposed to the waterfall's spray and was now a sufficiently hypothermic that he was not able to command the operation. Someone would need to watch over him until we got him back up and off the steep slope.

Bruce was MRT sergeant and the most likely candidate to take over command, but his radio battery had died. Several other strong leaders were focused on their specific assignments and hadn't recently seen the entire scenario from top to bottom as Olin and I had.

With no one else filling the leadership vacuum I jumped in to tackle at least the most pressing challenge of setting up the next raising station. I gathered all available ropes and determined that, tied end to end, they would be just long enough to reach the 150' of rope dangling from the raising station high up the slope. Olin and I hiked quickly and got the ropes connected in one continuous line. The upper station got to work raising the litter while several team members stayed with the litter.

The next challenge was the size of our victim. He was 6' 6" and weighed 300 pounds. Hauling him up the very steep slope made for hard work. We were somewhat short handed, and the upper team built a 5-to-1 system to get the job done. This meant that for every five feet of rope they pulled, the litter only traveled a single slow foot. Pulling the heavy load with a 3-to-1 was simply too hard for the limited number of workers at the station.

Passing the three sets of knots in both the main and belay lines added more temporary delays as additional systems were employed to safely move the raising system pulleys around the knots while maintaining two secure systems on the rope at all times.

By the time the litter reached the raising station, I'd never seen the team so tired. We still needed someone to run the ropes up the last 100' of snow and prepare the final anchor. For the first time ever, someone didn't eagerly jump up and volunteer. Lindsey was busy inserting an IV. I held the litter steady on the edge of the narrow cliff below our anchor and didn't dare let go. A minute or two passed before Shay finally stood and picked up the rope ends, then began kicking his way up the snow. Everyone else sat around, utterly thrashed, waiting for their strength to return.

The last slope was less steep than the 500' we had already covered. We raised our victim up it in good time, then lined up three rescuers on either side and carried the litter by its steel rail 200' through knee-high plants and marshy ground to the helicopter. We breathed a collective sigh of relief once we loaded him aboard and watched the chopper fly away.

After transporting our patient to a hospital, the helicopter returned to shuttle everyone down, starting with the coldest. Those waiting their turn made their way to a thicket of short pine trees that sheltered us from the wind and we shivered while watching the eastern edge of the dark sky begin to light up with a predawn glow.

The sky had turned a clear light blue by the time I flew away in the last shuttle. I felt sleepy and satisfied at a difficult job well done.

61 SECRETS OF
THE LOST CANYON

Native American ruins often get discovered during development projects, giving archeologists only days or weeks to excavate and explore before ancient villages and the hills they occupy get scooped away and replaced by interstate highways.

Range Creek Canyon, a remote mountain valley between the Green River and the Book Cliffs between Price and Moab, had no need (or possibility) of any major development, and it became the world's hottest archeology dig when, in 2004, the state of Utah bought it for two and a half million dollars from the a cattle rancher who had protected it for over 50 years.

Even by the second year of exploration, archeologists had located over 300 pit houses, granaries, ancient corn fields and other structures, and they still had all the time in the world to finish exploring the treasure trove.

Senator John Valentine, who happens to be a member of the Utah County SAR team, was involved in brokering the deal and arranged for our team to assist archeologists Renee Barlow, Duncan Metcalfe and others to rappel into ancient granaries built on high, sheer cliffs to study and date them.

The first year, the archeologists were ecstatic about the access we were able to provide. After a tour of some of the more exciting locations, we fixed ropes and lowered them into their first cliff-side targets - remote granaries whose wood core samples, tested in the lab later, dated back 900 years.

I brought along a small jade statue I bought at Honduras' Copan ruins and hid it repeatedly at every ruin we explored, waiting for someone to "discover" it. Finally, after hiking around all day long and rappelling three sets of cliffs to access the Rifle Granary (named for a massive hole in its wall shot out by a rifle years earlier), someone finally spotted the shiny green object and merely commented, "This doesn't look like it belongs here."

We returned the next year for more exploration, and Producer Nancy Green of the University of Utah's television station KUED came along and shot *Secrets of the Lost Canyon,* which became an award-winning documentary about the place and its history.

I got a brief moment in the film as Nancy and her camera got lowered over an 80' cliff to the Beehive Granary where Renee and I stood on a narrow ledge below, possibly the first humans there in nearly a thousand years. Nancy also graciously added me to the film's credits under "additional photography" for holding the camera to shoot the inside of the ancient storage bin.

Months later, several of us attended the film's gala debut screening at the KUED studios. After a long evening of fascinating speakers, presentations, awards, and the screening itself, Senator Valentine was called up and he called for me to join him. In my hands, I clutched two long, cylindrical packages.

"Our team was thrilled to have the chance to work with Renee, Duncan and the other archeologists in Range Creek," I said into the microphone after inviting Renee to join us in front of the large crowd, "and as a token of our appreciation, we found a limited-edition poster of an action hero that we'd like to give her."

I handed the first package to Renee. I assume that she, along with the entire crowd, was expecting to see Indiana Jones appear as she unrolled the poster. Instead, she found something even better.

The 48" poster showed a blue Jeep charging from a swollen creek with both front tires high in the air. I took it of Renee driving through Range Creek, swollen with spring runoff. An inset image showed her recording measurements at the Beehive Granary, another showed the Jeep half buried in the creek, and the caption read *Renee "Indiana" Barlow*.

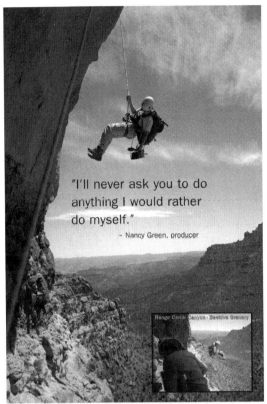

"I'll never ask you to do anything I would rather do myself."

— Nancy Green, producer

Next, we invited Nancy up and I handed her another action hero poster. In it, she dangled precariously on a thin rope amid a wide-open blue sky with a few light clouds, her camera pointed downward toward Renee and I as teams above lowered her to the granary. Across the sky were scrawled the words *I'll never ask you to do anything I would rather do myself.*

It felt rewarding to notice that neither of them could peel their eyes from their posters for the rest of the night, and Nancy later told me, "That's the best picture anyone has ever taken of me."

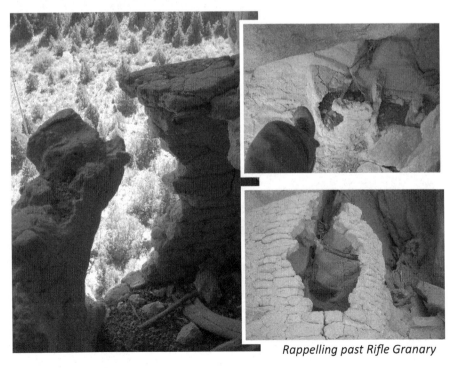

Rappelling past Rifle Granary

62 INTO THIN ICE

The lure and freedom of flight has captivated humankind's imagination since the beginning of time. Technology now carries us into the airy realm that formerly belonged only to birds and clouds. But long after Icarus fell from the skies with his waxen wings, human flight still continues to come with significant risks.

Gravity never sleeps, and nature often grows restless. There is no such thing as solid footing in the atmosphere, and the 10-12,000' mountain peaks that jut into the sky around Utah Valley claim several lives during the course of an average Utah winter.

Flying a small plane in stormy weather is like a game of blackjack. You count the cards on the table and decide whether to take another or hold. Take off or stay on the ground to wait out the storm. Sometimes you win, sometimes you lose. The dealer keeps dealing until you bust. Play long enough and take enough risks, and you'll eventually cash out with nothing left.

A dozen factors combined to stack the deck against Peter, a Utah County pilot, when he took off on a late January afternoon. The four dozen factors stacked in his favor that would come into play hours later all sported coats labeled "Utah County Sheriff Search and Rescue." Besides these, you could imagine a few other favorable factors equipped with non-waxen wings and white robes hovering in the background.

Factor 1: Low Visibility

A winter inversion kept the upper atmosphere clear while fog burned slowly away from the valley throughout the short winter day. Peter had just sat down to dinner when someone called and wanted to see the Cessna 152 Sparrow Hawk he had for sale. Pete left the table and drove to the airport to meet Joe in the clothes he had on – a light coat and boots with no socks.

The sun had already dropped below the horizon, temperatures had plummeted, and moisture condensed in mid air, filling the valley with a soupy fog. Against his better judgment, Pete took off into the mist and instantly lost his bearings. He could not find his way back to the airport.

Factor 2: Search and Rescue out of town

With the Salt Lake City Winter Olympic Games a year away, the seven counties involved in Olympic venues gathered to prepare for the estimated five daily call outs. Olympic visitors turned out to be spectators rather than participants, call outs were sparse or nonexistent during the games, but SAR had to prepare for the worst. A winter emergency scenario was staged at Powder Mountain, up Ogden Canyon, two hours north of Utah County, and half of the Utah County team attended, returning to Provo after 7:00 p.m.

As the Sheriff Department van carrying eight team members drove back through Provo, they passed another team member who had not attended the training. Robert rolled down his window and so did CJ in the front seat.

"Are you going to the call out?" Robert shouted over the wind.

"What call out?" CJ asked as everyone's eyebrows rose in surprise. Eight pagers immediately squawked out the answer. 02-39-58. Water Rescue – Provo Boat Harbor – Airplane Crash.

Factor 3: Force of Impact

The pilot dropped lower and lower through the fog in hopes of catching sight of Provo Airport's tower or runway lights. The ground came abruptly into view and he was relieved to find the plane gliding above flat fields with scattered clumps of weeds. He would land safely here and worry about his location later.

The ground rose harder than expected. Furthermore, it turned out to be not fields, but an icy marsh. The weeds they had seen from the air were reeds and cattails growing up through the ice.

The impact instantly snapped the Cessna's nose gear and both of the pilot's ankles. The plane lifted off again and when it touched down a second time, they lost control and skidded across the ice for 900 feet, gouging the ice with the broken landing gear as the plane slid along.

Factor 4: Thin Ice

As the plane slowed, it smashed through the ice, plunging nose-first into the frigid water. A large chunk of ice smashed through the windshield and struck the pilot, deeply lacerating his forehead, which bled profusely. The cockpit dropped completely under water and freezing water rushed inside.

Factor 5: Damaged ELT

Joe, the prospective aircraft buyer, smashed the cabin's rear window and climbed onto the top of the plane, where the tail section and one wing had come to rest above the water's surface. The area of Utah Lake south of Provo Airport is a shallow marsh known as Mud Lake. The broken landing gear touched bottom and saved the plane from complete submersion.

Joe dragged Pete, who could not move on his own, from the cockpit. Without the use of his legs, Pete reached out for something to hold onto, and found the Emergency Locator Transmitter antennae. When he went to pull himself from the cockpit, the antennae broke.

Our mountaintop ELT repeater requires a downed-aircraft signal for ten minutes before it sets off the alarm. This delay serves to weed out ELT radio checks and spurious false alarms. The broken antennae, along with the plane being mostly submerged, made the signal intermittent and prevented the alert from sounding. No one even knew a plane had crashed.

Factor 6: Distance

The plane crashed 1.7 miles south of the airport. Now below the low fog ceiling, Joe saw a light and went for help. He swam through the frigid water surrounding the plane, clambered onto the ice, and struck out toward the distant light, hoping to keep warm by moving steadily.

The light turned out to be a beacon on an old ski jump in the area. By the time he reached it, however, the Provo Airport lights came into view and he turned north toward them and continued on. The ice sometimes gave way and he fell through, but he always managed to clamber back out of the water.

After walking for over an hour, Joe reached the road embankment surrounding the airport and scrambled up the rocky dike. He forced his icy limbs to climb a chain link fence, now covered with hoar frost crystals nearly half an inch long. He traversed the wide, frozen ditch on the other side and reached the runway. After another hundred yards, he found an open hanger door and met airport technicians who immediately dialed 911.

Factor 7: Technical Difficulties

Life Flight was called, but wisely declined to fly in near-zero visibility. The Sheriff Department's Hoverstar hovercraft was in the shop with a blown piston. Chris Reed, still on his way south from the Olympics training scenario, called and asked Lieutenant Dave Bennett to pilot his hovercraft, but then arrived in time to don his dry suit and flight helmet and pilot the craft himself.

Six SAR members hefted the hovercraft off the trailer and carried it to the lake's edge. With a bit of teasing and battery-jumping, the engine started, but the throttle cable had taken in water during the summer, which now froze solid, making the throttle impossible to control.

Chris finally sliced through the cable with his dive knife, then cut away enough sheath to tie a loop in the cable's severed end. A short length of webbing was tied through this loop and Dave used it to run the throttle as he sat behind Chris inside the craft.

The craft and its two passengers finally rose above the ice, spun in a slow circle, and shot quickly away into the dark night. The smooth surface of the ice supported the craft easily and speed built up fast. Chris occasionally spun the hovercraft backward, the only way to reduce speed. He kept a sharp eye out for remnants of barbed-wire fences, driftwood, or other objects that could rip through the rubber skirts and disable the craft.

Chris and Dave stopped to take their first ELT reading when they caught up with teams 1 and 2 already walking across the ice. The signal was strong enough, but would occasionally stop for a second or two, probably because the ELT transmitter in the airplane was under water or the antenna was making poor contact.

Factor 8: Misinformation

While Chris and others worked on his hovercraft, three teams in wet or dry suits were already searching across the ice. A pair of two-man teams traveled quickly with ice sledges which enabled them to run across the ice and transfer their weight to the wide pontoons when the ice grew thin. With a maximum thickness of about two inches, the ice shot frequent cracks snapping out in many directions, but for the most part, it held. A third team of six rescuers removed the outboard motor from the Achilles inflatable raft and dragged it more slowly over the ice.

Somewhere between hasty assumptions and quickly communicated information, ambulance, airport and law enforcement personnel directed these teams toward the lighted ski jump buoy that Joe first reached, which was about 60 degrees in the wrong direction. Team One reached the jump first and reported the error. The RP (reporting party - Joe) was eventually contacted in the hospital where the story was clarified and ICS redirected the teams east, in the general direction of the sporadic ELT signals already DFed.

Factors 9 & 10: Time and Temperature

By this time, Pete had lain on the wing for nearly three hours, soaked and cold. His clothes froze solid against his skin. He spent most of the time huddled up, lying on his side, with his coat pulled up around his ears. He had given up hope of rescue and was only waiting for death. He had no way of knowing whether Joe had even reached the shore. He knew about the broken ELT antenna and did not expect it to work.

He removed his wet boots and pulled thin nylon gloves over his toes. He was in severe pain from his broken ankles, the gash across his forehead, the wet and extreme cold.

After suffering so long without rescue and recognizing the bad shape he was in, he contemplated igniting the fuel tanks to end the pointless suffering, but had no matches or lighter.

Temperatures had dropped well below freezing. Even with his remaining blood shunting to his core, the odds clearly predicted imminent death. Rescuers were now pointed in the right general direction, but Mud Lake spans several miles, travel over ice was slow, particularly for the team dragging the Achilles, and visibility remained only around 1/8 to ½ a mile.

Factor 11: Open Water

Chris continued steering across the ice while Dave swept a 50-million-candlepower spotlight beam back and forth around them. Dave suddenly spotted a deep gouge in the ice and shouted for Chris to follow it.

They turned and traced the scratch until it led them to the Cessna's tail jutting awkwardly from the ice.

Pete's first indication that help was on the way came when Dave's spotlight passed over him in the thick fog. He turned toward the light and sat up on the wing. "That's when I knew my angels had arrived," he later said, but the difficult challenges of rescue began where the search ended.

Chris set the craft down about 75 feet from the plane. He could see a man sitting on the fuselage with some kind of small penlight. The wings were still intact and the leading edge of the wings hung just above the water's surface. Dave hopped off the hovercraft and walked close enough to the plane to talk with the pilot, but open water surrounding the plane created a significant problem.

The hovercraft supports a 400-pound payload. Chris is 6'2" and weighs 220 pounds, and the victim was clearly at least 250. The ice's smooth, hard surface provided adequate lift, but once the craft settled into the water to load the passenger, it would become difficult or impossible to rise high enough to regain the ice.

Dave radioed GPS coordinates to command post in an attempt to hustle along SAR teams with ice rescue sledges while Chris experimented with a dramatic plan.

After a couple of trial approaches, he piloted his hovercraft straight toward the nose of the plane. As he rose onto the fuselage, he turned and let off the throttle just enough to settle onto the wing. The rear skirts just touched the water and the front skirts hung nearly a foot above the surface over the wing's trailing edge. As the craft's weight settled, the wing dipped closer to the water but did not sink.

The pilot was conscious and alert but had suffered serious injuries. A quick assessment revealed major trauma, significant blood loss, shock and hypothermia. His head laceration started above his left eye and continued across the top of his head. The cut was open to the skull and Chris feared an accompanying open skull fracture as well. Blood covered the wing and his clothing.

"Step onto the seat behind me!" Chris shouted over the roar of the engine and giant fan.

"I can't!" Pete shouted back. "My legs are broken!"

If Chris released the loop of webbing controlling the throttle, the hovercraft would slide backward into the water. He persuaded Pete to crawl to the edge of the hovercraft despite his obvious pain. Chris then grabbed his belt and lifted him across the seat behind him.

At this precise moment, Pete's luck shifted from bad to better. Just as everything had previously gone wrong, everything now went just right. The pilot's added weight on the craft dropped the left wing far enough to allow Chris to drive forward off the wing. They passed alongside the plane's fuselage, maintained a high bead on the water, and successfully flew back onto solid ice.

Factor 12: Hovercraft Difficulties

Out on the ice, Chris and Dave centered the pilot as well as possible, but could do little for his injuries, for which they apologized.

"I don't care!" he shouted back, "just get me the F@&* out of here!"

Chris quickly complied, leaving Dave with a radio and a GPS, awaiting the arrival of the first ice rescue sledge now only a few hundred yards away.

Chris now had to pilot the hovercraft, managing both the steering and improvised throttle on his own. He followed his tracks back the way he came, making good time and nearing the shoreline in a matter of minutes. The hovercraft's fans sucked freezing air past its passengers, and the wind chill dropped the temperatures another ten or twenty degrees. The pilot's exposed head and feet made the ride a miserable experience, but he wasn't about to complain.

When within a minute of reaching shore, with Chris working the awkward webbing-throttle and steering to control his speed, he got too close to some reeds and the hovercraft dropped through the quarter-inch ice surrounding them. Now he experienced the trouble he had anticipated in the open water surrounding the plane, and was unable to rise high enough to regain the frozen surface. Instead, the ice shattered and broke as the giant fan blades shoved the hovercraft slowly forward.

But Pete was on a roll and his lucky streak held intact. The second ice sledge team, concerned about not finding their own way back through the impossible conditions, had turned around. They met up with Team 3 and the Achilles, and now walked only fifty feet away. Chris plowed through the breaking ice toward them and they loaded the pilot onto a backboard and from there, into the raft.

The race against time continued as Chris radioed for more manpower and eight SAR members dragged the raft along as quickly as their slippery feet could propel them. Team members on shore hefted Gary from the raft and into the waiting ambulance while some members of the ice rescue team fell panting to their knees. The pilot's frozen clothing was cut away as the warm ambulance sped away over the pot hole ridden dirt road.

Aftermath

The following Monday morning, Rocky Mountain Helicopter, with support from SAR and other local agencies, hoisted the downed aircraft from the ice. Water drained dramatically from the tail section as the plane rose high above the surrounding fields of ice, looking like a rocket heading for outer space.

Three months later, the pilot entered our monthly meeting, rolling himself through the door in a wheelchair. The remaining pins in his ankles would be removed soon and he would learn to walk again. The scar running across his forehead was healing well.

Tears brimmed in his eyes as he thanked us for our efforts. "You are the only reason I'm alive today," he said, and reported that his doctor said he would not have survived another twenty minutes of exposure.

While everything eventually worked out for the best, we learned several important lessons from the call. We should have more quickly established contact with the RP and been more cautious about accepting second-hand reports. We were reminded of the importance of keeping all vehicles ready for immediate use, and have now installed battery-minders on our entire fleet of snowmobiles, four-wheelers, watercraft and hovercraft.

Other than those few details, meticulous training and quick response by team members, along with the miracle that kept the pilot alive for nearly four hours in the bitter cold, saved his life when seconds and minutes made all the difference in the world.

63 RAGING PLANET

In my third year on the team, I was made the Public Information Officer. It was a much smaller job than it sounds. I established contacts with news media to publicize recruiting, donations, and general information. My media contacts were more interested in hot-off-the-press information during rescue missions, and that wasn't the kind of data I was allowed to disseminate without approval from ICS. I gave a few television and newspaper interviews following newsworthy rescues that I participated on, but the most useful thing I did was build a team web page.

UCSSAR.org supplies basic information about the team and has been instrumental in recruiting new members, obtaining a few donations, and giving the public a place to submit questions and comments.

One such inquiry came from London. A production company shooting *Raging Planet* for the Discovery Channel wrote to ask if we knew any good blizzard stories. "We're keen to feature the Wasatch Range" in the *Blizzards* episode, Emma explained, due to the famous lake effect that creates our world-famous powder.

I wrote back with a few stories and the plane crash into icy Mud Lake captured their interest. With permission from the SO, I continued to correspond between Emma, the executive assistant, Alex, the director, and a few of the resources they'd need for the Utah shoot.

Alex and Emma dropped by my place on their way through town from the airport. I found them to be very pleasant, positive and energetic, and I looked forward to working with them. They were impressed with the glorious mountain shooting up 7,000' practically from my front yard and later claimed that Utah was the most beautiful and its people the nicest of the 48 states they had visited.

When the time came, a few of us headed up to Daniel's Summit where the shooting would take place on Strawberry Reservoir since Utah Lake had melted in the weeks before the company arrived. Chris borrowed a scrap airplane for the shoot, but rangers wouldn't allow us to cut a hole in the ice to recreate the dramatic rescue realistically.

The production company did their best under the circumstances and we all enjoyed watching them turn our story into a major production. In the end, despite being Alex's favorite story, the inability to recreate the most dramatic parts of the story as they actually happened meant that other stories in the *Blizzard* segment won more screen time with their more dramatic footage.

Emma and Alex obviously love their jobs

Lights, camera, action! Filming on the frozen lake

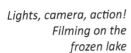

Chris and his hovercraft reenact the dramatic rescue

64 Point of No Return

I can't seem to stop shivering. I know, I know, I should have checked the weather report. Ah, hindsight. I also should have packed better emergency supplies in my Jeep for driving remote mountain roads in the middle of winter. At least I brought something. At least I kept a sleeping bag in the back and a little food in the glove box. Without those essentials, I would not be telling you this story.

When the storm began, I didn't think much of it. What's a little snow? I have good tires and four wheel drive. When the snow began to accumulate - piling up six inches deep - I was enjoying my little adventure. Winter is so beautiful! At one foot deep, I started wondering why the plows hadn't come by, and at eighteen inches, I decided I'd better turn around.

And I would have, if I could. Instead, I got stuck, and the snow kept piling deeper. After trying everything to get the truck moving and failing, I finally accepted my fate. I would have to spend the night in my car, or at least however long it took for the plows to arrive.

What I didn't realize - not for a day or two - was that the plows would not come. At least not for several months, not until spring. That was five days ago.

Now snow has piled up all around the car and I can't seem to stop shivering. My breath has fogged up all the windows, but I won't run the engine for more than fifteen minutes at a time. I have less than half a tank of gas and I have no idea how long it will have to last.

I turn my gaze upward and try to see through the frosted windshield. There must be a helicopter somewhere out there looking for me. It can't be much longer now. I reach up and scrape away the frost and peer upward at the sky, then bow my head again, wrap my arms tightly around myself, and resume shaking.

"Aaand...cut!" Alex says enthusiastically. I stop shivering and sit up straight in the driver's seat. "You're doing a fantastic job," he assures me in his charming British accent. "Let's have a bit more smoke inside the car," he requests and Phil climbs into the back seat with the smoke machine. It's too warm in the car to see my breath, so we have to make it up for the camera.

The Jeep is buried two hundred feet away from the Daniel's Summit lodge. I am now an actor for another story on the same Discovery Channel segment that we shot our ice rescue for.

Once Alex, Emma, and others passed through town and settled in at the lodge, they decided to shoot another story they had been researching. It involved a man caught by a blizzard in Washington State who spent two weeks trapped by several feet of snow in his Jeep Cherokee before a rescuer on a snowmobile located him.

They would need to fly in the victim, John, who now lived in Hawaii, to tell his story, and find an actor to play his part.

"You know who looks like John?" Emma asked thoughtfully. "Shaun," she answered when others looked at her questioningly.

They were hesitant to hire a non-actor for the part, but decided to take a chance. They seemed quite enthusiastic about my performance and I absolutely loved working with the crew. Everyone was unflaggingly positive and fun and it brightened my day just being around them. The five hundred bucks they paid me for two days' worth of shivering didn't hurt, either.

With the smoke ready inside the cab, we were ready to roll film again.

"I'm worried, Alex," I confided as I prepared for the fourth or fifth hour of taping me trapped inside the car. "I'm afraid I'm going to get type-cast as 'man who shivers a lot.'"

Tom checked the preview and assured us that the amount of smoke now looked perfect. "Okay, Shaun," Alex directed in his energetic yet soothing voice, "close your eyes and imagine you're really there, stranded in the blizzard." I had been cold plenty of times before. It wasn't difficult to remember. Alex paused for a moment to let me settle into my persona, then practically whispered, "When you're ready...."

I nodded and began to shiver.

65 THE SWAMP

Warm water sloshed half way up my shins. Giant cat tails towered four feet over my head, hiding everything but the dim, distant stars. I didn't know which direction I was walking anymore. Mosquitoes buzzed around my face and I swatted at them and slapped my neck and ears whenever I felt one poking its tiny proboscis through my skin. I was grateful for the wetsuit that protected most of my body.

My team of three had been slogging through the swamp for hours, hoping to find the last two survivors of a boat that sank in the lake's shallow waters about a mile off shore sometime after sunset.

By 'shallow,' of course, I mean ten to twelve feet of water. Even six or seven feet is deep enough to drown in. If people drown in bathtubs, then Utah Lake is more than adequate. It happens several times almost every year.

Fortunately, the boat sank near enough to shore that at least four of its six passengers were able to swim in. Unfortunately, the nearest shoreline was Powell Slough (pronounced *slew*), a disorienting expanse of ten-foot-tall reeds, ravenous mosquitoes, and a few trees, running three and a half miles long and almost a mile wide.

Three swimmers made their way to a narrower section of swamp near the north end, reached civilization, and sounded the alarm. Teams found the fourth wandering through the reeds not far from open water and my team drove the Achilles motorized raft in to pick him up. We coordinated by radio and whistle blasts, then half of my team stayed at the boat while the rest hiked toward the whistles and guided them back. Aware of the survivor's bare, bleeding feet, I did my best to stomp down any sharp reeds poking up in our path.

The raft returned to search the lake with a few passengers while the rest of us, encouraged by the latest find, joined the land search.

If you can call it land. It was more like land that sank. I didn't know whether to call it land or water, kind of like that mysterious moment when cookie dough in a hot oven suddenly becomes a cookie.

As we walked, we called out names of the missing passengers and paused to listen. Sometimes other search teams wandering a hundred yards away answered our calls and a moment of confusion would follow. We quickly learned to coordinate quiet times over the radio when everyone would blow whistles and shout and then keep quiet for at least thirty seconds afterward.

For one half-hour period, several of us on different teams all heard the same thing. A voice from the swamp, coming from the general direction of a single large tree growing in the distance. We worked our way that direction with high hopes of making another find.

As we drew closer, the voice quit calling out. Perhaps its owner was worn out. We hoped he hadn't fallen down and drown in shallow water that rarely rose higher than our knees.

We searched around the tree and found nothing despite being so sure we heard *something* out there. Perhaps it was a disembodied spirit unaccustomed to being disturbed so far out in the swamp. Maybe it belonged to a searcher on the water who wasn't paying attention to the radio commands to maintain silence after our calling out. More likely it was a waterfowl whose mournful cry, from a distance, sounded like someone desperately calling for help.

A helicopter joined the search periodically, flashing its spotlight across the slough and coordinating search team positions.

Having combed a long swath of swampland nearest the lake, and having heard other teams covering the terrain all around us, we decided to head deeper into the swamp and toward dry land. As we walked along, we veered right and left through any openings in the thick reeds that made the going easier. Sometimes we crawled over such large piles of dead reeds that they felt like logs and held us entirely above the water.

"Which way do you think is east?" a team mate asked once as I began to plunge through yet another opening. I pointed straight ahead. "Nope," he answered, holding up his compass and pointing behind us. I was completely disoriented without even knowing it.

Eventually, the water grew shallower and we spotted the tall power lines running along the edge of the golf course.

Meanwhile, a serious of miraculous events unfolded out on the lake. First, a team member with a high-quality FLIR camera (far looking infrared) went on a trip and planned to take the camera with him, but forgot. Somehow someone found out and picked up the camera on their way to the call. This person wound up in a boat and, as they ran search patterns, picked out a tiny white dot floating on the lake surface a hundred yards away or more.

Rescuers found the fifth swimmer hypothermic and completely unresponsive. Their bow wave washed over his face and his wide-open eyes didn't even blink. As is often the case on the lake, his PFD saved his life.

Rescuers jumped into the water and they hauled the man aboard as gently as possible, ever aware of the fragile heartbeat that accompanies hypothermia and cautious not to disrupt it.

After careful rewarming, the man explained his muddled mindset as the heat drained from his body. "I had completely given up hope," he told us. "If my hands weren't so cold, I would have taken off my life jacket."

By four a.m., the search ended for the night. We had searched as thoroughly as we possibly could. The sixth and final boater could not be found. Several days later when he floated, we understood why.

His body rose a mile in the wrong direction from where we found the sunken boat. He didn't have a life jacket though his friends reported that he had held onto a floating seat cushion after the boat sank. Hypothermia may have affected his judgment and sent him off in the wrong direction, and he was probably gone long before our initial search for him ended.

06/28/2002

A SAR member overlooks Mineral Basin from cliffs near Pittsburg Lake with a Life Flight helicopter, helping with the search for a missing hiker, in the background

Skiing backcountry powder near Mineral Basin

66 Brothers

Ron dove into Utah Lake's icy water without a second thought and swam toward the first man who had been floating there for at least two hours on this sunny November afternoon.

"H-help my b-brother!" the man stuttered, his words slurring together, referring to the second man. "I think he's gone!"

Another team member had already abandoned his watercraft and reached out for the brother. Rescuers swam and dragged both men onto thick foam rescue boards affixed behind the watercraft, shoving the trailing end of the board underwater, then letting it float up underneath them.

Once aboard, watercraft operators hit the throttle and the water flowing beneath the board lifted it still higher above the surface. Each attending rescuer knelt above the frozen men, doing their best to both hold onto the board's handles and keep their precious cargo from sliding off.

Over a mile away, the watercraft reached the rocky shore and waiting team members, sheriff deputies, and AirMed paramedics, their helicopter parked nearby with rotors spinning, helped carry the men ashore.

The brothers had been duck hunting on Bird Island, two miles out, in what looked like a bathtub-sized shallow-draft hunting boat decked out with blinds and a small outboard motor. Doug stood six-foot-three and weighed an intimidating 285 pounds. In comparison, his little brother Tad, at five-foot-ten and a lean 165 pounds, looked like he had been less effective at claiming his fair share of food at the table as a child.

After successfully bagging half a dozen mallards, ring necks, and pintail, they headed south for Lincoln Beach Marina. A 5-knot breeze had been blowing from the northwest, and foot-high swells rolled lazily toward shore.

Normally, such small waves would not present a problem even for such a shallow boat, but at one point almost half way to shore, a single wave interval changed slightly, with two waves slightly closer together than normal. The hull surfed down a wave face and the motor shoved the boat forward where it plowed into the back of the next swell. The boat speed slammed to a crawl.

This alone did not sink the boat, but Doug, sitting at the transom and steering, wasn't ready for the sudden stop and went flying forward toward his smaller brother. With the imbalanced weight all in the front, along with the momentum of the boat still trying to plow its way forward, the bow plunged underwater, emptying the boats contents as it rolled upside down.

The frigid lake swallowed the brothers whole. The initial cold slap to the face and scalp was nothing compared to water's icy fingers running down their chests and groins as the water poured into their coats and quickly soaked their clothing.

Their first thought as they came sputtering to the surface was to get out of the water as fast as possible, but there was nowhere to go.

"W-w-w-we g-gotta s-s-swim!" Tad stuttered frantically.

"We'll never make it," Doug objected. "And we should stay with the boat."

"A l-l-lot of g-g-good that'll d-do us!"

Tad was right. Only the bow of the boat floated now, and only an inch or two above the waves. Their decoys and dead ducks bobbed in the water around them.

"W-w-we gotta s-swim!" Tad repeated. "W-we gotta g-generate s-some heat!"

"Swimming will steal our heat faster," Doug explained. The cold didn't seem to affect him quite as much as his skinny brother. "We have to keep still and wait for someone to save us."

"N-n-nobody even kn-n-nows we're here!"

That thought had not yet had time to occur to Doug. What if no one found them? It was still early afternoon and could be hours before other hunters decided to return to shore from the island. Surely no waterskiers would come out on a cold day like this. He looked at his little brother and imagined them both dying just because of a stupid little accident.

No. He could not let that happen. He turned toward shore and shouted at the top of his deep voice. "Heelllp!!! Somebody heeeellllp!!!" Sound carries over water, and the breeze was blowing toward shore. Somebody just might hear them.

Somebody did.

A fisherman on the rocky low-water shore thought he heard a voice while the line whirred off the spool and his lure flew fifty feet out into the lake. When it landed with a distant plop, he didn't reel it in. He didn't spin the handle that would flip the bail over to recapture the line. He stood there, perfectly motionless in the lapping waves, holding his breath, listening.

He heard it again. A faint shout. Someone calling for help.

He spun the handle a few times to prevent more line from feeding out, then ran up the jetty for a better view, dropping his rod along the shore. A mile out into the lake, he saw a small crowd of objects bobbing on the surface. Shielding his eyes from the afternoon sun and removing his sunglasses, he squinted his eyes and looked closer. Two or three people floated there with no boat in sight.

The fisherman's brain slipped into high gear. It spun so fast that for a moment, it couldn't get any traction. He jumped up and down, his body desperately seeking an outlet for the unexpected surge of energy, and looked around. As his thoughts caught up, he looked up the marina for a boat he could send out to help. Nothing. He looked at the parking lot, but only empty trailers stood there.

He turned back toward the lake to make sure he wasn't seeing things, then dug frantically into his pocket and found his phone.

"911, what's your emergency?" the dispatcher inquired.

"H-help!" the fisherman blurted out. "Th-there's someone in the water!"

"What's your location, sir?" the dispatcher asked calmly, and soon the necessary details were collected.

SAR was dispatched and assignments were made to pick up watercraft from our hanger at the Sheriff's office. The first set of PWCs launched from the marina, but the water was so low at this time of year that the hulls scraped rocks as they moved down the channel. Because this was a desperate, life-threatening emergency, the operators paid no attention to normal protocol and ignored the rocks, hitting the gas instead to get up on plane.

Other watercraft were directed beyond the marina and down the rocky shoreline exposed by receding waters to a deeper-water launch point.

The first rescuers hauled the brothers to shore as quickly as possible, and shore teams immediately began CPR on Tad, whose heart had stopped during transit. They managed to resuscitate him and he sucked in a shallow breath, but only one. His heart stopped again and would not beat on its own. Tad was simply too cold.

Someone brought an AED and taped the pads to Tad's left side and right chest. "Clear!" a medic shouted and everyone backed away from the patient as the AED checked for a shockable rhythm. Everyone held their breath and waited for the outcome.

"Shock not advised," it droned in its robotic voice. "Continue CPR."

And so they did. Again and again, Tad's heart pumped a few beats and then ceased. The AirMed paramedic and pilot looked at one another. "May as well power down," the pilot said, shaking his head.

But Tom would hear nothing of it. "We're not giving up on him!" he shouted energetically. "Don't you, either!"

And so they didn't. They loaded him aboard the aircraft and flew him to a Salt Lake hospital, doing CPR off and on the entire way against standard protocol which calls for no CPR in a moving vehicle.

At the hospital, Tad's blood was sucked from his body, rewarmed at a single degree per hour, and pumped back in. His core temperature had dropped to a chilly 74 degrees. They added a sedative while he warmed, then waited to see if he would ever wake up.

He did.

As far as the doctors could tell, he recovered completely. Both brothers and their families visited our monthly business meeting to thank us in person for saving their lives. In the years to come, Tad's family sent us Christmas cards featuring photographs of the family standing together and smiling happily. We passed the cards around at our business meeting and smiled back.

The following year, at the annual Utah Emergency Medical Services Week awards ceremony, all agencies involved in the rescue from dispatch to the hospital were awarded the Air Rescue of the Year Award. The award was very nice, but the Christmas cards meant much more to us.

67 URBAN AIRCRAFT

An ELT triggered our West Mountain repeater and we set out to DF the downed aircraft signal and look for survivors. Vehicles were sent to various vantage points around the valley and reports began flooding in.

"88 degrees from Pelican Point, five microvolts, vertically polarized, confidence seven."

The degrees told the compass angle of the signal from each location. Microvolts told how strong the signal was, or rather, how low the ELPER could be turned without loosing the signal. Polarization told which way the antenna best picked up the signal, and confidence varied between zero and ten depending on how many buildings, wires, and mountain slopes might be bouncing the signal and providing misleading data.

"33 degrees from the northwest corner of Utah Valley University, three microvolts, vertically polarized, confidence five."

Reading by reading, crews raced nearer and nearer to the source. It wasn't long till one thing became obvious - the signal was coming from an urban area, somewhere in the middle of Orem.

Soon teams quit stopping to take readings and just drove with the ELPER antennas extended, listening for the signal to grow stronger or weaker, and hoping to locate the crash first.

When we reached a house with an airplane parked on its front porch, we put the ELPERs away.

The aircraft was a small jumbo jet.

Made of plastic with a handle for a child to sit on and steer. We took pictures of us tracking the signal to it before ringing the doorbell and asking the pilot there to check his ELT. Sure enough, his child had been playing with an ELT stored in a closet and accidentally set it off.

SAR and NFF carry an injured hiker down boulders and scree below Bridal Veil Falls

68 FLIGHT PLAN

The weather was overcast and grey, and a drizzling rain turned the world soggy as I drove through an overgrown field near Sandy Beach. An ELT signal had led us in this direction and we had a pretty good idea what we were about to find.

The wing had detached from the fuselage which lay in the grass nearby where it fell from the sky.

Medics leapt from their trucks and ran to the fuselage, searching for the six passengers listed on the flight plan. "There are only two people in here!" Jorge shouted. "Search the fields!"

We didn't wait for assignments from CP this time, but organized ourselves into rough lines and began to fan out through the tall grasses.

"I've got one!" someone yelled far off to my left. A moment later, his voice transmitted over the radio. "One female patient, approximately nine years old, unconscious but breathing, with severe lacerations."

"Where are you?" someone yelled, picking up a backboard and running in the general direction of the voice.

Soon we had located all six passengers. One was dead and the five living had suffered varying degrees of injury. We treated them the best we could in the field, then prioritized them for transport. The fatality was marked black. He could wait. Reds went first. Urgent attention needed. Next came yellows with non-life-threatening injuries, and we even found a green - dazed and confused but apparently uninjured.

"Let's wrap it up," Jared said over the radio around 11:30. "All teams report back to CP."

Our unconscious victims suddenly woke up. The injured we had not yet carried out sat up and unwound the bandaging from their heads, arms and legs. Chris towed in a twenty-foot trailer and asked for help lifting the aircraft parts onto it. He needed to return it to his friend at the junk yard who lent out the plane to make training more realistic.

Our sergeants take their training seriously. "Performance never rises above training," they sometimes quip. Realistic trainings help keep our skills honed, polished, and ready for the real thing when real lives are at stake and adrenaline complicates everything. It's all part of our team's commitment to high standards, and such preparation turns into increased confidence and job satisfaction.

"Hey, Shaun," someone said, waving me toward the fuselage where he stood. "Check this out."

I walked toward him, then bent over and peered into the fuselage where he pointed. There inside the narrow metal walls, someone had written a brief message. A pilot or passenger who crashed this plane must have crawled inside for shelter while waiting for rescue. Along the wall, they scrawled a message with a bloody finger tip:

"We're f#@ked."

69 GET YOUR HERO ON

What goes through your mind as you read these stories? Does your heart rate accelerate? Does your blood pressure rise? Do you think of ways you'd have saved people? Do you dream about it after you fall asleep and continue to dream long after waking? Do you want a piece of the action? Do you want to save dozens of lives or just help hundreds of people get safely off the mountain or lake?

Do you have the skills to do so? Do you have the time? What about the gear or money to buy it? Are you a good team player with a positive attitude, willingness to follow orders and safety protocols to the letter?

If so, we invite you to apply to our (or your local) search and rescue team. Call your sheriff department or look them up online and let them know that you'd like to volunteer. They'll send you an application or let you know how it works.

Looking down 600' of Stairway to Heaven

70 Save a Life Today

Can you imagine any pursuit more worthwhile than saving lives? How would you like to get in on the action?

Even if you don't have the time/money/desire or ability to be a full-time on-call volunteer rescuer, we still need your help! The following letter written by former Board of DIrectors Treasurer Brent Ripley tells how you can help us save lives today:

YOUR NEIGHBOR WENT FOR A SHORT ATV RIDE THIS MORNING, BUT SOMETHING WENT WRONG, AND NOW HE'S COLD, HUNGRY AND HURT.

WHAT WILL YOU DO TO HELP HIM?

Dear ...,

My name is Brent Ripley, and I'm writing you on behalf of the current officers and directors of the Utah County Volunteer Search and Rescue Team.

Our team is asking for donations to help buy critical rescue equipment. You are an important part of the fabric of Utah County and its citizens, and we thank you in advance for taking the time to read this letter and learn a little bit more about us and our needs.

What you do with this letter will have a very real impact in someone's life – someone who lives and works here in Utah County.

WHAT WE DO

In association with Utah County Sheriff's Department, our organization is involved in approximately 100 rescue efforts each year. Within the past 12 months, we've been involved in efforts surrounding avalanches, vehicle rollovers, missing children, lost hikers and hunters, fallen climbers, stuck cavers, lost Alzheimer patients, marooned boaters, and stranded snowmobilers. Many of these rescues involved serious, life-threatening injuries.

For example, late last fall, two brothers decided to go duck hunting at Bird Island, a small island off Lincoln Point in Utah Lake. On the way, their boat capsized leaving them stranded in 40° water. Our rescuers set out with wave runners that had rescue paddle boards affixed to the back.

(One thing many people don't realize is that cold water removes heat from the body 25 times faster than cold air. **Physical activity such as swimming, or other struggling in the water increases heat loss.** Strong swimmers have died before swimming 100 yards in cold water.)

When our rescuers reached them, one of the brothers was still conscious but the other was motionless and appeared dead. As our rescuers were in the water working to load the conscious victim, he told them, "take care of my brother first -- I think he's gone." In fact, in the words of Chris Reed, a longtime EMT and SAR volunteer, speaking of this other unconscious victim, they had a hard time maneuvering him on the equipment because "his arms were straight out in front of him, as stiff as a board." The rescuers took the victims straight to the nearest shoreline where they saw that the unconscious victim was not breathing nor could they feel a pulse. They began CPR and then used defibrillation paddles to try to revive him. This continued for nearly 20 minutes, with the victim occasionally attempting to breathe before seizing and going motionless again.

Once the transport helicopter arrived our rescuers insisted that CPR be continued since, in their opinion, the victim's color appeared improved. He was transported to the University of Utah medical Center where he underwent three hours of mechanical CPR, a heart bypass operation and gastric lavage to warm him, and three days of sedation in the ICU. The treating doctors said his core temperature was 75.2° when he arrived at the hospital. That anyone could survive a core temperature that low is astounding, but four days after arriving, he was interacting with his family and recovering very quickly. Miraculously, long-term medical effects appear to be negligible and he should lead a normal healthy life.

Needless to say, it was very satisfying when he, his brother, and his wife and child came to our monthly meeting to thank our team for its efforts.

We relate this example to show that a quick response by qualified and dedicated rescuers very often literally means the difference between life and death. These brothers certainly would not have survived much longer, and theirs is not the only example we could give.

We also want to impress upon you that our efforts are meaningful mostly to the residents of Utah County. The people we rescue are not far removed in a distant land, but are our neighbors, friends, and families. As much as we need to help victims of foreign disasters such as victims of the recent tsunami, we believe charity begins at home and relatively small donations by generous and dedicated citizens such as yourself go a long way toward saving lives of people you might run into at the local grocery store.

CHALLENGES WE FACE

Utah County is unique. We have mountain peaks rising to almost twelve thousand feet within only a few miles of a large, shallow lake. We have a large, outdoor-loving population within minutes of isolated wilderness and fast-flowing streams.

All of this provides us with serious challenges. **Unlike many search and rescue organizations which specialize in only one type of rescue** (such as technical mountain rescue or open water rescue), **our team must be very good at many types of rescue.** We have climbing specialists, SCUBA specialists, swift-water specialists, cavers, K9 operators, and medics.

It isn't *whether* someone from our valley will need us, it's *who, when* and *how* . . .

WHO WE ARE

Our organization is made up entirely of volunteers who donate their time, talents, and equipment not only to our rescue efforts but to the training which is so important to those efforts. We have between 40 and 50 members at any given time. In our day jobs, we are doctors, mechanics, lawyers, graphic designers, teachers, investment advisors, home builders, nurses, paramedics, and engineers. In fact, one of the founding members of our team is a prominent member of the Utah Senate.

Our volunteers are required to provide virtually all their own outdoor rescue and survival gear. This usually consists of just about any piece of outdoor equipment you can think of from SCUBA gear to climbing gear to cold water, snow and avalanche gear. In addition to providing equipment, members must commit to training and incident response throughout the year. This commitment of time and financial resources is considerable.

We are one of only five fully certified Mountain Rescue Association (MRA) teams in Utah. In addition, we are certified by the State of Utah as a Level I (intermediate) EMT organization, the same as most municipal ambulance services. We are also organized as a 501(c)(3) non-profit organization, so **any donation you make to us is tax-deductible** (you must see your accountant for further details).

WHAT WE NEED

We need gifts from community donors so we can purchase several pieces of team equipment that will greatly help us in rescue situations.

Rescues are demanding events. It's usually not a simple matter of finding the victim and bringing him or her out. Rough terrain, distance from roads, the safety of team members, and the victim's medical and emotional condition are all complicating factors. A winter rescue usually involves additional challenges such as snow travel, short days, and wet, freezing conditions, all of which can be deadly for victims who were not likely prepared for them.

Additionally, we must always plan for the safety of our team members by providing complete logistical support. For our sake and the sake of the victim, the less time we spend in the field – winter or otherwise – the better.

Removing victims from an incident scene and transporting them to an ambulance is especially critical and almost always the most time consuming part of a rescue event. Transport is usually complicated by darkness, canyons, steep hillsides, and cliffs where the accidents occur. Extrication can be slow and painful for a cold, tired, and injured person who is far from roads.

For example, a recent rescue involved a man whose four-wheeler tipped over backwards, landing on him and injuring his ribs and pelvis. He was deep in a side drainage up Spanish Fork Canyon. By the time we reached him, he was cold, tired, scared and in severe pain.

We treated him for his condition and then warmly packaged him in a rescue litter. By this time it was after 10:00 p.m. The trail was well-packed and somewhat rutted from other snowmobiles and four wheelers. Owing to his location and the time of night, no helicopter transport was available. We either had to carry him out or pull him on a litter behind an ATV or snowmobile. It would have taken hours to carry him out, so he was slowly pulled to a waiting ambulance at the mouth of the drainage.

While we did the best we could to steady his ride, it was a long and painful journey. Snow is not always soft!

Another example is that of a cross-country skier who, while skiing alone up the South Fork of Provo Canyon, fell and broke his femur (the thigh bone). A femur injury itself is often life threatening, and he was stranded alone in the snow for nearly 8 hours before he was found by another group of skiers. Needless to say, he was very tired and in a great deal of pain by the time our medical team reached him. We had to transport him from his accident location the same way as with the earlier example.

While we always take every measure to ensure that our victim is safe and stable before being transported, the circumstances of backcountry rescue sometimes make transport very difficult.

If either of the above victims had been more critically injured, it would've been even trickier to remove them from the accident scene in a timely fashion. **The bottom line is that we must enhance our ability to safely and comfortably transport victims when time is of the essence and helicopters aren't available. We need your help to do so.**

SPECIFIC EQUIPMENT WE NEED RIGHT AWAY

1)   We believe we can better transport backcountry accident victims by using an ambulance sled or trailer that we can pull with our snowmobiles and ATVs. The sleds have full suspension and plenty of cargo space, so they will also help us protect medical equipment and critical rescue gear that is often difficult to transport with a snowmobile or ATV. We need your help to purchase these sleds.

Use of these sleds will greatly reduce the possibility of further complicating an injury during overland transport. We need two of them. Each costs approximately $5,600 before shipping.

2)   We have another need associated with difficult and lengthy rescues. Many rescues are multi-day events requiring complex logistical support. For example, during the catastrophic avalanche that occurred near Aspen Grove last winter, our team spent many days working the scene and looking for victims.

Searching for victims of an avalanche is very difficult and tiring. It's critical to the rescue effort that searchers have enough food and drink to keep them healthy and energetic.

Each member brings sufficient food and water for 24 hours on any rescue, but for large multi-day events, **we need a medium-sized enclosed trailer within which we could store team food, drink, replacement gear, emergency shelter, our generator, lighting and extension cords, and other necessities such as large stoves for cooking and warming food.** This would allow our members to keep their packs intact and ready for backcountry rescues when they will be more isolated.

The trailer should not be too large for a medium-sized SUV to pull on any grade. The Wells Cargo Single-Axle Tote Wagon with V-Front, or similar trailer made by another company, would be an ideal trailer for our needs.

Of course, if your organization sees fit to donate the funds for any of this equipment, your company's name and logo would be prominently and tastefully situated on the equipment itself at no additional cost to you. As you must be aware, we get significant media coverage on many of our events. Citizens of our county would certainly appreciate your generous support.

3) Many of our members are very capable SCUBA divers, but unfortunately rescue SCUBA equipment is very different from recreational SCUBA equipment. We need a number of SCUBA helmets that will allow us to be in radio contact with our divers and maintain the proper safety threshold that we owe our volunteers. Each helmet costs between approximately $600 and $800, and we need a minimum of six.

<u>PLEASE HELP ANY WAY YOU CAN</u>

If you can't help us at this time with our larger equipment needs, cash donations of any amount are very helpful. The team provides some rescue gear such as ropes and webbing, litters, and medical gear. This equipment needs constant updating and monitoring.

We also consider in-kind donations of up-to-date reliable equipment, ranging from ATVs, snowmobiles, PWCs, trailers, and other devices.

Also, because we are MRA certified, we must send representative members to a multi-day re-certification and events and national meetings each year. We don't want our members to travel and lodge at their own expense if we can avoid it. This year, the event is being held at Brighton Ski Resort – a stone's throw away. Last year, it was in Anchorage, Alaska.

Cash is also helpful toward funding training exercises. Ongoing training is critical to our mission. We train every month, not only for rescue scenarios, but also for medical and transport scenarios. While training is not a large expense, we do need some equipment to keep it challenging and relevant.

Again, we appreciate any donation you see fit to make. We provide our donors with gifts that are suitable for their business entrance lobby or anywhere else in their home or facility so they can proudly show their support for our search and rescue organization. Donors at the highest suggested level will also receive an attractive fleece jacket with our organization's logo and a statement tastefully identifying them as generous donors.

We are confident that as your friends, clients and customers see your support of our organization, they will understand your commitment to our community.

Thank you, etc. etc.
Signed . . . .

P.S. It seems like everyone in Utah County knows someone we have helped. Your generosity and goodwill will be appreciated for years to come – and will, without a doubt, eventually help save the life of someone right here in our community. When was the last time you were able to do that?

P.P.S. Why do we ask for donations instead of charge a fee to those we rescue? This is a legitimate question and is the subject of some debate in the rescue community. Some believe that a rescue fee deters risky behavior. Many organizations, especially those associated with National Parks (such as Denali National Park in Alaska and Zion National Park here in Utah) will charge a fee in many cases.

While we acknowledge a potential rescue fee may deter risky behavior, **we know that it also deters requests for help,** even from people in dire situations. So far, we have been able to serve the citizens of our county without having them pay money for it. Whether we ever begin to charge a fee is ultimately for the Sheriff to determine, but we hope to continue to provide our services free of charge for a long time.

We sent this letter to three companies. Thanks to their generous response, we now have the snow ambulance and ATV trailer and have used them to save lives. We still need the rescue SCUBA masks and other equipment.

For example, better snowmobiles for more team members would help us access difficult locations on winter rescues, particularly when we must cover vast areas of wilderness to locate accident victims.

We also need high-quality FLIR (far-looking infrared) cameras. Our current cameras work fine once we get close, but they won't show us a boating-accident survivor a mile away on the lake.

If you prefer to help our volunteers directly, prepaid gas cards can ease the financial burden of responding to calls that cost each rescuer $10-40 just to drive up to 130 miles to the accident scene or trailhead and back. It's a great way to say, "Thank you for your dedication!"

We can't do this alone. We need your help. Your generous donations save lives.

Your purchase of this book provided a small donation to SAR volunteers. When the time comes to consider tax-deductible donations for yourself or your company, we hope you'll keep our cause in mind. Thank you!

THANK YOU for helping us protect Utah County.
Your generous donations save lives.

YOU

Utah County Sheriff Search and Rescue Volunteers
www.ucssar.org

71 DON'T TOUCH HER!

The moonless night was dark, cool and calm as we ran wide search patterns across the lake for a missing man and woman whose boat sank miles from shore.

Considering the water temperature and the length of time the couple had been in the lake, we weren't sure what condition we'd find them in, if we found them at all.

Pausing to shout out their names sometime after midnight, someone in the flat-bottomed Mud Buddy heard a response and called other boats toward them.

We were excited to find the couple alive and swimming toward shore, about thirty feet away from each other.

The mud buddy driver let off on the throttle and as the boat settled and glided toward the woman, a rescuer leaned over the gunnel and reached out a hand toward her.

That's when the man shouted frantically, "DON'T TOUCH HER!!!"

The rescuer didn't pause, but took her arm and others helped to lift her into the boat while the driver asked the man why not.

I hoped she didn't have some highly infectious and incurable disease. Perhaps he thought she was bad luck, blamed their boat sinking on her, and didn't want us to succumb to the same fate.

"How much is this going to cost?!" the man demanded. Apparently he wasn't interested in a three-thousand dollar boat ride when they could swim to shore just fine in another hour or two as long as hypothermia didn't set in and kill them both. I was relieved to know that the woman we had just taken into our boat wasn't a zombie or anything worse.

"It doesn't cost you anything," the driver assured him. "This is free."

"Okay, then," the man said after a pause, and another boat plucked him from the water and wrapped him in a warm blanket.

This is why the vast majority of volunteer rescuers feel so strongly about not charging for rescue. If people don't call, they may die. Even if the Sheriff charged a fee, the volunteers wouldn't see it anyway.

I've since wondered whether the man and woman were a married couple or out on a first date. If it was a first date, I'm guessing there wasn't a second.

72 Point of the Mountain

Topographical features of the valley influence weather patterns in various ways. Tall mountains create descending breezes as their cooler, denser air slides downslope on a hot afternoon. They deflect wind patterns of passing storms skyward, the air cooling as it rises, which sometimes maintains cloud cover over the peaks which dissipates as it blows away.

Storm fronts sometimes stall around Point of the Mountain, a narrow ridge dividing Utah and Salt Lake Valleys, and Lehi can pick up three feet of snow while other valley locations don't see a single flake.

One February afternoon storm brought rush-hour traffic to a standstill. I-15 became a parking lot with 50 accidents and 49 vehicles sliding off the road. Windows and windshields became encrusted with ice, and some commuters spent five hours on commutes as short at 11 miles.

Hundreds of children were returned to schools when busses were unable to deliver them home and many spent the night in classrooms.

Some motorists ran out of gas while idling the engine and cranking the heaters while 70 mph winds piled four-foot snow drifts against their car doors.

While residents were warned to stay indoors, SAR headed north to help out. CP was set up at an LDS chapel near major traffic arteries, and team members radioed information about routes that led there without encountering impassable snow drifts.

Once on scene, we unloaded snowmobiles and headed into the blizzard.

The snow fell horizontally and we sometimes couldn't see beyond fifteen or twenty feet, but we drove to the highways and worked our way along the rows of stranded cars to make sure everyone was okay. Some were cold and we brought them back to the chapel where they were given wool blankets for the night.

One man lived just up the mountain on Traverse Ridge. He grabbed his briefcase and held on while I gave him a ride up the hill, through residential neighborhoods, and across his front lawn to the front door. We waited to make sure someone let him in before riding away.

Sometime after midnight, the storm weakened and traffic got moving again. Many abandoned cars sat in the middle of road, waiting for their owners to return the next day.

73 A FALL FROM HEAVEN

Blake grinned ear to ear as he walked into the living room. His arm draped around Sheila's shoulders, and Sheila's eyes danced.

"Notice anything different?" Blake asked as his family glanced up from their game of Scrabble. Everyone had come home to spend Christmas together and meet Blake's girlfriend. Their eyes looked back and forth between the two happy faces, the family's expressions remaining blank. They considered the couple's haircuts and clothes, but only the happy expressions seemed to provide any clues.

Then Jenny's eyes shot wide open and she raised her hands to cover her mouth as she drew in a quick breath. "Oh, my gosh!" she exclaimed.

Everyone else in the room saw the shiny diamond ring immediately after, and the board game was forgotten as they stood up, examined the ring, and hugged their soon-to-be sister-in-law.

After several minutes of oohing and ahhing, Sheila was ready for some private time with her new fiance. She wrapped her arms around Blake's neck and whispered in his ear. "Let's go somewhere."

"We'll be back soon," Blake explained to his family, taking Sheila's hand and leading her from the room. They grabbed their jackets and headed for Blake's truck.

Just above the neighborhood awaited endless miles of world-class recreation opportunities. Good dirt roads climbed foothills and mountains and led to gorgeous views of the valley, lake, and the Wasatch Range stretching away to the horizon.

Blake loved his truck almost as much as he loved Sheila. He decked it out with all the features and accessories he needed for serious off roading in Moab and elsewhere. The challenging rocks he climbed there had scared Sheila at first, but she grew to trust his driving skills and enjoy the time they spent in the truck.

As they drove up the ridge named Jacob's Ladder, thick cloud cover moved in and obscured the road ahead. At a flat spot on the ridge, Blake turned off the key, and everything went silent except for a faint whisper of wind.

Blake and Sheila turned to each other and smiled. They understood. Words were unnecessary, but Sheila couldn't help but blurt out what they were both thinking.

"It's magical!"

"It's unreal," Blake agreed. "Enchanted."

He reached out and took her hand, and she undid her seatbelt, then leaned across the cab and kissed him.

"You're mine," she said with a mischievous smile. "I've got you forever now."

"And you're mine," Blake added, "so I don't want to see you looking at any other boys now."

"What other boys?" Sheila answered innocently. She pressed her forehead against his and they stared into each others eyes for a long time before Blake reached up and placed one hand behind her neck and drew her mouth toward his. Sheila closed her eyes and took his lips between hers in a long, soft kiss.

Outside the truck, snow began to fall. Small, wet flakes melted against the windshield and further blocked the world out. Blake and Sheila paid no attention as they wrapped their arms around each other and held one another close.

"I'm cold," Sheila finally whispered as a light shiver ran up her spine. The weather was nice for December, and they hadn't brought warm coats. Sheila slid back into the passenger seat and Blake turned on the key and cranked the heater, but the engine had cooled and only blew luke warm air. "Let's drive some more," she suggested.

"We'd better head back," Blake said as he peered through the windshield. Clouds still surrounded them, so thick they could barely see the ground outside. "I can't see a thing up here."

He put the truck in gear and began to pull forward until the front wheels started rolling over the edge of the hillside. Shifting into reverse, he backed up until the trailer hitch scraped against a rock. Shifting back to first gear, he cranked the wheel hard left and rolled forward again.

The right wheel dipped over the hillside, but Blake wasn't worried. One more time backing up should do the trick. He shifted into reverse and let out the clutch.

The right front tire slipped on a wet rock and the whole front end slipped sideways six inches. Sheila drew in a sharp breath and held it, then turned to Blake and smiled. She meant to communicate confidence in his driving abilities, but the spark of fear in her eyes asked, "You know what you're doing, right?"

Blake flashed a confident smile back that calmed her fears and she exhaled. This was his world, after all. This was nothing. Blake had hit the brakes when the front end slid around. Now he slowly let out the clutch again, pressing down on the gas pedal just enough to keep the engine from stalling.

Still on the same rock, the front end slipped again, this time eight inches, bringing both front tires over the edge. Sheila's eyes widened involuntarily. She looked out the window but could only see about thirty feet down the steep hillside. "Blake, you're scaring me," she admitted.

"Sorry," he grinned, then shifted into low range to turn the tires so slowly that he'd have plenty of traction to get fully back onto the road.

It worked. Letting out the clutch slowly again, the truck crept backward and was nearly back on stable ground when a loose rock tore loose from the ground and shot out in front of the truck. The sudden jolt made the wheels spin briefly and the truck lurched forward a foot. Both front tires now pointed nearly straight down hill now and Blake shoved in the clutch and slammed on the brakes. His knuckles had turned white now as he gripped the steering wheel. This was a little too close for comfort.

"Maybe you should get out for a sec while I finish turning around."

Sheila started to open her door when truck ground forward another five inches. "Blake, you could at least wait until I..."

"Get out!" Blake screamed frantically. "GET OUT NOW!" his foot pressed hard on the brake petal while pulling up against the steering wheel as if more pressure on the brake would do any good.

Sheila paused, he had never yelled at her before. Then she suddenly understood as the car lurched forward another foot.

This time the truck didn't stop sliding. It slid down the hillside, slowly at first, but picked up speed quickly and began to bounce like an untamed rodeo bronco.

Sheila desperately tried to push herself out of the door but the truck rolled over to the left and she fell back against Blake. She hit her head against his window and everything went black.

On the second roll, the centrifugal force threw Sheila from the vehicle. She landed on the rocky hillside and continued rolling, but never felt a thing.

The truck tumbled violently 200' down the steep slope with rocks flying and the sickening sound of metal crunching and breaking, and came to a sudden crashing stop, landing upside down, in the bottom of a narrow ravine.

Sheila rolled all the way down the mountainside following just behind the truck and came to rest atop the rear axle. A moment later, she opened her eyes. She expected to hurt all over, but she did not. She expected to feel cold in the chilly air, but she did not. In fact, she felt surprisingly good. She had never felt quite so light. *It must be the adrenaline,* she thought to herself as she sat up.

"I'm so sorry, Sheila," Blake said. He took her hand and helped her climb off the car. A charming ephemeral stream ran between mossy rocks and still-green grasses.

Sheila looked at him curiously. "Sorry for what?" she asked. Then she remembered rolling down the mountain. "How did you get out?!" she asked, her eyes blinking in astonishment.

Blake paused before answering. "I didn't get out."

Sheila sucked in a quick breath. And then she noticed. Blake's face had a strange glow about it. Pleasant but unusual. "Neither did you," he said. "I'm so sorry."

Sheila turned back and saw her body still laying across the rear axle. It looked so serene. Several seconds passed before the full impact dawned on her. She was dead. They were both dead.

"You mean it's all over?" she asked without taking her eyes from her body.

"I'm so sorry," Blake repeated.

Sheila turned toward Blake and their eyes met. She read the thoughts painted plainly across his face. He looked pained with regret. Just when everything was going so perfectly. Just when they had so much to look forward to. How could this happen?

Then she saw deeper than ever before. It was as if she could see straight through him. Straight into his heart. She saw the person she had fallen in love with. A wave of happiness of love more intense than she had ever before experienced washed through her. She stepped toward his glowing body and threw her arms around his neck and held him tightly.

He felt different now - less solid, less rough, but there nonetheless.

"At least we're together," she whispered into his ear. "I love you."

"I love you, too!" Blake whispered back, holding her tight.

"And everything will be okay. I don't know exactly how everything works now, but I know everything will be okay."

He began to feel better, too. More relaxed, and he noticed a deep peace that began to permeate his soul. *It had to happen eventually*, he thought, *and yes, everything will be okay.*

Back at home, no one thought to miss the couple too much until early the next morning when they realized they never came home. They called their cell phones but no one answered. They called Sheila's apartment, but her roommates were all out of town for the holidays. They called their friends, but no one had seen them.

The couple had been missing for two days when SAR was called out to search. We brought four wheelers and side by sides and prepared to search the area.

A news helicopter overflew the area and spotted the truck laying on its roof in the gully. Draper City Fire and Police arrived on scene first and verified no survivors. ATVs and a helicopter shuttled teams 5 miles to the crash site where they loaded Sheila into a litter and flew her out on a helicopter long line. The chopper sensitively lowered her near CP but behind a ridge and away from crowds of curious onlookers.

The crushed truck cab had folded around Blake and with the doors wedged against the hillside, it took firemen an hour to lift and shore the vehicle up enough to extract him. Clouds had settled in by then, and we put him in a litter and raised him up the hillside on a rope rather than flying a helicopter into the narrow ravine again. From the ridgetop, teams placed the litter inside the helicopter and waited for a break in the clouds to fly Blake down the mountain.

Edgar Allen Poe, the first literary critic, asserted that the greatest loss in any story was the death of a beautiful young girl, but he was wrong. This was worse, and we tried not to think about it too much.

Tomorrow is promised to no one. People die all the time. When the time comes, you can't cling to what's already gone. It sounds too trite, too cliche, to tell you to live every day to the fullest, but do it anyway. Just do it carefully.

74 GLIDER

A glider crashed in the Timpanogos foothills on a warm August morning. Observant citizens in town below spotted its long silver wings laying against the hillside above and phoned in the alert.

While SAR responded, Tom took a closer look through a spotting scope and found that it wasn't a glider at all, but a 40-foot-tall, skinny weather balloon.

Foot teams were preparing to head up the mountain and get it anyway, just to prevent more frantic reports from concerned citizens if nothing else; but when I showed up at the Dry Canyon trailhead with my motorcycle, Tom told them to stand by and sent me up to bring it down.

I happily complied. I hiked and mountain biked these trails often and always wished they weren't closed to motorcycles without some sort of emergency.

I rode around closed gates, up a dirt road to the Curly Springs trail, and continued along winding singletrack through scrub oak while Lieutenant Bennett flew overhead and guided me toward the balloon.

When I left the trail and the hillside grew too steep to ride without digging troughs in the ground with my rear tire, I stopped the bike and hiked. When I reached the balloon, it was about half filled and would have floated away if the camera, batteries, and a set of wooden fins hadn't caught in the brush.

Carrying it through the thick scrub oak was awkward, but I managed to get it back to my bike and rode slowly down the trail as the balloon bounced its way between branches above the trail.

A phone number was written on the balloon offering a reward for its return, and back in the parking lot, we got busy emptying the balloon's helium for transport. Television crews had arrived, and it must have been a slow news day, because we made the evening news. The anchors seemed to enjoy the story, including the part where I took a deep breath of helium and staggered away while speaking in a cartoon-like high-pitched voice.

Driving down the Curly Springs Trail with an errant weather balloon in tow

75 CHILDREN FIRST

The darkness of the December night only added to the confusion as a twelve-foot aluminum boat and its passengers - three men, two dogs, and a skinny young teenager - came to an abrupt halt when its bow plunged into a wave face.

With too much momentum to merely stop, the bow dove deeper into the cold water and the transom, complete with an 80 hp outboard motor, rose into the air.

The boat slowed and the duck hunters momentarily wondered if it would flip all the way over, but quit wondering when they were ejected and went flying through the air and into the cold lake.

The boat fell, upside down, on top of them, and they pushed away from it and swam, choking and sputtering, to the surface. Even if the sun hadn't set hours earlier, the water would still have been a deadly forty five degrees, and the air wouldn't have been much warmer.

"Where are the life jackets?!" Gary demanded as the group gathered around the upside down hull, whose bow still floated and provided a few square feet of surface above the waves.

"I put 'em in the front o' the boat," Gerald answered.

Gary thought this over. They could flip the boat over and get them, but then the air trapped inside the bow might escape and boat might sink. He glanced at his nephew Percy and decided against it. If the skinny child didn't have a place to sit out of the water, he would freeze to death in half an hour.

The dogs had scrambled atop the overturned boat and Gary told Percy to climb up with them, which he managed to do with some help. As the dogs continued to scamper back and forth across the hull, they threatened to tip it and send Percy back into the water.

"We gotta shoot 'em," Gary declared.

"Wait ain't gonna shoot Percy!" Gerald objected. "Are you outta yer frickin mind?"

"Not Percy, you idiot! We gotta shoot the dogs!" Gary bellowed back. "If they keep running around like that, they're gonna knock Percy off. What's the matter with you?!"

"Oh," Gerald muttered. The cold was really digging into his skin now, along with the seriousness of their predicament. No one would know they capsized the boat. No one would expect them back for hours. *What's the point?* he thought to himself. *We're all gonna die out here anyway.*

"Gimme the gun," Gary directed. Gerald was cradling his new Remington 20 gauge when the boat flipped and he had somehow managed to hang on. He would miss the dogs, but they could be replaced. He handed the shotgun to Gary. When he felt Gary grab the double barrel underwater, he let go.

"Gimme the gun, Gerald," Gary commanded again. "No use putting it off. It's gotta be done."

"I already gave it to you," Gerald said.

"You mean after you poked me with it?" Boyd asked.

"I never poked you with it!" Gerald objected, and it dawned on everyone at the same time what happened. Gerald thought Gary had the gun and simply dropped it into the lake.

Gary sighed. "Everybody grab onto the boat an' hold as still as you can," he directed. "Try to keep the warm water against you like a wet suit." Smooth two-foot swells rose and fell in an endless procession. Soon the dogs calmed down and stopped threatening Percy's precarious perch.

Hours passed as the men passed through from one stage of hypothermia to another. Chattering teeth became violent shivers and then those stopped. Warm blood shunted to protect their core organs. Questions about what would become of them and preparing to die faded as level of consciousness dropped and all thought blurred slowly into a dim, distant haze.

Around midnight, Boyd blinked his eyes and tried to focus his thoughts. Half a dozen stars shone in the distance, but they seemed too bright. And too low. And they seemed to be moving across the water toward them.

"Wha's that?" he drawled slowly.

Gary and Gerald didn't turn to look. Their muscles were all too cold to move. They merely looked at Boyd and waited for him to answer his own question.

Percy, still shivering violently atop the boat, turned toward the lights skipping quickly toward them across the lake. Somewhere in the back of his mind, he knew what they meant - boats - but he didn't dare believe they were coming for them. They were spread apart, about fifty yards between each one, and most, if not all, would pass right by and never notice the tight clump of dying men floating just above the lake surface.

Percy tried to shout but his voice came out high and weak, they would never hear it over the sound of their own motors. Boyd tried to shout as well, but his lungs felt frozen and he could hardly make a sound.

Sure enough, all the boats passed by; but then the nearest one, about twenty yards away, let off the gas and slowed. The headlamp on the driver of the PWC turned toward them, and then the watercraft followed.

"Hello?!" the driver called out without much certainty. Light bounces off water and makes it hard to see far at night, but something had interrupted the pattern of city lights reflecting from the east as he drove past.

While Boyd tried to shout back, Percy began to cry. He felt ashamed but he couldn't help it. He couldn't shout back and they wouldn't get found and they were all going to die and it would be all his fault.

But the driver did see them. He punched the throttle and shot toward them while speaking frantically into his radio. "I found 'em! Everybody get back here!"

The next thing the men knew, a watercraft had pulled alongside them and a man had jumped into the water next to them. His headlight blinded them as he looked around, assessing who to help first. "Are you okay?" he asked.

"I think I'm gone," Gary mumbled as he pried his fingers away from the boat and tried futilely to swim toward the rescuer. He felt his face sink below the waves, and the cold water felt warm against his neck and chin. The swimmer reached out and grabbed his coat collar, then swam him over to the watercraft and pulled him onto the rescue board attached to the back as other PWCs pulled up and loaded up the others.

"Can you climb onto the seat?" a rescuer asked, but other than Percy and the dogs, none of them could move much at all. "Let's get 'em to shore!" a team leader decided, and rescuers straddled the men and did their best to hold them on the rescue boards as the group sped off across the water.

A mile later, the squadron of watercraft entered the harbor without slowing and fresh hands waded down the boat ramp to pick up the frozen victims and carry them up to waiting ambulances.

It turns out that the men's families began to worry when the men didn't return by 11 p.m. Their husbands and brothers had already spent four hours in the water when the call went in to 911. Miraculously, all of them survived to deliver heartfelt, tearful thanks at our next team meeting.

*A SAR member swims for an eddy
on the Provo River during training*

76 SQUAW PEAK

One benefit of living near Provo Canyon is the proximity to many call outs. The cliff-covered mountains on either side of the canyon attract a high percentage of the trouble people get themselves into, and arriving on scene early increases the chances of getting sent up on a hasty team or being assigned another useful job.

Such was the case the night I needed one more story to complete this book. The page came out at 1:41 a.m., just as I was falling asleep. Two BYU students had gone hiking without flashlights and ended up caught above high cliffs in Little Rock Canyon in mid-May.

Camel Pass Road would have taken us within a mile of where the girls had built a small fire along the ridge, but it was still closed with snowdrifts and avalanche debris covering it in spots, so we drove to the Squaw Peak overlook instead.

Bruce was made team leader for the hasty team with Matt and I, and we loaded our packs with supplies for possibly cold, injured, hungry or dehydrated victims, along with light technical gear in case we encountered small cliffs, then struck out on the trail traversing the mountainside.

The trail was steeper than we remembered, and it became apparent that Bruce's frequent back country ski trips had kept him in better shape than me over the winter as we rushed along and my legs began turning to jelly. I occasionally paused for fifteen or twenty seconds to rest, determined not to slow the team down. Despite my temporary fatigue, it felt good to move fast and get the job done well.

We finally reached the top of Little Rock Canyon and dropped down a steep ridge, jumped over a small stream where we spooked some large animal that went crashing away through the trees, then over another ridge and stream toward the coeds. I enjoyed finding our way up steep hillsides through thick brush, grabbing branches and avoiding thorny roses, and making good time to our destination.

Olin's team was dropping in behind us and Bruce suggested that they keep a few members on the ridge with enough elevation to see both our headlamps and the girls' fire and guide us directly to them.

Emily was local and, other than not bringing flashlights, warmer jackets, and more water, seemed comfortable and like she knew pretty well what she was doing. She had lit the fire that kept them relatively warm and helped us find them. Without the firelight to guide us, we'd likely have spent another hour or more spreading out and searching the entire area more thoroughly.

Emily's cousin Jessika had moved to Utah from Chicago for school last fall, and the steep mountainside had freaked her out a bit (according to Emily's mom who we met an hour or two later). She was chilled and I pulled a jacket from my pack for her to wear. She was lucky to have chosen the warmest night of the year for their little adventure.

We gave them headlamps and guided them down the steep mountainside, picking a route around the tallest cliffs down to a faint trail in the bottom of the canyon. Before leading them over tiny cliff bands, I scouted ahead. "Wait here while I make sure this route goes," I directed, "so we won't have to climb back up if it's a dead end."

As we reached the canyon bottom, Team One met us and we proceeded to pick our way down canyon. It turns out the toughest challenges lay ahead as the ephemeral stream sometimes filled the narrow canyon from wall to wall, forcing us to wander back and forth over boulders, cliffs, and scree fields to find for the best route down.

Team Three came up from below and met us after we dropped below the trickiest parts of the canyon. We then noticed that Jessika was stumbling along. The long, challenging hike had worn her out. She didn't want to stop and drink water or rest, but we made her sit down for a few minutes now and then rather than risk a twisted ankle or a forty-foot tumble into the stream below.

At 5:30 a.m., the narrow trail dropped into a Provo residential area and we found Emily's mom there waiting for us. Tom gathered a few details for his report and had a little chat with the girls about being prepared, and Team Three gave us rides back to our vehicles at the overlook.

Because we had a team training coming up in just an hour, several of us went to breakfast together rather than going home and to bed.

"Were they cute?" someone asked who had been stuck in the parking lot all night without an assignment.

"Yeah," I answered, "but they were 20 years old. That doesn't do me any good."

Everyone turned to 23-year-old Matt who was also on the hasty team.

"No, thanks," he declined. "As soon as I heard they were BYU students, I lost all interest."

Ah, school rivalry. At least another West Side Story or Romeo and Juliette was averted by prejudice.

77 THE DEER HUNTER

Mike shivered in the predawn chill, but he didn't care. He had lost twenty pounds in the last few months, and his light jacket didn't provide much warmth. Normally, he would be waking up for school about now, but he hadn't slept all night, huddled and shivering in a thicket of scrub oak in Dry Canyon where he often hiked with his family. He probably should have picked a higher spot, somewhere that didn't funnel the cool breeze from the tall mountain behind him, and where the sun would reach sooner.

But he didn't care. He wasn't about to go home. Not to his stupid family. He was sick of them telling him how he should be and what to do all the time. It was none of their darn business if he wanted to play video games instead of making friends. He was seventeen years old - nearly a legal adult. He could make his own decisions! Why couldn't everyone just leave him alone?

The sound of cars driving up the road and stopping in the trailhead parking lot surprised him. People in matching red coats gathered together in a clump, then broke into groups and walked away. One group headed up the canyon toward him. He didn't want to be seen, so he scooted deeper into the brush and found a rock to sit on.

Soon he heard the group walking the trail above him, the small rocks grinding below their feet. "Mike!" one of them called in a loud voice.

What? Mike asked himself, startled. *How do they know my name?* It didn't take him long to figure out. All the hikers must be out searching for him. *And they want to make me go home. Well, I don't want to.* Mike carefully, quietly crawled even deeper into the brush.

As the day wore on, others passed by along the trail above. They stopped and peered into the bushes. At one point, someone seemed to be looking straight at him. Mike could barely see out through the branches, but he felt so vulnerable. How could they not see him?

When the searchers left, Mike crawled up canyon to get farther away from the parking lot and all the activity. He knew that the foothills go on forever with criss-crossing trails everywhere and plenty of places to hide. *They'll never find me,* he thought. Escaping became something of a game.

A while later, he heard a group moving down the hill toward him. They made lots of noise and Mike heard them coming from half a mile away. They would be easy to avoid. Mike moved down and across the mountainside, always staying hidden in the thick brush.

After two hundred yards of scrambling and just as Mike was about to settle into a new thicket and stay for a while, Another group of searchers came thrashing through the woods toward him. They made lots of noise but didn't move very fast. Mike dropped down a ravine and soon crossed a trail and followed it for a ways.

Down in the parking lot, Tom gazed up at the foothills, then spoke into the radio. "He's moving northwest now. Team Two, keep going the same direction. We'll flush him out soon."

Tom couldn't see the boy, making his way stealthily through covered ravines, but he could see the deer who stopped munching grasses along the ridges and watched Mike scramble through their normal daytime hideouts. They telegraphed his location with perfect clarity.

Mike found himself at the neighborhood and decided he could hide in town as easily as in the foothills. He'd just blend in with other people taking afternoon walks until the bothersome searchers gave up and went away.

As he stepped onto the street, a pair of Orem police offers stepped around the corner of the house and walked toward him. Mike froze. He could run, but which way? He couldn't decide fast enough, and soon the officers each had a hand on his arms.

"Good afternoon, Mike," one greeted him in a friendly tone. "We've been looking all over for you! Your family's been worried."

A helicopter takes off during a search from the Dry Canyon trailhead

78 DEER-SIZED LEDGE

"I'm stuck on a deer-sized ledge in Battle Creek," the distressed caller reported to dispatch, "I'm clinging to a sagebrush branch. I think I'm gonna die!"

Thus began an urgent response to the narrow, cliff-filled canyon. *Yeah! I thought when I read the page. This is what I live for!* Adventure, challenge, and making a difference.

As team members reached the parking lot and quickly packed for technical rescue, CP gave a victim description of a blond teenager wearing a green shirt and blue jeans, and dispatched teams up canyon to locate our imperiled climber.

Instead of sending Bruce and I up the canyon with the others, our assignment involved climbing the north canyon wall to gain elevation and perspective in case we could spot our victim from there.

"We see someone in a green shirt," Bruce radioed to CP, "but he's not stuck on a ledge."

Far from it. The hiker we spotted sat on a rock the size of a small car on a relatively flat scree slope near the top of the southern slope just below an 80' cliff.

CP called our victim's phone and told him to wave.

"Yeah," Bruce radioed back, "he waved."

Despite the abrupt dissipation of urgency, a Life Flight helicopter that responded to help the search flew a team member to the top of the upper cliff. He walked two hundred yards around the cliff and strode comfortably right up to our victim. They appeared to chat for a moment, then the rescuer turned and walked back across the easy scree slope and up the hill, leading the way as our victim walked behind him, crouched over near the ground like a gorilla.

I met the boy in the parking lot and couldn't tell why he had such strange judgment about the safety of his surroundings.

Maybe he had climbed something truly steep below and got freaked out and wouldn't recover till he got off the mountain. It reminded me of a Florida girl we once "rescued" from a steep scree slope in the Primrose Cirque. Her boyfriend led her up a "shortcut" between trail switchbacks, and, unaccustomed to steepness of any kind, she got overwhelmed. Though not technically necessary, we attached a rope and belayed her back to the trail, where she suddenly felt better and the couple continued hiking up the mountain.

On the other hand, the boy may have had some sort of substance-induced altered mental state. We'll never know for sure.

79 ELIZABETH SMART

The galloping unicorn slowed to a trot as color drained from the rainbow stretching across the bluebird sky. Pixies paused midair, then abruptly scattered and hid behind trees and rocks. A black dragon with red eyes and dagger-like fangs reached out a clawed paw and clutched the front of Elizabeth's shirt.

Then she opened her eyes. The dream vanished and a nine-month nightmare began.

"Get up quietly or I'll kill you and your family," threatened her kidnapper, a self-proclaimed prophet who called himself Emmanuel and was later diagnosed with narcissistic personality disorder, pedophilia, and anti-social personality disorder.

The alarm was raised the next morning, and thousands of volunteers searched Salt Lake County neighborhoods. National media picked up the story and dozens or hundreds of searches across the region took place.

Searches with no place last seen (PLS), frequented locations, or vehicle to provide clues as to where to start make searches next to impossible, but Utah County checked places along major highways anyway where a body may have been dumped.

Elizabeth and her captor remained in the area for four months, during which time my friend Chantal met them in a Salt Lake City park. Their obviously religious dress - robes with hoods and veils for the women - caught her attention and sparked her curiosity.

"Hi," Chantal said in her typical friendly, energetic manner. "What religion do you belong to?"

"Jesus Christ," answered Emmanuel. Chantal thought he looked 'kinda crazy,' which only increased her curiosity.

"Oh yeah?" she probed, "What's the name of your denomination?"

At that, Emmanuel blew his top. "That *is* the name of the religion!" he said angrily. "It doesn't need more of a name than that!"

Chantal thought it wise to let the conversation end there. Only many months later did she realize who she had spoken to.

The group later fled to California for five months, and a week after returning to Utah, Emmanuel was recognized by a passing biker - Elizabeth's knight in shining armor - who had seen his sketch on *America's Most Wanted* the night before. Police arrived and the nightmare ended at last.

80 The Bike Thieves

The beautiful blonde BYU coed had been missing five days when local authorities finally called on search and rescue for assistance.

There weren't many clues. Camille had gone for a bike ride and never returned. Her last credit card transaction purchased a fruit drink at a nearby gas station. Her bike could not be found. With nothing better to work from, we organized our search around places she was known to ride. We hiked and motorcycled every inch of trails along the mountainside above Provo and into the canyon, logging GPS tracks which ICS saved to a single map to reveal any unexamined gap.

Search teams and citizens, hundreds of whom showed up to help with searches organized by a local organization who passed out printed photos of Camille and her bicycle, reported unrelated clues that would nonetheless make gripping plots for television detective shows. A mechanic noted strands of blonde hair in the back seat of a car that came in to get a fender bender repaired. A long skidmark on Slate Canyon Road may have marked the place where Camille was hit, then stuffed into the car and disposed of elsewhere to avoid any trouble about the crash.

Ongoing media coverage finally paid off. Someone dialed the police tip hotline and confessed.

The confession had nothing to do with Camille directly. It was about the bike. After seeing the purple Schwinn parked in the same spot along the River Trail for several days, some boys had cut the lock and stolen the bike. When they found out whose bike they had taken and realized that it could be hampering the search, their consciences got the better of them and they phoned in.

We followed up on the confession and found the destroyed lock in the river right where the thieves reported having thrown it. The boys were not prosecuted, and the search area focus instantly shifted to the area surrounding Bridal Veil Falls.

Teams combed thousands of acres of cliffs, ledges, pine forests, and steep slopes choked with scrub oak and other vegetation. The terrain made searching difficult, and after searching the entire slope, we still hadn't found Camllle.

"I want you to search that area again," Tom told a search team, pointing to an area far up the slope and blanketed in thick growth. "I'm just not comfortable that we checked it thoroughly enough."

And that's where we found her. She had fallen from a steep cliff ramp above while hiking, and judging from the position where she stopped, she was dead long before her body came to rest.

If SAR had been involved sooner, we may have found the bike before it got stolen and located her body sooner, but the final outcome would have been the same.

81 MRA

When MRT Sergeant Bruce R. asked if I was willing to submit my name for a leadership position in the Mountain Rescue Association's Intermountain Region, I consented. The former leadership had served for many years and they decided to give someone new a chance.

I wrote up a short SAR bio and Bruce forwarded it to the region's team MRA reps to vote on. That's how I wound up as region secretary. That position lasted less than a year.

The new region chair was a friend from Salt Lake County SAR; a skilled, experienced, dedicated and enthusiastic rescuer and strong leader, but also a busy entrepreneur whose business success meant that he didn't have the time to devote himself to the office as fully as he wished. When he announced that he would step down, he recommended to the team reps, who voted on behalf of their individual SAR teams, that I take over his position. The votes came in and made it official.

Since then, I've made a few contributions, such as submitting a few reports, improving communication avenues for the region, organizing a recertification exercise for region teams (a major undertaking, as anyone who has taken this on knows), and moderated a few minor disagreements, inserting my best people into the situation to help smooth out any differences. Soon we'll reexamine our region bylaws and update them. We've decided to change the way we handle recerts to better serve our teams and reduce the burden on the teams that host the event and others who travel great distances for it.

As for my major goal, however - recruiting more teams to join the MRA, I haven't made much progress. It's not just about getting in touch - new teams require significant attention by mentors to get them up to speed and ready for certification. As a volunteer, there's just not enough time to do everything. Bills must be paid. More urgent obligations come first.

One county is seriously considering joining, and I recently heard about interest from another team in Montana who inquired about the benefits of MRA membership. Here's what I wrote in response:

...In my experience, MRA membership offers four primary benefits and several lesser ones.

Major benefits include:

1. High safety & effectiveness standards

Because search and rescue often occurs in very dangerous terrain and requires technical systems, it's crucial that teams practice the safest and most up-to-date techniques to protect their own safety and that of the victim. These standards may be maintained through diligent vigilance and thorough training, but can be significantly enhanced through interaction with other MRA teams.

Every two years (alternating between winter & summer rescue skills), our teams meet with other teams & evaluators in practical scenario tests to ensure that safe standards are being met. Occasionally, an important safety issue is pointed out during these evaluations, but certainly the preparation for such recertification evaluations provides significant benefits.

In the first place, veteran members brush up on their skills to give the best possible performance. They pass along a significant amount of training to newer members, and the high standards required for the recertification test filter throughout the entire team. In my mind, this benefit alone is enough to validate MRA membership.

2. SAR association & mutual support

Those who participate in recertifications and other regional or national events form satisfying associations with SAR members from around the country. MRA members may join the email lister and participate in discussions about many aspects of SAR. They become well informed on issues facing the wider community that they may otherwise never hear about. All this can make their volunteer service even more rewarding.

By getting acquainted with nearby teams and their skill sets, mutual aid becomes easier and safer to coordinate. Team members know they can trust systems as they get lowered off a cliff, for example, by another MRA team, and mutual respect and camaraderie helps operations to run more smoothly.

3. Training information

The MRA has developed some training information available online and more is under development. This allows teams and individuals skilled in specific areas to spread a wealth of knowledge and experience that would otherwise take decades to accumulate as an individual team.

4. Lobbying and influence in the wider SAR world

The National MRA organization is well-connected to government and other SAR organizations and acts as a strong voice for ensuring that regulations remain functional and supportive. Any MRA member who wishes to participate at this level is welcomed with abundant opportunities, and those who aren't still benefit from others' efforts.

Lesser but valuable benefits of MRA membership include:

1. Prestige

Not only does the MRA patch on a uniform denote the highest standards in search and rescue, but it creates a sense of team pride from knowing that your skills and dedication make you the cream of the crop. This may sound like an insignificant matter, but in a volunteer organization, that's far from the case. Volunteers will give more of themselves, remain active in the organization longer, recruit others better, and seek donations more effectively when they enjoy the satisfaction that comes from excellence and a job well done.

2. Indirect legal protection

The MRA does not provide any sort of direct legal support, but religiously following technical standards approved by a prestigious regional organization like the MRA can make a cogent argument for competence should you ever face a lawsuit. (You set all your own team protocols, by the way; the region merely requires that they be safe).

If you're ready to look at the specifics of how to join the MRA, you can find the official documents at http://www.mra.org/about/how-to-join. Also feel free to give me a call to discuss any questions you may have. Note that regular membership means that your team trains and certifies to a 4-season standard in skills such as snow travel & anchors, avalanche search and recovery, search, low angle, and high angle rescue. Associate members may train and certify to a lesser degree, and Ex-officio membership is for non-volunteer teams like NPS.

Let me know if you have any further questions and if you're ready to begin the membership process. We'd love to add you to our MRA family! I'll let Ravalli County know about your interest and we'll be in touch.

Looking back at Hogsback Ridge while climbing
Mount Hood during the MRA 50th anniversary annual
meeting where it all began at Timberline Lodge

82 Rock Canyon

May's monthly SAR training took place in Rock Canyon on a gorgeous Saturday morning. Following an extended winter and cold, wet spring, the good weather drew crowds of valley residents outside and up the canyon. Some rock climbed the popular routes in the lower canyon. Groups of geology students strolled up the rocky road and wrote their observations of the dramatic folds in the quartzite rock layers for class.

"You really should be wearing helmets," Chris said as he passed some sport climbers on his way to a medical scenario above.

"Ah, nothing ever falls around here," the belayer answered. He was right. The Appendage was bolted decades ago, and any loose rock had long since been pried away.

Forty five minutes later, our training was winding down. I stood on the road a hundred feet down-canyon when a loud sound caught our attention and made us all spin around at once.

A thousand feet up Squaw Peak, a rock the size of my living room, which had formed an overhanging cliff for probably the last thousand years, broke free. It fell a hundred feet, where it struck a twenty-foot-wide ledge and burst into pieces, erupting in a huge dust cloud and shooting car-sized rocks in every direction. These rocks dropped another two hundred feet over the next cliff, then bounced and rolled a quarter mile down the mountainside, sweeping away trees like a hand moves through a column of smoke. Several boulders made it all the way down and struck the far side of the canyon within feet of the dirt road where geology students scattered frantically for safety.

The dust didn't settle for several minutes, during which time we radioed teams still on that side of the mountain to make sure everyone was safe, then proceeded to check for other injured hikers or climbers. We were relieved to find that no one was injured.

"I told them they should wear helmets!" Chris exclaimed, but I disagreed.

"I doubt that would have made much difference."

83 Without a Paddle

Kyle and Eddie hadn't sailed far into the lake when the wind picked up. Their small Hobie 14 took off and their paddle fell into the lake.

"I got it!" shouted Kyle. "Come back and pick me up." With that, he dove off the boat and swam for the paddle. After all, if he didn't get it now, they might not be able to spot it between the waves once they turned around.

Eddie tried to come about but he hadn't sailed long and it took a minute to figure everything out. In the mean time, he sailed maybe a hundred feet away.

Once he got turned around, he couldn't see Kyle anywhere. The waves must be hiding him. He sailed closer, and when he still couldn't see him, he called out.

Now he was confused. They were a little too far from shore for Kyle to have swum that far. Was he playing some sort of joke on him? That would be like him. He looked under the trampoline mat in case Kyle was holding onto the dolphin catcher and grinning, but found nothing there.

He continued searching, looking back and forth, going over everything in his mind when it finally dawned on him. Kyle was underwater.

Eddie looked down but could barely see an inch through the murky depths. He pointed the bows into the wind to stall the boat and sat for several minutes, too stunned to do anything.

Once he realized that there was nothing he *could* do, he raced back for the marina as fast as the little craft would take him. Rather than sail all the way around to the harbor mouth, he ran aground on a narrow concrete ramp on the river side of the marina, then ran up the jetty shouting for someone to call 911.

He couldn't identify an exact PLS, but we began a search anyway in the general area where Eddie pointed. The water was cool enough that it could take up to a week for the body to float.

The next day, we gathered a few boats with side scanning sonar and used GPS to run a grid search patterns across the flat lake surface, trying to distinguish anything that could be a body from among piles of rocks and other irregularities dotting the lake bottom. The weather cooperated with flat, windless days as the sun beat down and burned our skin.

Three days later, Kyle floated and someone spotted him near the eastern edge of our search area.

When you're up a creek, a PFD is much more important than a paddle. As in all other drownings on the lake, a PFD would have saved Kyle's life. Learn from others' losses and wear yours!

84 Ledged Out

The third rescue of the day called us to the cliffs a quarter mile down canyon from Bridal Veil Falls. Night had fallen and caught three boys in their late teens or early twenties between cliffs ranging from 40 to 150 feet high. They had downclimbed exposed slopes to reach their spot and were afraid to go back the way they came - for good reason.

This corner of Cascade Peak has a ridiculous amount of cliffs. Cliffs stacked on cliffs for thousands of feet, yet people still climb all over and go places they don't belong. We would return to the same spot two more times this summer, and other nearby cliffs two or three other times. Even so, responding to ledged hikers beats scraping up fallen hikers, and we typically tell these hikers that they made the right decision by calling. We get them down the mountain and let them chat with Tom about how they did the wrong thing by going there in the first place.

By flashing their cell phone down toward the highway, we spotted their exact location, and I felt sure I knew how to get there. A passage through cliff bands around the mountain from their location led to steep dirt and an even steeper stone ramp that terminated 200' directly above our hikers. I thought we could make our way down from there.

Others disagreed. Kevin and Bruce wanted to try a direct approach. They would start up the Great Western Trail that cut across the slope, then pick the right ravine and climb the scree slope which created a break in thick scrub oak to the base of the cliff. From there, they hoped to find a passage up the cliff to retrieve our victims.

ICS listened to both groups and settled the matter by splitting us into two teams. I was assigned to lead Team One my roundabout way, while Team Two took the direct approach.

I glanced around to see who was available for my team. I picked Olin, whose mountaineering skills I knew and trusted, and then saw a proby standing nearby, just outside the tight circle gathered around CP. He stood still and acted calm, but I wasn't fooled. His eyes told the real story, practically bursting with the plea "Pick me! Pick me!"

I knew something about his extensive climbing experience and turned back to CP. "And I'll take Curtis," I told them.

"You've got a 70 meter dynamic?" I asked him, then instructed him to "Pack it up" when he assured me that he did. The dynamic rope would come in handy for our climb up the steep ramp. Our normal static lines didn't have enough stretch to safely catch a lead fall. Again, his eyes told the unspoken story. Excitement. Gratitude. Eagerness to get going.

Once we were all packed and ready, someone gave us a ride up the river trail and we started up the boulder-filled gully below Stairway to Heaven. We reached the first cliff band and turned right, and continued hiking as fast as our lungs would allow across the mountainside, climbing steep slopes, hiking through patches of thorny wild roses, traversing mossy waterfalls, and finally reaching a cleft in the cliff.

Steep rock and hard dirt above the cleft made us cautious and slowed our progress a bit, but we pushed onward. The ground was so hard that even my stiff-soled mountaineering boots barely dug in and I never felt completely stable. It was bad enough to be a little scary. If I slipped, I would probably be able to catch myself, but I couldn't be sure, so I tested every rock I grabbed and placed every step carefully.

I trailed a 75' rope behind me and secured it to a small tree for the rest of my team and others who might follow later to use as a handline up to that point.

Meanwhile, everyone who didn't get an assignment stood in the parking lot, listening to our radio traffic and waiting to find out which team would win. We never actually said so, but we all knew the race was on. Except for Bruce, everyone on both teams was at least mildly competitive.

At the base of the 200' ramp, Olin tied a belay around a large pine tree away from potential rock fall, and I tied onto the sharp end of the rope with a handful of pro dangling from my harness. My pro, or protection, consisted primarily of aluminum chocks - rectangular blocks of varying sizes with wires passing through them - which I would wedge into constricting cracks as I went and then clip the rope to. If I fell, these pieces - theoretically - would catch me.

I started up the stone ramp, tapping with my fist on jutting corners of rock to make sure they sounded solid before wrapping my fingers around them and pulling myself upward. I stepped onto small blocks or ledges and let my legs - which are much stronger than arms - do most of the work.

Though somewhat exposed, which means it's a long way down, the climbing was relatively easy, and I only set pro every twenty or thirty feet, where cracks made placements possible.

At last I reached the twenty-foot-wide flat spot at the top of the ramp and called down on the radio to let Olin and Curtis know. I tied a 20' length of webbing around a giant boulder and clipped the rope to it, then called for my team to clip their ascenders to the rope - which only slide one direction and make a continuous hand hold - and follow me up, cleaning my pro from the cracks as they went.

Now all we had to do was hike or rappel a hundred and fifty feet to our stranded victims and then retrace our steps. We had accomplished the toughest part of the mission already and it only took forty minutes, to the amazement of some team members in the parking lot as they later told me.

I also heard that Team Two was somewhat put out at coming in second. They made their way to the cliff band but had not yet found a way up it. This news only made our "win" that much more satisfying, though In the end, competition never gets in the way of a mission. Victim safety and comfort always comes first and we all know it.

Having turned the corner around the exposed ridge, a light breeze now blew past and the mild wind chill dropped temperatures enough that we took jackets from our packs and put them on. As for the victims, a helicopter had hovered over them and dropped blankets, food, and sports drinks long before we arrived. When we rappelled down and met them, they were all in good condition but eager to get moving and get off the mountain.

The slope back up to the top of the ramp was mild enough that we didn't mind hiking it, and put climbing harnesses on our victims and gave them our ascenders while we guided them back up. Olin then rappelled back down the ramp to receive our victims who we would lower one by one while Curtis wrapped one of their ankles, which the boy had sprained, with athletic tape for support.

With all three victims in harnesses, I attached one to the rope and instructed him in how to get lowered. "Lean back and let the rope take your weight, and keep your feet up high in front of you. Then just walk backward down the rock. If you let your feet get down below you, they can slip - which isn't a big deal because you're totally secure with this rope," I added reassuringly. The boy nodded.

"You can hold onto this rope," I continued, indicating the knotted line attached to his harness, "but keep it straight. Don't pull yourself up with it, because any slack in the line can let you fall a little bit." If the ramp were more vertical, I wouldn't have to explain that last part, because pulling himself up the rope would be next to impossible. 11mm climbing ropes are too thin to get that good of a grip on - nothing like the 2" hemp rope you used to climb in gym.

"711, 727," I called into the radio - Olin's number, then mine at the time, like saying "Olin, this is Shaun." "We're ready to lower our first 85." A 10-85 means a victim. 85 for short.

"Go ahead," he replied. "We're ready down here." Once our team reached the victims first, Team Three followed us up the mountain and began setting additional ropes to get the 85s off the mountain safely.

The boy began to walk backwards over the edge. At first, I held the rope tight as it wrapped through the friction-creating bars on the brake rack. I wanted him to feel secure. "You tell me if you want to go faster," I said as the rope began to slide through the bars.

"A little faster," he nodded, and I complied. We reminded him to keep his feet high against the wall when he instinctively tried to put them down and get his hands and body closer to the rock. He stood up straight again and continued down smoothly.

"You can spread your feet wider apart for more stability," I coached as his two friends took mental notes.

When the boy reached Olin's station, they attached him to another rope and then called "Off rope" over the radio for us to send down the next boy. After sending the third one down, Curtis rappelled, and I folded the rope in half through a steel rappel ring tied to the webbing and double rope rappelled - running both strands through my rappel device - for as far as the rope would take me.

Doubled over, it wasn't long enough to get me all the way to the next anchor, so when I reached the rope ends, I stayed attached to one end of the rope and continued downclimbing. The single strand didn't hold me securely, but provided some support as the other end slid back up the mountain to the rappel ring which would be left on the mountain. Now that I knew the route, I felt comfortable enough down climbing the last section without more support.

Team Three had already led two of our victims back to the River Trail and we followed. At the parking lot, we sorted gear to make sure we didn't leave with someone else's carabiners, and got home shortly after 2 a.m.

Evening sun illuminates the Old Glory area on Cascade's NW corner

85 WHITE WEDDING & FLOWERS

If ice farmers had their way, the north end of Cascade Peak would turn into a solid sheet of crystal from November till March. By installing thin PVC pipes from water sources high on the mountain to formerly dry cliffs, below-freezing temperatures can transform a tiny trickle of water into a glorious spire of ice seemingly overnight.

Ice farming creates new routes to climb by swinging ice tools - miniature axes with picks affixed - and kicking crampon front points into frozen-in-time waterfalls, temporarily marring these endlessly self-renewing recreational resources.

Sheriff deputies once asked a team member to help them access an area around Upper Falls where they had noticed pipes being installed and suspected a narcotics operation of operating there. "They're probably just farming ice," the SAR member told them, then added, "Real ice - frozen water - for ice climbing," he further explained when he saw their puzzled expressions.

Uninitiated bystanders shake their heads at the utter foolishness of ice climbing. Perhaps they're right. After all, ice is inherently slippery. How many Utah residents have never bruised their tailbone after slipping on the sidewalk? How many of us have never slid our car off icy roads?

Add to that information like the way ice gets brittle in extreme cold and every swing of a pick can shatter away giant chunks called "dinner plates." Or that if you move your tool shaft back and forth after a placement, it can work its way loose.

Next comes the problem of protection. There are no pre-placed bolts or pitons in the ever-changing ice. When lead climbing, stopping and hanging in the leashes (unless you climb leashless) attached between wrists and ice tools to drive a screw into the ice to attach the rope and - hopefully - catch you if you fall, is tiring. Therefore many climbers run the route out - leaving wide spaces of twenty feet or more between screws. That means the potential drop after a fall is forty feet or more, and the chance that a screw will fail also increases.

Move into mixed climbing - moving back and forth between ice and rock - and you experience the challenge of ascending tiny rock edges with tinier steel points lacking the sensory feedback of fleshy fingertips during summer rock climbing. Once when I encountered a smooth cliff with no adequate edges to hook, I jammed my axe head into a shallow, horizontal, flared crack and pressed all my weight down on the shaft to elevate myself high enough to reach the next hold. Miraculously, the placement held, but a crampon point sketched off its rock and I fell five or six feet before, luckily, catching myself. If I hadn't, the rope would have caught me twenty feet later.

On the other hand, with the right conditions and the right training, ice climbing can be relatively easy and safe, and one of those life experiences

- like going skinny dipping in a warm, moonlit lake or visiting Yellowstone - that every adventurer should try at least once.

With temps just below freezing, the ice becomes "plastic" and tools stick with a satisfying and secure *thwack!* You can swing your tool and kick your way straight up one of the most stunningly beautiful sites you'll ever see. Think of a three-story-tall crystal chandelier extending a hundred feet into the sky as you cling to its center like a fly.

Provo Canyon has world-renown ice like *Bridal Veil Falls, Stairway to Heaven, The Fang*, and many other routes. Considering the volume of climbers who regularly scale its cliffs, a few accidents are bound to occur - like Mike's.

Mike didn't mind being a little late for work. He usually arrived right on time at 8 o'clock sharp and did good work, and if a quick jaunt up the ice meant he arrived at 9 once in a while, no one would complain.

On this particular morning, he and his climbing partner Neil chose *White Wedding* - a 60' spire of farmed ice a stone's throw from Bridal Veil Falls, except, of course, for the fact that all the stones were frozen beneath a glassy-smooth six-inch sheet of clear ice at the sloped base of the route.

"It's plastic!" exclaimed Mike with delight after roping up and swinging his first tool placement into the wall. "Climbing!" he declared, and swung his other tool as Neil responded with "Climb on!"

"Don't ya think it's time for a screw?" Neil asked as Mike neared the half way mark thirty feet up the route.

"If you say so, honey," Mike joked, then detached a chromoly steel screw from a harness gear loop and jammed its sharp teeth against the ice. By twisting it back and forth, the teeth dug away the ice and pressure built up that sent the ground ice out through the screw's hollow core.

Once the screw dug in half an inch, the threads wrapping around the outer edge caught, and Mike twisted the handle clockwise as a white stream of chopped ice poured out like a piña colada snowcone. When the screw sank all the way flush to the handle, he clipped a quickdraw - two 'biners connected by a short dogbone sling - to it and clipped the rope to that.

"Happy now?" Mike shouted down.

"Yes, sweetie," Neil shouted back with a grin.

Mike continued kicking and thwacking his way up the route, and when Neil suggested he place another screw, he was within ten feet of the chains bolted to an exposed rock buttress to the right of the ice flow.

"I'm almost there," he replied. "I'll just clip the chains instead. The ice is good, so no worries."

Once even with the chains, Mike set his right tool with a solid swing into the ice and detached his leash. He unclipped a quickdraw from his harness and reached toward the chains to clip it there.

As he reached, his left tool twisted ever so slightly to the right. And popped free.

Mike had no time for anything more than a quick, sharp breath. "Falling!" he screamed as he toppled over backward, pivoting around his crampon front points still poking a quarter inch into the ice.

Mike's body plunged downward, rotating through the cold morning air, past his first screw and toward the deck where Neil stood with his mouth wide open in shock.

The rope caught Mike's fall, but not until after he hit the deck, landing face-first on the ice.

Statistics reveal that climbers have a 50/50 chance of surviving a 50' fall, and lucky for Mike, the face seems to be a good thing to land on. It absorbs momentum as sutures between major skull pieces - closed since infancy - crack and jaw and orbit bones around the eye shatter.

I was already at my desk at work when the page came. 7:50 a.m. I was working the morning shift on the technical support desk for the newspaper software company where I worked. My reluctance to leave - in case some newspaper had a publishing-critical emergency and needed my help - was all but erased by the knowledge that other tech support engineers would arrive within ten minutes. I closed my computer cover and left.

When I arrived at Bridal Veil Falls, someone had opened the gate and I drove up the river trail, then parked and quickly geared up. A small team of medics had just reached the victim and I heard Mike's loud groans every time they keyed their radio mics to call down patient condition and report what gear they needed sent up the mountain next.

I took a litter from Tom's truck and stood waiting for someone to arrive and be assigned to accompany me up the frozen mountain. Every moan heard over the radio sent an uneasy queasiness squirming through my stomach.

Finally someone arrived and we started up the trail. My teammate wasn't in as good of shape as me at the time, and we didn't get far before he had to pause and catch his breath. He had tried his best, and now stopped and bent over double, gasping for breath.

Soon my proby trainer caught up with us - a fragile-looking sixty-something-year-old who ran hundred-mile marathons over rugged mountain passes - and took the other end of the litter. We took off up the trail again at a fast clip.

When we reached Bridal Veil Falls, the ground became a solid sheet of ice sloping smoothly down the mountain, and we stopped to put on our crampons. As my companion finished attaching his, I took the litter across the slope to the waiting team where we attached it to a set of ice screws drilled into the ground with equalizing webbing to distribute the weight evenly across them, and loaded Mike into it.

Mike's moans didn't bother me anymore. I had switched into rescue mode and his pain didn't much matter to the task at hand.

From the time the litter attendant at Mike's head called "Down slow!", commencing our journey over ice and boulders and flowing water from the falls, to the moment we stepped onto the River Trail's snow-covered pavement, only eleven minutes elapsed.

We lifted him into the ambulance which sped him away. We had done all we could and could now only wait and hope for the best.

Helping to expedite the litter up the trail felt like one of the few times that I made a personal difference on a rescue. As a team, we make a significant difference up to a hundred times per year. As an individual, that experience is more rare.

Later on at the hospital, his face heavily bruised and jaw wired shut, Mike hit the call button, and when a nurse entered his room, he looked frantic. Unable to speak, he used hand signals to mime a pen and paper. The nurse handed him her clip board, and Mike scrawled a quick note and handed it back to the nurse whose adrenaline now coursed through her veins, ready for the worst.

"It's my girlfriend's birthday!" the note read. "I need to make sure she gets flowers."

Yeah, he's gonna be just fine.

A climber prepares to toprope an ice route

A ice tool set in the ice

86 ORI

Two teens went river biking late one autumn in the Spanish Fork River near where it pours into Utah Lake. River bikes are made by taking a normal bike and putting it into the river. Because river biking can lead to rust, the boys decided to use stolen ones.

When the boys didn't come home after dark, we went looking.

The dirt bank a hundred yards from the lake showed where two sets of tire tracks led into the water. We sent a hasty team quickly down river to search for survivors, another team to more carefully cut sign and identify where anyone left the river, and another team donned wetsuits and dry suits and clambered into the river.

So near the lake, the water ran slower than upstream, and deeper than we anticipated - almost over our head in spots. Teams formed a chain and did their best to step on every square foot of the riverbottom while watching out for dangers like barbed wire fences and other debris.

The river team had covered about a hundred feet and located the first abandoned bike when the hasty team made their first find. A large teenager lay on the bank at the river mouth, hypothermic and, judging by his incoherent cursing and babbling, inebriated.

"I don' know what...you're talking about," he declared randomly when we hadn't so much as spoken to him, and "Get yer effing hands off me," when a rescuer checked his pulse.

We moved him carefully into a litter and off the cold ground and began working at rewarming his core by placing heat packs around his neck, arm pits, and groin.

"You...stupid...punk," he slurred, seemingly unaware of his surroundings.

The river team finished their search and, failing to find any tracks leading from the river, a few team members headed out the delta formed as the lake level drops throughout summer to where it meets the lake.

Sure enough, we found our second victim half bobbing, half standing in five feet of water two hundred feet from shore. Like his friend, he was cold, drunk, and alive. We sent a four wheeler towing our ambulance trailer recently bought with generous donations from supportive community businesses and soon had him back near the road with his friend.

"Jumbo, this is Moonbeam," a team leader said over the radio and reported on our progress. "We're 10-24." Mission completed.

"Report to Hobble Creek Canyon," ICS responded. "We have a report of a downed aircraft."

With that, our teenage victims stood up and began to remove their wet suits. They no longer looked like teens, but men in their twenties or thirties.

"You're so funny," a team member said to one of the "inebriated" men. "And very convincing."

Before long, all the probies had packed up their gear and left the scene.

Their final exam - the ORI - would continue all night long and into the following afternoon.

The Operational Readiness Incident was designed loosely after one of Commander Alan Wakefield's favorite movies - *A Gathering of Eagles* - a Rock Hudson film about training an Air Force wing to deploy with perfect precision on a moment's notice. That's where the uncommon terminology like "jumbo" and "moonbeam" originated.

In earlier years, proby tests were designed by their proby trainer or the board and consisted of shorter written or practical exams. The trainer then presented the first year members to the board and team for approval.

The fact is, most newbies who don't survive their first year flunk out long before the ORI by failing to get the required gear or being unwilling or unable to commit to the demanding schedule of call outs, team meetings and trainings, plus two extra monthly trainings for the probies. We've found that if new members can't commit to the first year's demanding schedule, they probably won't make dedicated and productive team members in the future, either.

Now the secretive ORI gets talked up and strikes fear and excitement into the hearts of probies. They train hard all year long and know that they'd better know their stuff for the big test. They approach it with either trepidation or excitement to prove themselves as totally qualified team members.

The probies never know what time the pager will go off Friday night. When it does, they rush up the canyon to find a baby (or a doll) in the river, or track a child who wandered away from a campsite, or raise a fall victim up a cliff, or use any number of the skills they've trained for throughout the year.

They may get a few hours sleep in the middle of a search to test whether they brought sufficient supplies for an unexpected bivouac and teach them a lesson if they didn't.

The operation ends sometime Saturday afternoon with a delicious BBQ cooked by the Jeep Patrol's (now VIPS - Volunteers In Police Service) expert chefs, and to which their spouses are invited - without whose support they'd never have made it through their probational year nor the many demanding years to come.

87 Fast & Light

Telling all these stories has proven more taxing than I expected. Remembering the dark times of all the disasters I tried to block out, and then reliving them in sufficient detail to record them here, has made me wonder whether such events have affected me more than I realized or care to admit.

That's why I want to end this book on a happy note, and I know just the rescue story to tell. It's one of my favorites and was simple, easy and fun. It was not technical nor tiring, nor did the victim's life depend on us. In fact, the teenage boy was already hobbling down the Primrose Cirque toward Aspen Grove when we found him half way down the switchbacks below Hidden Lakes on one of the dozen-or-so times I climb half way up Timpanogos every year.

It's the way this rescue played out that makes me love it, and it makes me feel happy and light just remembering the smooth, effective teamwork and excellence that characterizes this story.

The skinny teenager had twisted his ankle. A dozen rescuers responded with our wheeled litter, or Timpanogos Taxi as I sometimes call it. We split the litter and its handles and wheel into four parts, dividing the load to carry up the mountain, then assembled it once we reached our victim and, after a quick assessment of his ankle, strapped him in.

Two team members took the handles - one in front and one in back - and began rolling the litter down the trail. The front attendant frequently called out "Four inch drop" or "Lift six inches" to the rear attendant whose vision was mostly blocked by the litter. Others preceded the litter and kicked loose rocks out of the way or followed behind holding a length of webbing to use as a tag line brake on steeper sections of trail.

The day was a perfect early autumn afternoon. The sun had dipped behind the mountain and temperatures were refreshingly cool but not uncomfortable. Skies were clear. Leaves remained green and a few wildflowers still bloomed.

After traversing half of the long Heber Switchback, the attendants agreed to switch out and let others take their place, and CJ and I stepped in - me in front and him behind.

From then on, all the way down the mountain, over rock piles and around corners, under giant pines and trees whose root systems made nice seating, past Second and First Falls, and over the flat, rocky trail to the parking lot, our team ticked like clockwork.

CJ and I moved quickly with such a light load that we barely felt it at 160 pounds, yet every time we reached tiny cliffs where we had to lift the litter down six foot drops, team members would already be there, standing alongside the cliff and ready to help lift, steady, and protect our load from tipping over. Every time we passed particularly exposed spots where the trail had worn away, two or three team members were already in place like a protective police escort lining a parade route.

And all the while in between, CJ and I moved fast and light, bringing our young patient down the mountain in record time. When we reached the flat trail far below, we jogged.

Something about the operation of this well-oiled machine felt extremely satisfying. I felt grateful for the opportunity to play a part, to be a cog in the gears, and it felt even better, when I looked in CJ's eyes, to know that he felt the exact same way. We didn't have to say it out loud, which is convenient because we wouldn't have known exactly how, but in this small, relatively insignificant way, for a brief moment on a blissfully beautiful autumn afternoon, we attained excellence. Life doesn't get much better than that.

For me, this experience sums up the Utah County Sheriff Search and Rescue volunteer team. We quietly go about our business; day or night, winter or summer, rain or shine or sleet or worse; willingly, optimistically, expertly getting the job done.

88 AFTERWORD

In closing, I want to say one last thing about volunteering: it matters. Do it. Sometimes it seems that the One Great Truth of life is that it is hard. Though it may not show, it's hard for everyone at times. When we share one another's burdens, they grow lighter. Miraculously, other people's burdens usually feel light to the helping hands pitching in, as do their own when they return to their lives after serving.

Volunteers comprehend that civilization means that we're all in the same boat. We rise or fall together. We can't do everything for everyone everywhere, but we can always do something, and blessing someone else's life blesses our own in immeasurable ways.

To all my teammates, past, present and future, and to volunteer rescuers everywhere - whether you venture into the clouds to bring injured people home, or deliver hot meals to senior citizens who would otherwise go hungry, or build houses for the homeless, or donate funds to charitable organizations, or any other of the myriad silent services that Americans are so famous for: I respectfully salute you.

People like you make our world a far better place. Your efforts may seem small to you, but in others' eyes, you are heaven-sent angels.

Keep up the good work.

About the Author

Shaun Roundy was born in New Jersey and moved to Massachusetts, California, and Brazil before growing up in the Rocky Mountains in Logan, Utah. He later lived and worked around the world in Spain, Taiwan, China, Honduras, and elsewhere.

He earned a Master of Arts degree from Utah State University and taught writing there and at Utah Valley University for over a dozen years. He has published half a dozen books including an innovative writing textbook, all of which can be found on the University of Life website: UofLIFE.com.

His father, a former member of the Cache County Search and Rescue team, taught him to camp, ski, ride motorcycles, and other outdoor pursuits which shaped Shaun's life and prepared him for saving lives in Utah County's extreme terrain.

Shaun joined Utah County Sheriff Search and Rescue in December of 1999 and has since participated in hundreds of rescues, many of the most memorable of which are detailed in this book.

He has served as UCSSAR Public Information Officer, Webmaster, Board of Directors Secretary and Vice President, Mountain Rescue Team Sergeant, and Mountain Rescue Association Intermountain Region Secretary, Chair, and Vice Chair as well as MRA Education Committee Webinar Training Subcommittee Chair.

For his last words, Shaun wishes to express his heartfelt gratitude and admiration to all his amazing teammates who make the team work so well.

The author crawls out of Nutty Putty Cave following a successful rescue

Like us and get rescue story updates at Facebook.com/RescueStories

Made in the USA
Lexington, KY
02 December 2017